Key Words or Phrases that
Unlock
SUBJECTS *of* THE BIBLE

Carl Verner Cederberg

◆ FriesenPress

Suite 300 - 990 Fort St
Victoria, BC, V8V 3K2
Canada

www.friesenpress.com

The original Manuscripts of the Holy Bible

Strong's Exhaustive Concordance

In this book we have strived to bring forth the "seek and you will find"; the full stories as we peace together Scriptures that relate to a subject as found written by 6 various Authors in the Original Masoretic text or The Original Manuscripts Other references:

Smith's Bible Dictionary
The Companion Bible
KJV 1611 edition
NIV Bible
The subject Bible
Strong's Exhaustive Concordance
The Apocrypha
Wikipedia Encyclopaedia

ISBN
978-1-4602-9109-2 (Hardcover)
978-1-4602-9110-8 (Paperback)
978-1-4602-9111-5 (eBook)

1. RELIGION

Distributed to the trade by The Ingram Book Company

Contents

This book or commentary is based on a copy of the Original Manuscripts or the Masoretic Text. Using copy and paste of various Scriptures from KJV, NIV, reprinting from Strong's Exhaustive Concordance and information found online from the Wikipedia Encyclopaedia.

vii   Preface

2   Chapter 1: Opening Statement, Dedication, The Bible and You and Who Agrees with the Holy Bible?

12   Chapter 2: Who Is Satan and What Are the Three Earth Ages?

54   Chapter 3: God's Verbal Drawing What is it? An elephant? A hippopotamus? A giraffe?

67   Chapter 4: Noah's Flood

84   Chapter 5: Understanding the inspired Word Of God

131   Chapter 6: Who Did Cain Marry?

138   Chapter 7: The Garden of Eden and Apple or the Truth

165   Chapter 8: Paul, Our Sinful Nature, Rapture, Christ's Second Coming

174   Chapter 9: Where Did All the Races Come From?

179　Chapter 10: Did the Races Survive Noah's Flood?

184　Chapter 11: History of the Bible and Moses

192　Chapter 12: Rightly Dividing the Word

200　Chapter 13: What Is Judaism, Who Are the Jews, Why Did They Reject Jesus?"

211　Chapter 14: Does the Holy Bible Teach Discrimination or Racism?

219　Chapter 15: Who Was or Is Jesus? Why Did He Come?

228　Chapter 16: Is Jesus Coming Again? Is There a Rapture First?

236　Chapter 17: What Is Born Again or From Above and Baptism?

244　Chapter 18: Which Church Is Best? Is Tithing Required by Christians?

251　Chapter 19: What Foods Are We to Eat or Reject?

256　Chapter 20: The Real Easter Story

262　Chapter 21: The Christmas Story

272　Chapter 22: Final Word

281　About the Author

The
Key
Turned
And
The Truth of Understanding was Revealed.
My Eyes Were Opened I could
See
And
Hear
The
Words
Of
God
My
Soul
Jumped
For
Joy

Amen.

Carl Verner Cederberg

Special Thanks to many Evangelists.

Billy Graham
Oral Roberts
Rex Humbard
Garner Ted Armstrong
Allan Dunbar
Charles Price
Arnold Murray
Denis Murray

Preface

The words of the Bible will be *in Italics* as well as words of Jesus, Strong's Dictionary, Smith's Bible Dictionary and quotes from the Apocrypha.

Ephesians 6: 17. And take the helmet of salvation, and the sword of the Spirit, which is the word of God: John 1:1 In the beginning was the Word, and the Word_was with God, and the Word was God 14. And the Word was made flesh, and dwelt among us; this is Emanuel or Jesus the Christ.

When Jesus was twelve years old it is recorded in the New Testament of the Holy Bible; *Luke 2:42. And when he was twelve years old; 46. And it came to pass, that after three days they found him in the temple, sitting in the midst of the doctors, both hearing them, and asking them questions. 47. And all that heard him were astonished at his understanding and answers.*

Jesus only had their Scrolls of the Old Testament as his reference. Later in: *Matthew 19: 4. And he answered and said unto them, Have ye not read, that he which made them at the beginning made them male and female;* By this very verse Jesus validated the OT all the way back to the beginning.

Jesus stated in; *Matthew 5:18. For verily I say unto you, till heaven and earth pass, one jot or one tittle shall in no wise pass from the law, till all be fulfilled.*

Revelation 22:18. For I testify unto every man that hears the words of the prophecy of this book, If any man shall add unto these things, God shall add unto him the plagues that are written in this book: 19. And if any man shall take away from the words of the book of this prophecy, God shall take away his part out of the book of life, and out of the holy city, and from the things which are written in this book.

Paul who also had only the Old Testament to reference wrote to Timothy in a letter *3:15. And that from a child you have known the holy scriptures, which are able to make you wise unto salvation through faith which is in Christ Jesus. 16. All scripture is given by inspiration of God, and is profitable for doctrine, for reproof, for correction, for instruction in righteousness: 17. That the man of God may be perfect, thoroughly furnished unto all good works.*

Some of the newer printed Holy Bibles have removed or changed that Jesus, was Gods Son and any reference to *John 3:16. "For God so loved the World that he gave his only begotten Son, that whosoever believeth in him should not perish, but have everlasting life".* They may not contain the <u>Key words or phrases</u>.

This study of the Word is based on a copy of the Original Manuscripts known as the Masoretic Text, with the Strong's numbering system enabling the reader to <u>look up alternate translation of a word from Hebrew or Greek to English</u>.

Some of my critics have said: You have taken the Bible scripture's far too literal in your writings! My reply; Jesus said several times *"Have you not read"* validating every word or phrase found in the scriptures. He later said*: Mark 13:23. So be on your guard; I have told you everything ahead of time. Paul wrote: 2 Thessalonians 2: 17. Encourage your hearts and strengthen you <u>in</u> every good deed and* *word. 2 Timothy 2:9. Wherein I suffer trouble, as an evil doer, even unto bonds; <u>but the word of God is not bound</u>. Every word is sacred!*

This book may not be well received by those Preachers or Churches that have been taught religion based on a single verse here and a verse there or a prescribed doctrine or dogma that they must follow. Many take one verse and then spin a story to make you feel good! Hopefully these writings will help you find the key to understand the Word be it literal or just fact. The Word or writings of the 36+ God inspired authors on three continents; Africa Asia and Europe over a period of 1500 years; hold a key or like a piece of a jigsaw puzzle when we connect a subject as revealed by various scribes or authors, we see the whole picture or a deeper truth. All we need to do is seek and recognize key phrases. It is free.

Jesus only approved two out of seven churches in Revelation chapter 2 and 3, the Church in Smyrna and the Church in Philadelphia.

Those who have felt there must be more to what they have been taught or only read the Bible once are the ones I hope this book will offer the inspiration to look for the deeper complete story and truth and be able to follow the various subjects recorded by the thirty-six different inspired writers of <u>God's letter to us</u> found in the pages of the Holy Bible.

I have used a copy of the Original Manuscripts, the 1611 KJV, the NIV, Smith's Bible Dictionary, and the Strong's Concordance to unlock the deeper story to the best of my ability, but realize I have only begun my journey.

I fully endorse the Ten Commandments including the fourth regarding the Sabbath or day of rest. Because of His work on the cross, Jesus became our Passover or day of rest Christians now revere God any or every day of the week.

Matthew 11: 29. Take my yoke upon you, and learn of me; for I am meek and lowly in heart: and ye shall find rest unto your souls.

As a Christian, my thirst for truth began in earnest in 1989 when I went to Israel and was baptized in the Jordan River.

This Book is not a Novel. Chapters may be read out of order [To get an insight you could skip ahead to Chapter 6 and read the first page] some scriptures may be found in every chapter tying all the subjects together.

Romans 11:8: (According as it is written, God hath given them the spirit of slumber, eyes that they should not see, and ears that they should not hear ;) unto this day.

1 Corinthians 2:10: But God hath revealed them unto by his Spirit: For the Spirit searches all things, yea, and the deep things of God.

AND THEIR EYES WERE OPENED AND THEY BEGAN TO HEAR THE WORD OF GOD.

Matthew 7: 7: Ask, and it shall be given you; seek, and ye shall find: Knock and it shall be opened unto you.

Romans 3: 22-25. This righteousness from God comes through faith in Jesus Christ to all who believe. There is no difference, for all have sinned and fall short of the glory of God, and are justified freely by his grace through the redemption that came by Christ Jesus. God presented him as a sacrifice of atonement, through faith in his blood. He did this to demonstrate his justice, because in his forbearance he had left the sins committed beforehand unpunished—

Chapter 1

Opening Statement, Dedication, The Bible and You and Who Agrees with the Holy Bible?

Carl Verner Cederberg presents a book that has Key words or Phrases that Unlock subjects of the Bible to better aid believers in Christ to understand the deeper truths utilizing the Scriptures to answer questions such as: What or why: is the scripture telling us? Hopefully this book will open up Scriptures overlooked or not taught in traditional Dogma. Thus proving only with the inspiration of God could the 39 + different Authors and scribes collectively reveal to those with eyes to see asking for wisdom find the deeper truth in the letter or the Holy Bible written to us. Jesus validated the Old Testament.

For the contentious reader and those searching for a deeper understanding and truth, the student must search out and find a copy of the original manuscripts and rightly divide the word. To show how hard the translator's task was let us start with a few pages; a direct translation, it will be a challenge to understand.

The literal translations of scripture from the original manuscripts are as follows. Genesis *1:11. And said God Let sprout the earth tender sprouts, {the} plant seeding seed {and} of tree fruit producing fruit after its species, which it {is} in it on the earth. And it was so. 12. And gave birth to the earth tender sprouts {the} plant seeding seed after its species, and tree producing fruit which its {is} in it after its species. And saw God that {it was} good.* [Below we will read 2:5 certain shrubs were not created at this time which raises the Question! Why or what is the deeper truth?]

We now read of the creation of Mankind *1:27.And created God the mankind in His image, in the image of God He created him; male and female He created them.* [we read]*1:29 And said God, Behold, I have given to you every plant seeding seed which {is} on the surface of all the earth, and every tree which in it {is} fruit of {the} tree seeding seed. To you will it be for food,*

The Original Manuscripts had no chapters but for reasons why the printers started the 2nd chapter where they did seems to contradict the end of subject of creation. This is questionable to the astute reader rightly dividing the word. *Genesis 2:4. These are the generations of the heavens and of the earth when they were created, in the day that the Lord God made the earth and the heavens:* [This possibly should be the end of the Chapter.] the man whom he had formed in verse: 29. And caused to spring Yahveh God from the ground every tree pleasant to the sight and good for food. And the Tree of Life {was} in the middle of the garden and the Tree of the Knowledge of Good and Evil.

We read in verse 2:7. God creates the man Adam 'eth-'Ha' 'âdhâm and while he is sleeping he creates Eve from his rib, curve or DNA

With these verses and the other writings in this book the advanced student can glean that there is a creation of Mankind [male and female and like the creation of different trees animals and flowers the different races of Mankind would have also been created and lived on the whole dominion of the earth and were fruit pickers, hunters and fishermen] and then there is a formed man who is placed in a planted Garden on earth; a husbandman, a farmer/rancher. [This will be explained in the opening verses in Chapter 6.]

The subject will now change from a Creation to the forming phase. To help the student grasp the significance of what we are about to read let's consider: For clarification if we buy property in a city we build a home erect a fence plant grass and in a spot usually in the rear create or plant a vegetable Garden. God had created the trees and all living on the face of the earth or Eden up to Verse 2:6 but now as we return to scripture we read:

Genesis 2:7. And the Lord God formed man of the dust of the ground, and breathed into his nostrils the breath of life; and man became a living soul.

8. And the Lord God planted a garden eastward in Eden; and there he put the man whom he had formed.

It is very important and a key that unlocks the truth: God has planted a Garden in an area East of Eden. It will be referred to as the Garden of Eden but Eden was the whole earth. With this knowledge we could assume a new subject will begin and a new chapter would be more feasible starting with (again the Literal translation) *2:5. And every shrub of the field not yet it was on the earth and every plant of the field not yet it had sprung up, because not had rain sent Yahveh God on the earth, and a man was not to till - the ground.6.and a mist went up from the earth, and watered all the surface of the ground. 7. And formed Yahveh God the man {out of} dust from the ground, and blew into his nostrils {the} breath of life; and became the man a soul, living. 8. And planted Yahveh God a garden in Eden to the east; and put there {the man Adam}.*

I dedicate this book to those who ask: "Why was I born" "Is God real" and those who believe there is more to Gods word than taught in church and thirst for the truth.

NIV Genesis 1:1. In the beginning God created the heavens and the earth. : 2. Now the earth was* formless and empty, darkness was over the surface of the deep, and the Spirit of God was hovering over the waters.

Having purchased a New International Version of the Holy Bible I noticed that the word (was) had an * or asterisk, the second was in the same scripture had no asterisk. Looking at the bottom of the page, there was written * "or became."

Note! in the original manuscript there was no second "was" some Bibles correctly *italicize the second was* to denote that it was added for clarity.

This, along with various scriptures, caused me to think (what?) or question (why?) as an example KJV *Genesis 1:26. And God said, Let us make man in our image, after our likeness --. 27. So God created man in his own image, in the image of God created he him; male and female created he them. 28. And God blessed them, and God said unto them, be fruitful, and multiply, and replenish the earth, and subdue it: and have dominion over the fish of the sea, and over the fowl of the air, and over every living thing that moves upon the earth. And God said, Behold, I have given you every herb bearing seed, which is upon the face of all the earth, and every tree, that has fruit of a tree yielding seed; to you it shall be for meat [or for food].*

Why do we read later? *Genesis 2:5. -- "and there was not a man to till the ground* (Key)? Why is there a need for a farmer? This is a phrase that unlocks the Word to search for the deeper or rest of the story to those who have eyes to see and ears to hear.

Why is after Noah's flood in Genesis 10:1–7 the list of descendants of Noah is interrupted by verse 10:5 that mentions "the Gentiles divided in their lands"? Then we read Jesus in the Gospel of *John 8:44: "You are of your father the devil, and the lusts of your father you will do."* Were there other survivors of Noah's Flood? The Bible written by thirty-six inspired authors is like a jigsaw puzzle. When correlated, they can provide the Key or answer to a question or the solution to understanding.

Many scriptures or subjects may be repeated throughout the various chapters of this book to help tie the subject being covered with the rest of the book. The word small word (Key) may appear after a Key word or a Key revealing phrase helping to unlock important information later revealed to fully understand the deeper truth.

The Bible and You; the best way to start this study is to read a few scriptures [for these verses we will use for clarity the NIV] *1 Thimoty1: 3. As I urged you when I went into Macedonia, stay there in Ephesus so that you may command certain men not to teach false doctrines any longer 4. nor to devote themselves to myths and endless genealogies. These promote controversies rather than <u>God's work-- which is by faith</u>* (Key). (Gods letter to you). His letter has a simple truth from the beginning <u>that must be understood or the rest of the letter can become confusing</u>.

We read God created Mankind KJV *Genesis 1: 27. So God created man in his own image, in the image of God created he him; <u>male and female created he them</u>.* (Key)

In the original Manuscript the word for Male and Female or mankind is 'eth-'âdâm as opposed to just man 'âdâm we will read of The man Adam 'eth-'Ha'âdhâm (Key)later.

The created Mankind male and female have the whole earth to roam and their every need is provided for and they have dominion over everything.

Genesis 1:28. And God blessed them, and God said unto them: Be fruitful, and multiply, and replenish the earth, (Key) and subdue it: and have dominion over the fish of the sea, and over the fowl of the air, and over every living thing that moves upon the earth. 29. And God said, Behold, I have given you every herb bearing seed, which is upon the face of all the earth, and every tree, in the which is the fruit of a tree yielding seed; to you it shall be for meat.[or food]

Now a statement that most preachers gloss over but it holds the key to the truth and understanding of the beginning; *Genesis 2: 5. And every plant of the field before it was in the earth, and every herb of the field before it grew: for the Lord God had not caused it to rain upon the earth, and there was not a man to till the ground. (Key)*

Why would there be a need for a Husbandman or farmer? As we read for our self the scriptures of the Holy Bible we will find the answer to this Question.

Mankind has the whole earth that could well be identified as Eden the garden of God. Reference is found in *Ezekiel 28:13. Thou hast been in Eden the garden of God; (KEY)*

We now read in *Genesis 2:7. And the Lord God formed man of the dust of the ground, and breathed into his nostrils the breath of life; and man became a living soul.* [Here we read God formed The Man Adam 'eth-'Ha'âdhâm] [This formed man has no gender (Key) but we will read his DNA is split to form a helpmate Eve.]

: 8. And <u>the Lord God planted a garden</u> <u>eastward in Eden;</u> [Key] *and there he put the man whom he had formed.* [This man is restricted to a protected area as opposed to the created male and female 'eth-' âdâm who roamed the whole earth]

There are a few true Church's that teach this truth and is part of their Dogma. This will be discussed in depth several times in the various Chapters.

One of the main writers of the New Testament was Paul. Although he had never met Jesus [Jesus was crucified April 3, 30 AD] Paul before his name change from Saul and his conversion to Christianity in 37AD had persecuted the Christians and was part of the Group who stoned to death Steven who was the first Christian martyr 35 AD. Acts 6:5 and 10; -- They chose Stephen, a man full of faith and of the Holy Spirit -- These men began to argue with Stephen, but they could not stand up against his <u>wisdom or the Spirit by whom he spoke</u>. Steven in his last words in Acts chapter 7:1- 59. gives a brief history of the Old Testament.

In *1 Timothy 1:3. -- so that you may command certain men not to teach false <u>doctrines</u> any longer.* This gives us the perfect Segway to understand that the Holy Bible is a letter addressed from God directly to you.

Where most Christians go wrong is when they read the Bible they rely on the dogma of a church to explain the Bible whereas the bible explains or interprets itself to the reader who can rightly divide the word.

In this Book we will take up a subject and let the Bible a letter written by 36 + various inspired by God writers who may deal with a common subject and much like a jigsaw puzzle we must let the word explain itself to reveal the picture or the full story or truth.

The Holy Bible as stated above was written by various authors on three different continents with no contact with one another. *1 Timothy 2:3. This is good, and pleases God our Saviour, who wants all men to be saved and <u>to come to knowledge of the truth</u>. 2 Timothy 3:16. <u>All Scripture is God-breathed</u> and is useful for teaching, rebuking, correcting and training in righteousness, Revelation 1: 3. Blessed is the one who reads the words of this prophecy, and blessed are those who hear it and take to heart what is written in it, because the time is near.*

With this being said; my hope with the help and inspiration of the Holy Spirit; is that this book may help you find the truth in Gods letter to you for yourself.

Most scientists and archaeologists tend to agree that the earth is billions of years old and that there was an age when there were plants, trees, and huge animals, some capable of flying. They claim that the Dinosaurs, along with plant life from which we get coal and oil today, were destroyed by a huge comet that struck the earth. This also knocked the earth off its axis. We now have a true north and a magnetic North Pole. This slight shift in the axis has also created our four seasons. The striking of this huge comet on earth is thought to have caused a great cloud of dust that blotted out the sun and moon from the earth. The earth cooled and ice covered the earth and all forms of life perished. The dust took a long time to settle.

Some biblical scholars claim that the earth is only about seven thousand years old and that the Dinosaur, along with the plant life from which we get coal and oil, was destroyed and is the product of "Noah's flood". The evolutionists or atheists seem to want to believe in the scientists up to a point but claim that life then started from a single cell that split and ended up as mankind. [Here again you may want to Jump ahead to Chapter 6 and read the first page]

In this book, we will attempt to follow a subject and the connecting subjects in other chapters, searching for the deeper wisdom, written by the different authors who penned the inspired words of God to find the deeper truth. In Jesus's name we pray.

Father we ask for understanding and wisdom to present a deeper truth to these our readers. Thank you Father. Amen.

This book will not be well received by those who only have been taught religion by a preacher of a church that base their teachings on a single verse here and a verse there or a prescribed doctrine. Jesus only approved two out of seven churches in Revelation chapters 2 and 3. Those who have felt there must be more to what they have been taught or only read the Bible once are the ones I hope this book will serve as an inspiration to look for the deeper story and truth and be able to follow the various subjects recorded by the thirty-six different inspired writers of God's letter to us.

I have used a copy of the Original Manuscripts, the 1611 KJV of the Bible (words like thou have been changed to you etc.), the NIV is used to clarify scriptures but must follow the truth found in the O.M., Smith's Bible Dictionary, and the Strong's Concordance to unlock the deeper story to the best of my ability. I fully endorse the Ten Commandments including the fourth regarding the Sabbath or day of rest.

Jesus said in *Matthew 11:28*, *"Come unto me, all ye that labour and are heavy laden, and I will give you rest."* Jesus became our Passover or High Sabbath in *1 Corinthians 5:7*: *"For even Christ our Passover is sacrificed for us: as a true Christian every day with Jesus and the Holy spirit in our heart and mind is our Sabbath Day"* and in *Luke 23:54*, *"It was Preparation Day, and the Sabbath was about to begin."* Then we learn in *John 19:31*: *"Now it was the day of Preparation, and the next day was to be a special Sabbath. Because the Jews did not want the bodies left on the crosses during the Sabbath, they asked Pilate to have the legs broken and the bodies taken down. "They pierced Jesus's side and blood and water flowed so they knew he was dead and no need to break his legs.*

As a Christian, my thirst for truth began in earnest in 1989. In 1995, I traveled to Israel and was given the title "JERUSALEM PILGRIM" by the Jewish mayor. I was baptized at the traditional baptismal site of Jesus in the Jordan River by total immersion. Two pastors were present and laid hands on me. I did not receive the gift of tongues, but we all receive a gift: 1 Corinthians 12:4–11. I believe mine was *"To one there is given through the Spirit the message of wisdom, to another the message of knowledge by means of the same Spirit."* At this printing, I am eighty-one years + of age.

Chapter 2
Who Is Satan and What Are the Three Earth Ages?

Before we start our study of the main subject of this chapter, consider this scenario based solely on the preponderance of basic logic having hopefully rightly dividing the Word. Once we have come to the conclusion there are three earth ages recorded we may make the assumption that God has no gender and the angels were created without gender and were in angelic bodies roaming the first earth age with the Dinosaurs. Reference:

1. 1 Corinthians 15: 38. But God gives it a body as he has determined, and to each kind of seed he gives its own body. Verse: 40. There are also heavenly bodies and there are earthly bodies; but the splendour of the heavenly bodies is one kind, and the splendour of the earthly bodies is another.

2. Job 40: 15. "Look at the behemoth, which I made along with you and which feeds on grass like an ox. [This is covered in chapter 3. Gods verbal picture]

In the second earth age God created the 6th day mankind with gender male and female but in his basic image; *Genesis 1:27. Then he formed The Man Adam 'eth-'Ha' âdhâm and while he slept he took part of his DNA and formed Eve Genesis 2:21. And the Lord God caused a deep sleep to fall upon Adam, and he slept: and he took one of his ribs, and closed up the flesh instead thereof;*

We read the following in the book; *Revelation 20:1–2: "And I saw an angel come down from heaven, having the key of the bottomless pit and a great chain in his hand. And he laid hold on the dragon, that old serpent, which is the devil, and Satan, and bound him a thousand years."* We can tie this to a verse in the Old Testament—*Isaiah 14:12–13. "How you have fallen from heaven, O Lucifer, son of the morning! How you are cut down to the ground, you who did weaken the nations! For you have said in your heart, I will ascend into heaven, I will exalt my throne above the stars of God."* This name Lucifer for Satan will be validated as we continue with our study. In Genesis, we learn that Satan was referred to or represented by a tree:

Genesis 2:9. And the LORD God made all kinds of trees grow out of the ground—trees that were pleasing to the eye and good for food. In the middle of the garden were two trees the tree of the knowledge of good and evil representing Satan and the tree of life representing Jesus

Genesis 2:15-17. And the Lord God took the man, and put him into the Garden of Eden to dress it and to keep it. And the Lord God commanded the man, saying, of every tree of the garden you may freely eat: But of the tree of the knowledge of good and evil, you shall not eat of it: for in the day that you eat of it you shall surely die

Satan used his good side to attract Eve then his evil side take over; here we can ask the question.1. Why was that old serpent, the devil or Satan, related to evil? Was he the reason for the end of the first earth age?

For years, I was confused by the word Tyre, which was used three times in the NIV and only once in KJV. In the NIV; *1 King 5:1. "When Hiram king of Tyre"*; then in *Ezekiel 28:2, Son of man, say to the ruler of Tyre and in Ezekiel 28:12 "Son of man, take up a lament concerning the king of Tyre and say to him: This is* *what the Sovereign LORD says: You were the model of perfection, full of wisdom and perfect in beauty. 13. You were in <u>Eden the garden of God</u>.'" Was the whole earth a garden? 14. You were anointed as a guardian cherub, for so I ordained you. You were on the holy mount of God; you walked among the fiery stones.*

Then we read in verse: *15. "You were blameless in your ways from the day you were created <u>till wickedness was found in you</u>."* As we continue our study we will learn this was Satan and God had put him in charge or as a ruler a King of the first age. In the KJV, *1 Kings 5:1 says, "And Hiram king of Tyre"; in Ezekiel 28:2. "Son of man, say unto the prince of <u>Tyrus</u>"; and in Ezekiel 28:12, "Son of man, take up a lamentation upon the king of <u>Tyrus</u>."* Looking up the word Tyre in the Smith's Bible Dictionary and then the Strong's Concordance, we find that the two words are related to the word platypus or old <u>Tyre</u> and are interchangeable, but the student of the Bible must rightly divide the word.

Strong's no. 6865 Transliterated: Tsor Phonetic: tsore Text: or Tsowr

{tsore}; the same as 6864; a rock; Tsor, a <u>place in Palestine</u>:—<u>Tyre, Tyrus</u>. tsur. See 6697. Strong's Number: 6697 Transliterated: tsuwr Phonetic: tsoor Text: or tsur {tsoor}; from 6696; properly, a cliff (or sharp rock, as compressed); generally, <u>a rock</u> or boulder; figuratively, a refuge; also an edge (as precipitous):—edge, X (mighty) <u>God</u> (one), rock, X sharp, stone, X strength, X strong.

When the word Rock is capitalized it is reference to <u>God</u>. Just "<u>rock</u>" is reference to a false or manmade <u>god</u> It is now quite evident that "Tyre" in 1 Kings is referring to a king of a place in Palestine. We will later connect the word <u>Rock</u> to God and an evil rock to Satan. When we read of "Tyre" in the NIV, Ezekiel 28:2:

"Son of man, say to the ruler of Tyre, 'this is what the Sovereign LORD says: In the pride of your heart you say, <u>I am a god</u>; I sit on the throne of a god in the heart of the seas. <u>But you are a man and not a god</u>, though you think you are as wise as a god.'"

Then in *Ezekiel 28:12–18: Son of man, take up a lament concerning the king of Tyre and say to him: This is what the Sovereign LORD says: You were the model of perfection, full of wisdom and perfect in beauty.*

<u>You were in Eden, the garden of God</u>; every precious stone adorned you: ruby, topaz and emerald, chrysolite, onyx and jasper, sapphire, turquoise and beryl. Your settings and mountings were made of gold; <u>on the day you were created</u> they were prepared. <u>You were anointed as a guardian cherub</u>, for so I ordained you. You were on the holy mount of God; you walked among the fiery stones. <u>You were blameless in your ways</u> from the day you were created <u>till</u> <u>wickedness was found in you</u>. Through your widespread trade you were filled with violence, and you sinned. So I drove you in disgrace from the mount of God, and I expelled you, guardian cherub, from among the fiery stones.

Your heart became proud on account of your beauty, and you corrupted your wisdom because of your splendour. So I threw you to the earth; I made a spectacle of you before kings. By your many sins and dishonest trade you have desecrated your sanctuaries.

Here we have read that Satan was created and was in <u>Eden; The Garden of God</u> this could be the first age as the whole world is a garden. We also read in Genesis that Satan was recorded as being in the smaller confines of <u>the planted Garden of Eden</u> created in the second age! The whole earth at one time was; <u>The Garden of God</u>? Reference to the 2nd age; *Genesis 2: 8. Now the LORD God had <u>planted</u>* (Key) *<u>a garden in the east, in Eden</u>;*

We can also glean from scripture <u>the word rock</u> which when used in the song of Moses, *Deuteronomy 32: 3 "I will proclaim the name of the LORD. Oh, praise the greatness of our God! 4. <u>He is the Rock</u>, his works are perfect, and all his ways are just. A faithful God who does no wrong, upright and just is he"* and *Deuteronomy 32:30 "How should one chase a thousand, and two put ten thousand to flight, except their Rock had sold them, and the Lord had shut them up?31 For their <u>rock</u> is not like our rock.* We can now safely assume <u>their "rock" is not God but is the rock or Satan, the evil one.</u>

With this information, we can rightly divide the word and move on to the study, "The Three Earth Ages." To help understand what we have read above "on the day you were created," Satan was "anointed as a guardian cherub, for so I ordained you. You were on the holy mount of God [in "The Garden of God" the first age!]; you walked among the fiery stones." There are no fiery stones recorded in "The Planted Garden of Eden" in the second earth age where God placed the man he had formed 'eth-'Ha' âdhâm "The Man Adam" who had no gender.

We can also reference the creation of Satan in the first age by a statement in Job: "Look at the behemoth, which <u>I made along with you</u> and which feeds on Grass like an ox." We will learn later that this had to be a Dinosaur. Satan was in charge of the first age, *Ezekiel 28: 14. You were anointed as a guardian cherub, for so I ordained you. You were on the holy mount of God; you walked among the fiery stones.* <u>But when he wanted to take the place of God, God destroyed the first age.</u> One-third of the inhabitants followed Satan; we can read of them in Revelation! 12:4 and 9: *"His tail swept a third of the stars out of the sky and flung them to the earth"* and *"The great dragon was hurled down—that ancient serpent* *called the devil, or Satan, who leads the whole world astray. He was hurled to the earth, <u>and his angels with him</u>."* Jesus also said, *"On this rock I will build my church."* By rock, he meant on this truth. With this brief bit of information, we can begin our deeper study of the three earth ages.

Jesus validated the Old Testament when He said, *"Have you not read?"*

Proverbs 1:7: "The reverence of the Lord is the beginning of knowledge: but fools despise wisdom and instruction."

In this research and study of the Three Earth and Heaven Ages and other subjects or writings contained in this book, I will copy and paste actual biblical verses from the KJV (editing the KJV by only substituting you for thou, etc.) and the NIV of the Bible, notes from Strong's Exhaustive Concordance and excerpts from the online Wikipedia Encyclopaedia. The teaching of Jesus will be copied and pasted in black.

The Holy Bible is translated from the writings of thirty-six various God-inspired persons at different periods of time on three separate continents having way of direct communication. It is a very complex work of various subjects supporting one another with scriptures expanding throughout the Bible, thus explaining or revealing the whole truth.

Isaiah 28:10: "For precept must be upon precept, precept upon precept; line upon line, line upon line; here a little, and there a little." We must look for and follow the subject in the various writings and scriptures; this can be best understood when we realize God is the true Author while Moses, Matthew, Paul, and the others are the scribes or God-inspired writers.

As we study and assimilate the subjects written by these thirty-six Authors, we will glean that there is one heaven and one earth. The Bible also records that the earth is divided by major happenings or periods of time, thus revealing that there are three earth ages revealed within the writings.

The greater revelation: This study of scriptures should expel any truth to the theory of evolution. God has left us some evidence of the first age. Scientists and archaeologists continually now confirm his Word to the believers, but this confuses the atheists who waste his or her time trying to disprove God's Word.

When the Holy Bible was canonized, it was divided into a collection of books that were then divided into chapters and numbered verses. However, unlike a novel, the Bible is full of different subjects that reoccur throughout the Word. In order to follow the subject of the ages or eons, we will start with the first subject found in the Bible, "In the Beginning," the first hint of the first earth age. The second verse, we will learn, relates to the end of the first age.

KJV, *Genesis 1:1. "In the beginning God created the heaven and the earth .2. And the earth was* (Key) *without form, and void; and darkness was upon the face of the deep. And the Spirit of God moved upon the face of the waters."* We can verify that there was a first age by reading *Psalm 104:30: "You sent forth thy spirit, they are created: and you renewed* (Key) *the face of the earth."* For clarification is *NIV 30: "When you send your Spirit, they are created, and you renew the face of the earth."* This renewal of the face of the earth could be our first clue! As we get deeper into this study, scripture will reveal more evidence of the three ages.

Then a new or second subject starts *in Genesis 1:3: "And God said, 'Let there be light,' and there was light."* With this scripture, we enter a new subject; God has begun his work and started the "Creation," the beginning of the second earth age. In this second age after the creation, we are born of women with a free will. Could our soul and spirit have existed in the first age in a spiritual form? We will be given an earthly physical body in this age! The answer that is revealed will astonish some.

We find Dinosaur bones with even their flesh, but no human remains from this age! Were we in angelic form? We can find an answer by reading in *Job 40:15, KJV, "Behold now behemoth, which I made with thee; he eats grass as an ox"* and *NIV "Look at the behemoth, which I made along with you and which feeds on grass like an ox."* In the *NIV, 2 Corinthians 4:4: "The god of this age has blinded the minds of unbelievers so that they cannot see the light of the gospel of the glory of Christ,* [Notice that god is not capitalized; therefore it represents Satan and take note *of "this age"* in the KJV it is *"the god of this world"* both the NIV and KJV support there was a separate first age.] The verse continues: *4:4 who is the image of <u>God</u>."* God here was capitalized. This subject is also covered in the study "God's Verbal Picture."

We read in Genesis *1:27. "So God created man in his own image, in the image of God created he him; male and female created he them. 28. And God blessed them, and God said unto them, be fruitful, and multiply, <u>and replenish the earth</u>.* (Key)" The word replenish is only found in the KJV. The following appears in Strong's Concordance Dictionary:

Strong's no. 4390 Text: or malae (Esth. 7:5) {maw-law}; a primitive root, to fill or (intransitively) be full of, in a wide application (literally and figuratively):—accomplish, confirm, + consecrate, be at an end, be expired, be fenced, fill, fulfill, (be, become, X draw, give in, go) full(-ly, -ly set, tale), [over-]flow, fullness, furnish, gather (selves, presume, replenish, satisfy, set, space, take a [hand-]full, +have wholly.

Most people would concede that the word replenish would mean that there was something before suggesting a previous age? KJV Genesis 1:28 says, *"And replenish the earth."* Could this use of the Hebrew word be our second clue to the truth of the three earth ages? Some biblical scholars' say that the earth is only about seven thousand years old and the deeply buried Dinosaur along with the plant life produced the coal and oil and is the product of Noah's flood that took place approximately five thousand years ago?

Most scientists and archaeologists tend to agree that the world is millions of years old and at one period of time there were plants, trees, and huge animals and that the Dinosaur, along with plant life, decayed and produced coal and oil. They have also agreed or concluded that they were destroyed by a huge comet that struck the earth. The dust blotted out the sun's rays that heated up the earth. The temperature dropped, and the earth froze up and ended the age. This tremendous impact rocked the earth off its axis, thus explaining why we now have a true north and a magnetic North Pole.

The evolutionists and the atheists seem to want to believe in the scientist up to a point but claim that life started from a single cell that split and ended up as the various animals. Some stayed the same, but one animal, the ape/monkey, kept evolving into mankind. All of their findings of the missing link have been debunked and discredited, but they still hang on to this theory and search for answers. We still have monkeys, apes, and humans that for centuries have not evolved but remained the same. Perhaps they should look into the oceans and looking for a mermaid. [Here again you may want to Jump ahead to Chapter 6 and read the first page].

In this exploration of His Word, we will follow a subject or subjects, unraveling and piecing together the information from various scriptures or writings by the various God-inspired authors of the Holy Text, thus revealing the reason for the three earth ages much life a jigsaw puzzle. One last thought: how long does it take to produce real diamonds?

<u>We now can ask the question:
Does the Bible support a teaching
of the three earth ages?</u>

The Holy Bible will reveal this to those who seek and connect the information about the ages. There is much written about the past, the present, and the future. The past (first age) was billions of years ago. The present (second age) is our time on earth in our physical earthly bodies. The future (third age) is the new heaven and earth age (Rev. 21:1).

Part 1. Follows the subject "In the Beginning."

Part 2. The fall of Satan and the end of the first age.

Part 3. We start a new subject, "Creation," the start of the second age.

Part 4. We read of the third Age.

Part 5. Varies scriptures of the various ages.

Part 6. I hope to show that the Holy Bible teaches in this second age that we are born of women with a free will, to choose to love as taught by God and his Son Jesus, or follow Satan's way of lies and deceit, our sinful nature.

Before we actually get into our deeper study, let's first get a brief outline of the subject—the three earths and heaven ages and glean some deeper knowledge by connecting the various scriptures written throughout the Word. This should lead us to consider or understand that all souls were part of the first age, possibly angelic or spiritual beings, and that Satan was put in charge of the first age. We will learn from the scriptures that Lucifer/Satan had become so overcome in his beauty and his standing that he wanted to be equal to or even replace God.

Was this the main cause for the end of the first earth age? At that time, one-third of the souls followed Satan to await their faith until in this second age:

Revelations 12:3.And there appeared another wonder in heaven; and behold a great red dragon [one of many names for the Serpent or Satan] *having even heads and ten horns, and seven crowns upon his heads. 4. And his tail drew the third part of the stars of heaven, and did cast them to the earth*

Revelations 12:9. And the great dragon was cast out, that old serpent, called the devil, and Satan, which deceives the whole world: he was cast out into the earth, and his angels were cast out with him.

These three verses speak of Satan and his followers. Satan is presently held in heaven, but a part of Satan's spirit still roams this second earth age to deceive many. As false prophets, scholars, and as teachers, they will deceive many until the antichrist appears and will take them under his wing.

The first verse of Genesis covers the beginning of the first age; the second verse speaks of its end, which was a total destruction, as we will uncover, and not just a cleansing of the first earth age. We have read or will read of Noah's flood, which only killed the Nephilim's and their offspring who tried to taint the seed line to Christ in the second age, but life continued (Gen. 6:4).

At this point in our study, may we ask the Father for wisdom to open our eyes, to lead us into his deeper truth, rightly dividing his Word, in the name of Jesus Christ we pray. Amen.

2 Timothy 2:15. Study to show yourself approved unto God, a workman that needs not to be ashamed, rightly dividing the word of truth.2 Tim 3:16. All scripture is given by inspiration of God, and is profitable for doctrine, for reproof, for correction, for instruction in righteousness Psalms 19:14. Let the words of my mouth, and the meditation of my heart, be acceptable in your sight, O Lord, my strength, and my redeemer.

Genesis 1:1. <u>In the beginning</u> God created the heaven and the earth. This was a time before the first earth age. As we learn by reading;

In *Proverbs 8:12, "I wisdom dwell with prudence, and find out knowledge of witty inventions." To understand that this was before the first age, Proverbs 8:22 to verse: 29. The Lord possessed me <u>in the beginning</u> of his way, before his works of old. I was set up from everlasting, <u>from the beginning</u>, before <u>the earth was</u>. When there were no depths, I was brought forth; when there were no fountains abounding* *with water. Before the mountains were settled, before the hills was I brought forth: While as yet he had not made the earth, nor the fields, nor the highest part of the dust of the world.* <u>*When he prepared the heavens, I was there:*</u> *when he set a compass upon the face of the depth: When he established the clouds above: when he strengthened the fountains of the deep: When he gave to the sea his decree that the waters should not pass his commandment.*

We can read of the first earth age in the book of *Job. Job 38: 4–7. Where were you when I laid the foundations of the earth? Declare, if you have understanding. Who laid the measures thereof, do you know? Or who had stretched the line upon it? Whereupon are the foundations thereof fastened? Or who laid the corner stone thereof; when the morning stars sang together, and all the sons of God shouted for joy?*

The sons of God could be angelic beings and were present in the first age, along with the Dinosaurs, as we can read in *Job 39:15:* *"Look at the behemoth,* <u>*which I made along with you [the behemoth or dinosaurs had flesh-and-bone bodies]*</u> *and which feeds on grass like an ox."* Man was in spiritual bodies, not physical bodies in this first earth age. For reference see the index: "God's verbal picture."

We now follow the subject to the New Testament, *John 1:1–3: In the beginning was the Word, and the Word was with God,* <u>*and the Word was God.*</u> The same was in the beginning with God. All things were made by him; and without him was not anything made that was made.*

This relates to the first and second earth age. We now must divide the Word as we have a new subject, *John 1:6: "There came a man who was sent from God; his name was John. He is born of women and is in a flesh body. He came as a witness to testify concerning that light* [Jesus], *so that through him all men might believe.*" We now return to the previous subject, *John 1:14: "And the Word was made flesh, and dwelt among us."* This confirms that Jesus was Emanuel or God among us in this second earth age born of women in a physical body.

The apostle Paul wrote *2 Corinthians 12:2: "I knew a man in Christ about fourteen years ago, whether in the body, I cannot tell; or whether out of the body, I cannot tell: God knows; such a one was caught up to the <u>third heaven</u>* [or the coming third age]." Our first thought is, who might it be? How many times did God create the heaven and earth? <u>Answer:</u> We will, hopefully, through searching the scriptures find that the answer is that there are three different ages written about of both heaven and earth.

<u>Prelude to Heaven and Earth: A Deeper Study</u>

First age: <u>heaven and earth are linked together</u>. In Scripture, we find the first earth age became without form and void due to the rebellion or fall of Satan. There was no light, sun, or heat. Without light or heat, all living things perish: *"I looked at the earth, and it was formless and empty; and at the Heavens, and their light was gone" (Jer. 4:23)*. <u>The light was gone?</u> The earth is cast into total darkness—no sun, no moon or stars. Some scholars interpret this as part of the final tribulation, disregarding the earth that has become formless and empty! When Jesus returns according to Revelation 19:19–21, he will be at war with those who are alive and who have the mark of the beast. This is one more validation of the earth ages.

Second age: <u>earth will be restored and once again linked to heaven</u>. *Genesis 1:2. "And darkness was upon the face of the deep. And the Spirit of God moved upon the face of the waters.3. And God said, Let there be light: and there was light".*

God creates the physical man male and female to roam the earth, <u>but in the planted garden east of Eden</u>, (Key) God places the formed man 'eth-'Ha' 'âdhâm The Man Adam. Adam had close contact with God, but is separated after "the Sin." Adam was banished from the Garden and his direct relationship with God and now has to roam the earth. He and his descendants will become the Adamic race, and later <u>God will chose Adam's pure seed line or descendants as his chosen people from whom Jesus will be born</u>. [Here again you may want to Jump ahead to Chapter 6 and read the first page].

Genesis 2:7. And the Lord God formed man of the dust of the ground, and breathed into his nostrils the breath of life; and man became a living soul. 8. And the Lord God <u>planted a garden eastward in Eden</u>; and there he put the man whom he had formed.

Genesis 3:23. Therefore the Lord God sent him forth from the Garden of Eden, to till the ground from whence he was taken (Key). [Notice he was formed from the ground of Eden where the six day had been created and placed in a planted garden] *24. So he drove out the man; and he placed at the east of the garden of Eden Cherubims, and a flaming sword which turned every way, to keep the way of the tree of life.*

Jesus, who was the tree of life in the Garden, would sit on the right hand of God until God decides to give mankind a new hope when Jesus returns by a virgin birth, in a flesh body for thirty-three years, then sheds his blood on the cross, and returns to sit once again at the right hand of God; *1 Peter. 3:22. Who is gone into heaven, and is on the right hand of God; angels and authorities and powers being made subject unto him.*

Third age: <u>heaven and earth are once again linked together</u>. We must understand and rightly divide the word. Some preachers of the rapture theory falsely claim that "come up hither", in Revelation is the church being called up, but it was the disciple John who is called: *Rev. 4:1. After this I looked, and, behold, a door was opened in heaven: and the first voice which I heard was as it were of a trumpet talking with me; which said: Come up hither, and I will show thee things which must be hereafter.* [This is near the end of the second age]. *2. And immediately I was in the spirit: and, behold, a throne was set in heaven, and one sat on the throne.* How can they assimilate John's calling to their church being Raptured!

In: *Revelation 21:1. "And I saw a new heaven and a new earth: for the first Heaven and the first earth were passed away* [this might confuse some, but we must remember that John came from the second age]; *and there was no more sea."* The sea or water is the earthly flesh people of the second age.

To clarify this; *Revelation 17:15: "And he said unto me, the waters which you saw are peoples, and multitudes, and nations, and tongues." Revelation 21:2: "And I John saw the holy city, New Jerusalem, coming down from God out of heaven, prepared as a bride adorned for her husband."* New Jerusalem is in the third age. We can now begin an in-depth study and search the scriptures for the deeper truth God wants for those who seek.

Part 1
In the Beginning

The original manuscripts and the literal translation of verses are as follows: *Genesis 1:1 "In the beginning created God the heavens and the earth 2. And the earth was [Strong's number for was is1961] without form, and void; and darkness was upon the face of the deep. And the Spirit of God moved upon the face of the waters.* Note! That the number 1961 is inserted after the word was (Key); it is referring to a lexicon or a Strong's number. We will do an in-depth look into this word later.

The first earth age—"in the beginning"—could well be billions of years or more ago; we will glean the deeper truth as we study the word was depicted by the number 1961. It holds a very important key to understanding!

It will become clearer as we discover. God created Lucifer (Satan, the devil) and all the angels in the first earth age: *Ezek. 28:14–15 "You were anointed as a guardian cherub, for so I ordained you. You were on the holy mount of God; you walked among the fiery stones.* [The fiery stones reflect to a world of wonder the whole earth was a Garden at that period in time]. *You were blameless in your ways from the day you were created till wickedness was found in you"* This relates back to verse Gen. 1:2.

Ezekiel 28:2. Son of man, say to the ruler of Tyre, "This is what the Sovereign LORD says: 'In the pride of your heart you say, "I am a god; I sit on the throne of a god in the heart of the seas." But you are a man and *not a god, though you think you are as wise as a god."* "Seas" here is not water; it is a reference to the angelic people; here we can safely say Satan was put in charge of the first age. This period can relate to *Job 40:15. "Behold now behemoth, (Dinosaur) which I made with thee; he eats grass as an ox"* The reference to water is people*: Rev. 17:15. "The waters which you saw, where the whore sits are peoples".*

We can find another clue to the first earth age in the NT in *1 John 3:8: "He who does what is sinful is of the devil, because the devil has been sinning from the beginning.* We can also read that the whole world was a Garden." Also in Ezekiel 28:8 is the following*: "You were in Eden, The Garden of God."* Satan or the serpent was represented as a tree in the newly planted Garden of Eden that God had created in the second age. Adam was formed from the dust of the earth to till the soil. Satan is offered as a tree, but his fruit is lies. This is covered in depth in the study "Apple or Truth."

To help us in our journey for the deeper truth, we can glean a deeper insight by asking if Satan walked on earth in the first earth age: *Job 1:7 "The LORD said to Satan, 'Where have you come from?' Satan answered the LORD, 'From roaming through the earth and going back and forth in it".* Later we read in *Job 40:15: "Look at the behemoth, which I made along with you and which feeds on grass like an ox."* We will learn later the behemoth is a Dinosaur.

We can read in the New Testament that Satan's presence is an influence in this second age: KJV *1 Peter 5:8. Be sober, be vigilant;*

because your adversary the devil, as a roaring lion, walketh about, seeking whom he may devour: NIV *"Be self-controlled and alert. Your enemy the devil prowls around like a roaring lion looking for someone to devour"*

This behemoth had a huge tail as described in *Job 40:17. His tail sways like a cedar.* We find no animal in this second age with a long tail that looks like a Cedar tree, but we find the remains of these creatures labeled Dinosaurs and preserved in the earth. This is covered in the study "God's verbal picture."

As we dig deeper into the Word, we find another clue to the ages: KJV *Ps. 104:30 "You send forth your spirit, they are created: and thou renewed the face of the earth"* To better understand this verse we take a look at NIV*: "When you send your Spirit, they are created, and you renew (Key)the face of the earth."* This is a key verse. Looking back to KJV, Genesis 1:28 are we closer to considering or accepting the word replenish, as opposed to just the newer translations where the word fill is used? Were they to replenish or fill the earth and subdue it?

The Holy Bible was written by thirty-six or more different inspired scribes or authors at various periods of time located on three different continents. They were all inspired by one God, and each author provides a piece of the deeper truth much like a jigsaw puzzle. In this study, we will seek out the subject as recorded throughout the Bible and rightly divide the word and piece the information together to see the whole picture or deeper meaning.

This next segment will be a little repetitious, but we must be persistent to understand the deeper truth in His Word. The following writing is a copy as it would have appeared in the original manuscript, with Strong's numbers to enable the reader to check the translated words used that would have been written in Hebrew. To read, you must do so from right to left.

The word "was" #1961 will be part of our deeper study. Genesis Chapter 1:2 Strong's # 776 853 8064 430 1254 7225

: earth the and heavens the God created beginning the In .1

592 2822 92 8414 <u>1961</u> 776

on darkness and; <u>empty</u> and <u>form</u>

<u>without</u> <u>was</u> earth the and .2

5921 7363 430 7307 8415 6440

on gently moving God of spirit the and, deep the of face the

4325 6440

.waters the of surface the

Note! There is not the second was in the manuscript. The numbers work with Strong's Concordance, a Hebrew-to-English and Greek-to-English dictionary. Let's examine the three under-lined words above: Was, without form, and empty.

1. The word was: *Strong's. 1961 hayah, haw-yaw'; a prim, root [comp.1933; to exist, i.e. be or <u>become</u>, <u>come to pass</u> (always emphatic. and not a mere copula or auxiliary): -beacon, X altogether, be (-come accomplished, committed, like), break, cause, come (to pass). continue, do, faint, fall, + follow, happen. x have last pertain <u>quit</u> (one) self, require, x use*

   The words "come to pass" and "quit" suggest an end! But the end of what? Answer: The first age.

By all reasoning, the word *was* should be translated to the verb *become* or *became*.

2. without form: *"Strong's ref. no. 8414 Romanized tohuw Pronounced to'-hoo from an unused root meaning <u>to lie waste</u>; a desolation (of surface), i.e. desert; figuratively, a worthless thing; adverbially, in vain: KJV—confusion, <u>empty place</u>, <u>without form</u>, <u>nothing</u>, <u>(thing of) naught</u>, vain, vanity, waste, wilderness.*

   You cannot <u>lie waste or make desolate something</u> <u>unless</u> at one period of time <u>it had existed</u>! Again, *Genesis 1:2. "And the earth was (became) without form and empty."*

3. Empty: *Strong's no. 922 Transliterated: bohuw Phonetic: bo'-hoo Text: from an unused root (meaning to be empty); a vacuity, i.e. (superficially) <u>an undistinguishable ruin</u>—emptiness, <u>void</u>.*

   There had to be more than a flood or some other serious catastrophe to cause the earth to become empty or void—an empty place, without form, a nothing! In the beginning, God had formed the earth to be inhabited "not in vain" or void. In the book of Isaiah, was he in the following verse alluding to a deeper knowledge that he understood or possessed and was trying to share?

   Isaiah *45:18: "For thus said the Lord that created the heavens; God himself <u>whom formed the earth</u> and made it he established it, he created it <u>not in vain</u>, he formed it <u>to be inhabited</u>: I am the Lord; and there* *is none else."* This verse may have influenced the translators to use was instead of became as both are verbs, but which one leads to the truth.

Vain: *Strong's 8414 (in the Hebrew, tohuw, to-hoo;) from an unused root mean. to lie waste a desolation (of surface).i.e. desert; figs worthless thing; adv. in vain;—confusion, empty place, without form, nothing, (thing of) naught, vain, vanity, waste, wilderness.*

In the New Testament, we read KJV *2 Peter 3:5. "For this they willingly are ignorant of, that by the word of God the heavens were of old, and Standing out of the water and in the water: 6. whereby the world that then was, being overflowed with water, perished."* Note the phrases "the world," "that then was," and "perished. In NIV *3:6. "By these waters also the world of that time was deluged and destroyed."* This is and was plainly the end of the first age.

At this point, it might help to read *Genesis 6:5. And God saw that the wickedness of man was great in the earth, and that every imagination of the thoughts of his heart was only evil continually.6. And it repented the Lord that he had made man on the earth, and it grieved him at his heart.7. And the Lord said, I will destroy man whom I have created from the face of the earth; both man, and beast, and the creeping thing, and the fowls of the air; for it grieved me that I have made them.* [This was Noah's flood].

What we have just read what could be gleaned as two parallel scriptures. Genesis and 2 Peter. But God totally destroyed the first age when Satan tried to replace or be god. The next verse in Gen. God has second thoughts about his new creation. *Genesis*

6:8. "But Noah found grace in the eyes of the Lord. God saves two of every flesh"

Noah's flood takes place in the second earth age: we read that the world continues. As further proof, we can read of two separate floods: Noah's flood, which <u>receded slowly</u>, *Genesis 8:3. and the waters returned from off the earth continually: and after the end of the hundred and fifty days the waters were abated."*

Now read of the first-age flood or total destruction in *Psalm 104:6. "You covered it with the deep as with a garment; the waters stood above the mountains. 7. <u>But at your rebuke the waters fled,</u>*[(Key)] *at the sound of your thunder they took to flight."* The waters took flight, indicating not slowly but very rapidly! To clarify is *Psalm 18:15. "The valleys of the sea were exposed and the foundations of the earth laid bare <u>at your rebuke, O LORD, at the blast of breath from your nostrils.</u>"* The sea or waters fled.[(Key)] Once we can separate these two floods, the new open-minded reader will find several times where the first age is revealed as they read through the Bible. We can even read of God's verbal picture, the description of the Dinosaurs in Job with its tail like the huge Cedar tree of Lebanon, Solomon used these cedars for beams so they had to be long, not curly or short as false teachers preach, claiming the behemoth was an elephant or hippopotamus or a giraffe. In *Job 40:15. It says, "Behold now behemoth, which I made with thee; he eats grass as an ox."* In NIV is as follows: *"Look at the behemoth, which I made along with you and which feeds on grass like an ox."* You can find the truth in the chapter; "God's verbal picture."

When or if Moses was inspired to write the book of Job it is hard to decide if this was in the first or the second age as Job has a wife. Was Job in a flesh body and married; hinting it could be in the second earth age. Satan and the sons of God are in spiritual bodies. *Job 1:6. Now there was a day when the sons of God came to present themselves before the Lord, [here this would be in the spiritual realm] and Satan came also among them. 7 And the Lord said unto Satan, where have you come from?* [Satan tempted Jesus in the wilderness and on roof of the temple]. *Then Satan answered the Lord, and said, from going to and fro in the earth, and from walking up and down in it. 8. And the Lord said unto Satan, have you considered my servant Job, there is none like him in the earth, a perfect and an upright man, one that fears God, and shuns evil?*

As we read this inspired story, Satan will try to redeem himself from his actions or failure in the first earth age by eluding that no one could be perfect. Satan then challenges God, claiming that He had isolated Job from the pressures of the world. God accepts his challenge: Job has no knowledge about what is about to happen.

Job 1:12. And the Lord said unto Satan, behold, all that he has is in your power; only upon Job put not forth your hand. So Satan went forth from the presence of the Lord. Satan will even try to get Job's wife to convince Job to denounce God. *Job 2:9. His wife said to him, "Are you still holding on to your integrity? Curse God and die!"*

The serpent/Satan in the planted garden east of Eden had tempted and beguiled Eve and brought forth the sinful and disobedient nature to mankind. Satan is allowed to torment and influence Job's friends in his attempt to try to break Job's faith in God in the next thirty-six chapters, trying to get Job to denounce God and thus follow a sinful nature as Satan had done in the first earth age. Satan loses his freedom to roam after he tempts

Jesus. In Matthew 4:10, Jesus said to him, *"Away from me."* In Revelation 12:7, Satan will return to the earth.

Part 2
The Fall of Satan and the End of the First Age

We have read *Genesis 1:2 "And the earth was (became) without form and void,"* the end of the first earth age, *and "darkness was upon the face of the deep and the Spirit of God moved upon the face of the waters."* This was caused, as we will read, by the rebellion of Lucifer or Satan—<u>a total destruction of the first earth age</u>. Satan and one-third of his followers end up somewhere in the heavenly realm. In Jude verse 6. "And the angels who kept not their first estate, but left their own habitation, he has reserved in everlasting chains under darkness unto the judgment of the great day." Or when they war with Michael in Revelation 12:7, they will be cast out with Satan, as recorded in *Revelation 12:4: "And his tail drew the third part of the stars of heaven and did cast them to the earth."* His tail can be considered his lies; a third had believed him and followed him in the first age. *Rev. 12:9. "And the great dragon was cast out, that old serpent, called the Devil, and Satan, which deceived the whole world.* In this verse, it is confirmed;. The dragon, old serpent, the devil, and Satan are one.

Satan deceived the whole world? This validates the first earth age. In this second age <u>he will be cast out into the earth and his angels</u> were cast out with him".

We now return to the Bible account of Satan's demise and the end of the first earth age in *Isaiah 14:12*. *"How are you fallen from heaven* [today we pray "on earth as it is in Heaven"], *O Lucifer, son of the morning! How are you cut down to the ground* [the verse continues speaking of how Satan had caused the end of the first age]. *But here which didst weaken the nations!"* In the NIV, this part of the verse reads, *"You who once laid low the nations!"* In the OM, this part of the verse reads, *"Who weakens on the nations."* We might need some help here to get the true meaning.

Weakens; *Strong's no. 2522 Phonetic: khaw-lash' Text: a primitive root; to prostrate; by implication, to overthrow, decay:—discomfit, waste away, weaken.*

With this information, we can understand "who weakens the nations." Satan was the cause for the overthrow or the wasting away or the destruction of the nations or the first earth age.

Let's look at the KJV version again with this information in *Isaiah 14:12. How you are fallen from heaven, O Lucifer, son of the morning! How you are cut down to the ground, which didst weaken* (wasted away) the nations!" This was the downfall of Satan and caused the end to the first earth age. This will become more evident as we rightly divide the Word. It is written verses *14:13. For thou hast said in your heart, I will ascend into heaven, I will exalt my throne above the stars of God: I will sit also upon the mount of the congregation, in the sides of the north: 14. I will ascend above the heights of the clouds; I will be like the most High. 15. Yet thou shalt be brought down to hell, to the sides of the pit. 16. they that see thee shall narrowly look upon thee, and consider thee, saying, Is this the man that made the earth to tremble, that did shake kingdoms; 17.*

That made the world as a wilderness, and destroyed the cities thereof; that opened not the house of his prisoners?

Having read this last verse, can there be any doubt that Lucifer or Satan had caused the end of the first earth age? This is not Noah's flood as some might teach. This also can be found *in Jeremiah 4:24. "I beheld the mountains, and, lo, they trembled."* We will cover this in depth later.

We now need to look at some other supporting scripture that speaks of Satan's creation and fall and the reason behind the end of the first earth age. Who is "the king of Tyrus/Tyre"? It will become evident later that this is Satan, but for now, we can learn from a word study:

> *Tyre. Strong's ref. no. 6866 Romanized tsarab Pronounced tsaw-rab' a primitive root; to burn: KJV—burn.*

We can now identify and realize that he is the "king of burn"; he will also become the king of the lake of fire. *Rev. 20:10 "And the devil that deceived them was cast into the lake of fire and brimstone, where the beast and the false prophet are"*

Our search for truth will continue as we read more of "the king of Tyrus/Tyre" or Satan's creation and downfall in *Ezekiel 28:11–13: "Moreover the word of the Lord came unto me, saying, "Son of man, take up a lament concerning the king of Tyre and say to him: 'This is what the Sovereign LORD says: "You were the model of perfection, full of wisdom and perfect in beauty. <u>You were in Eden, The Garden of God</u>; we can assume and now confirm that the whole world was a Garden."*

God will recreate or plant a garden in the second age: (Gen 2:8) <u>*"And the Lord God planted a garden eastward in Eden; and*</u>

there he put ('eth-'Ha' 'âdhâm) the man whom he had formed."
Rightly dividing the Word, we can realize in the Garden of Eden
that Satan is depicted as a tree leading some preachers to falsely
teach about an apple. This is covered in depth in the study of
the chapter "Apple or Truth." Back to; *Ezekiel 28:12. "You were
the model of perfection.* [This was the creation of Satan.] *Every
precious stone adorned you: ruby, topaz and emerald, chrysolite, onyx
and jasper, sapphire, turquoise and beryl. Your settings and mountings
were made of gold; on the day you were created they were prepared."*

The whole earth was a Garden. The king of Tyre or Satan
had every part of the beauty God had created. Here, Satan is on
earth in the first age, along with the Dinosaurs. We will read of
them in Job 40:17. This is fully covered in the chapter, "God's
Verbal Picture."

In *Ezekiel it is written: 28:14. You art the anointed cherub that
covers and I have set you so: you were upon the holy mountain of God;
you have walked up and down in the midst of the stones of fire. 15.
You were perfect in your ways from the day that you were created, till
iniquity was found in thee. 16. By the multitude of your merchandise
they have filled the midst of you with violence, and thou have sinned:
therefore I will cast you as profane out of the mountain of God: and
I will destroy you, O covering cherub, from the midst of the stones of
fire. 17. Your heart was lifted up because of your beauty; you have corrupted your wisdom by reason of your brightness: I will cast you to the
ground. I will lay you before kings, that they may behold you.* [The
next 2verses are related to the end of the second earth] *18. You
have defiled your sanctuaries by the multitude of your iniquities, by
the iniquity of your ways; therefore will I bring forth a fire from the
midst of you, it shall devour you, and I will bring you to ashes upon*

the earth in the sight of all them that behold you.19. All they that know you among the people shall be astonished at you: you shall be a terror, and never shall you be any more.

These last 2verses are related to the end of the second earth age when Satan Rev. *20:2. "the dragon, that ancient serpent, who is the devil, or Satan"* Rev.(20:10) *was thrown into the lake of burning sulphur.* This is speaking of the final lake of fire. This will be the final end or demise of Satan.

Let us continue our study of the end of the first age caused by Satan's rebellion by examining 2 Peter 3:5–13. These verses speak of <u>all three ages</u>. As a general guide: Verses 5 and 6 covers the first earth age*: "But they deliberately forget that long ago by God's word the heavens existed and the earth was formed out of water and by water. Whereby <u>the world that then was</u>, being overflowed with water, <u>perished</u>."* Pay attention to the word perished. It is absolute, nothing left. Also note *"the world <u>that then was</u>."* These two verses speak of the end of the first age. Let's do a word study:

Perished; *Strong's no. 622 Transliterated: apollumi Phonetic: ap-ol'-loo-mee Text: from 575 and the base of 3639; to <u>destroy fully</u> (reflexively, to perish, or lose), literally or figuratively:—destroy, die, lose, mar, perish.*

We once again return to Genesis 1:2[a supporting scripture relating to the end of the first earth age:] *"And the earth was (became) without form, and void; and darkness was upon the face of the deep, And the Spirit of God moved upon the face of the waters".* We can now relate to *Jeremiah 4:23. "I beheld the earth, and lo, <u>it was without form and void</u>; and the heavens, and they had no light.24. I beheld the mountains, and lo, they trembled, and all the hills moved* *lightly.* <u>There was no shaking or trembling of the mountains in Noah's flood.</u>"

We find further proof of the end of the first age *in Jeremiah 4:27. "For the Lord said, the whole land shall be desolate; <u>yet will I not make a full end.</u>* [The earth only becomes dormant.] *For this shall the earth mourn, and the heavens above are black because I have spoken it, I have purposed it, and will not repent, neither will I turn back from it.* <u>The Heavens are Black; there is no LIGHT.</u> Thus any organisms <u>that require light die, light creates heat.</u>" Had this been Noah's flood, everything including Noah would have <u>frozen</u>. It can only be an end of the first age! <u>It definitely is not Noah's flood.</u>

Part 3
New Subject: "The Creation" of the Second Earth Age

Genesis 1:2: "Now the earth was/became formless and empty, darkness was over the surface of the deep, and the <u>Spirit of God was hovering over the waters</u>." We can find the deeper understanding and truth of this verse by considering *Psalm 104:30. You sent forth thy spirit, they are created: and thou renewest the face of the earth. NIV: 30. When you send your Spirit, they are created, and you renew the face of the earth.*

Genesis 1:3. "And God said, Let there be light: and there was light." We now read of the return; the change from total darkness after the destruction of the first age. This is the beginning of the second earth age, same earth and heaven; just being renewed.

Genesis 1:4. "And God saw the light, that it was good: and God divided the light from the darkness.[we read in *Jeremiah 3: 28. Therefore the earth will mourn and the heavens above grow dark, because I have spoken and will not relent, I have decided and will not turn back."] Gen. 1:5 And God called the light Day, and the darkness he Called Night. And the evening and the morning were the first day."* This subject is explored in greater depth in the Chapter 5; "Understanding the inspired Word of God".

It is important to compare the end of the ages. Again we read of the end of the first and second age *in 2 Peter 3:6. "Whereby the world that then was (Key) [the past] being overflowed with water, perished [end of first earth age]."* We can now read of the next age in *2 Peter 3:7. "But the heavens and the earth, which are now,* (Key) [the second earth age] *by the same word, are kept in store, reserved unto fire* [the second age will be destroyed by fire] *against the Day of Judgment and perdition* [death] *of ungodly men."* Again, this is not Noah's flood! The flood of Noah's time did not totally destroy the world, only cleansed the age.

Here we found the words "that then was" (past); we also find the word "perished," then the words "which are now" (present), this second earth age is destroyed by FIRE! Let's once again do a word study:

Perished: *Strong's 622, "to destroy fully," KJV, "destroy," "die," "lose," "mar," "perish"*).

2 Peter 3:8: "But, beloved, be not ignorant of this one thing, that one day is with the Lord as a thousand years, and a thousand years as one day". Time is actually forever with our Father in the heavenly realm but on earth time in the second age is limited to us because we will suffer the death of the flesh body.

2 Peter 3:9. "The Lord is not slack concerning his promise, as some men count slackness; but is longsuffering to us-ward, not willing that any should perish but that all should come to repentance." Our Lord is longsuffering or patient because He wants to bring as many of the rebels back into his loving hands as possible.

2 Peter 3:10. "But the day of the Lord will come as a thief in the night; in which the heavens shall pass away with a great noise, and the elements shall melt with fervent heat, the earth also and the works that are therein shall be burned up." This is the end of the second age.

2 Peter 3:11. "Seeing then that all these things shall be dissolved, what manner of persons ought you to be in all holy conversation and godliness. 12. Looking for and hasting unto the coming of the day of God, wherein the heavens being on fire shall be dissolved, and the elements shall melt with fervent heat". Jesus has returned, the millennium or one thousand years of preparation for the new final age is complete. Satan has been cast into the lake of fire." The day of God is not the same as the day of the Lord. The day of God marks the Great White Throne Judgment and then the start of the third and everlasting age.

Part 4
New Subject: We Read of the Third Age

We now will get an insight of the third age starting with Revelation 4:1–2 and 21:1.

Revelation 4:1.After this I [John] *looked, and, behold, a door was opened in heaven: and the first voice which I heard was as it were of a trumpet talking with me; which said, <u>Come up hither</u>, and I will show you things which must be after this. 2. And immediately <u>I was in the spirit</u>.* [Possibly an angelic body] *And I saw a new heaven and a new earth: for the first heaven and the first earth were passed away; and there was no more sea.* This might have confused some teachers. John was alive in the second age in an <u>earthly body</u> but was taken and changed to a spiritual body into the third age. He said <u>I saw</u> or to his knowledge the age had passed away [but he had come from the second age]. This helps us understand that, when we were in the first age we had an angelic or were in a spiritual body.

We read that Paul related the following in *2 Corinthians 12:1.I: must go on boasting. Although there is nothing to be gained, I will go on to visions and revelations from the Lord. 2. I know a man in Christ who fourteen years ago was caught up to the third heaven. Whether it was in the body or out of the body I do not know--* God knows. If we go back to the creation or the planting of the Garden of Eden, we read about two trees in the midst of the garden that were <u>not for food</u> but were in fact the tree of life (Jesus) and the tree of knowledge of good and evil (the serpent or Satan). Satan had the ability to take on an earthly form; he appeared to Eve in the Garden and again in the N.T. to tempt Jesus in the wilderness.

Mark 1:12. At once the Spirit sent him out into the desert, 13. And he was in the desert forty days, <u>being tempted by Satan</u>. He was with the wild animals, and angels attended him.

We read in *1 Peter 5:8. "Be sober, be vigilant; because your adversary the devil, as a roaring lion, walking about, seeking whom he may devour."* In a spiritual form but before the end of the second earth age, Jesus returns to put his enemies under his feet and save the second age for another thousand plus years as written in *Revelation 20:1. "And I saw an angel come down from heaven, having the key of the bottomless pit and a great chain in his hand. 2. And he laid hold on the dragon, that old serpent, which is the devil, and Satan, and bound him a thousand years."*

This is basically the entity or spirit of Satan that causes Mankind's sinful nature. Jesus took control and preached and cleansed the second age for a thousand years (millennium). Then as written in *Revelation 20:7. "And when the thousand years are expired, Satan shall be loosed out of his prison, 8.and shall go out to deceive the nations which are in the four quarters of the earth."* Some of the so-called religious teachers and scholars will again fall for his lies as they did at Christ's first coming. We all in this second age have free will and must now choose! *9. "And fire came down from God out of heaven, and devoured them. 10.And the devil that deceived them was cast into the lake of fire and brimstone, where the beast and the false prophet are, and shall be tormented day and night for ever and ever."* This will be the end of the second age. Then God sends down a new heaven and a new earth age, *Rev. 21:1. Then I saw a new heaven and a new earth, for <u>the first heaven and the first earth had passed away</u>, and there was <u>no longer any sea</u>* (Key). *"*

Here again we must rightly divide the word and remember ["I was" this is John in a spiritual Body] a clue is "there was <u>no longer any sea</u>" There are no longer any <u>Earthly Bodies;</u> we learn in *Revelation 17:15. Then the angel said to me, "<u>The waters</u> you saw, where the prostitute sits, <u>are peoples</u>, multitudes, nations and languages".* The second earth age we were in Earthly bodies described as seas, these earthly bodies are gone - changed. Validating the passing of the 2nd age, the age John came from. The third age will be an everlasting time of peace.

2 Peter 3:13. "Nevertheless we, according to his promise, look for new heavens and a new earth, wherein we live in righteousness." The eternal third age begins anew; our Father will restore the heaven and earth to their youth. We will also reside in incorruptible youthful spiritual bodies. There will be no sinful nature or death. Satan and his followers have been blotted out for good.

We can read of the third age in the Old Testament: *Isaiah. 65:16. "That he who blessed himself in the earth shall bless himself in the God of truth; and he who takes an oath in the earth shall swear by the God of truth; because the former troubles are forgotten, and because they are hid from mine eyes. For, behold 17. I create new heavens and a new earth* [the third and final age]: *and the former shall not be remembered, nor come into mind."* Both the first and second age are blotted out. Then in verses *18–19, "but be glad and rejoice forever in that which I create: for, behold, I create Jerusalem a rejoicing, and her people a joy. Now the great promise of God. And I will rejoice in Jerusalem, and joy in my people: and the voice of weeping shall be no more heard in her, nor the voice of crying. Peace on Earth."*

Part 5
Varies Scriptures as They Relate to the Various Ages

We will now look into some correlating scriptures of the various ages: Jeremiah 4: 1–18. Is in the second age in verses 19–29. We read of the first age; and verses 30–31. Speaks of Satan.

Reading with care, we will be able to rightly divide the word, following the different periods of time or the subject as written in Jeremiah 4:1–2, which is written to or about Israel who are now the ten tribes. Then in Jeremiah 4:3–18, is written to the two remaining tribes, Judah and Benjamin, who will be attacked by Babylon. This is also covered in 2 Kings 25:1–12. Note that this was a period of approximately <u>ten years</u> and will take place in the <u>second earth age</u>. In this chapter we find the subject changes.

We can read of the end of the <u>first earth age</u> and its total destruction; this is recorded in Jeremiah 4:19–29. Here again we must rightly divide the word as we are starting <u>a new subject within this chapter</u>: *Jeremiah 4:19. "My bowels, my bowels! I am pained at my very heart; my heart makes a noise in me; I cannot hold my peace, because you hast heard, O my soul, the sound of the trumpet, the alarm of war. 20. Destruction upon destruction is cried; <u>for the whole land is spoiled</u>: <u>suddenly</u> are my tents spoiled, and my curtains <u>in a moment</u>."* We read that this destruction <u>does not take ten years</u> as written above in Jeremiah 4:1–18. This is detailed or covered in 2 Kings 25:1–12. <u>This happens instantly</u>. In *Jeremiah 4:21 it is written, "How long shall I see the standard, and hear the sound of the trumpet? 22. For my people is foolish, they have not known me; they are foolish children, and they have none understanding: they are wise to do evil, but to do good they have no knowledge. 23. I beheld the* *earth, and, lo, <u>it was without form, and void; and the heavens</u>, and <u>they had no light</u>.*" No Light, only darkness and <u>completely void</u>. This cannot be <u>Noah's flood</u>.

This verse explains and confirms what is written in *Genesis 1:2:* "*And the earth was [became] without form, and <u>void</u>; and darkness was upon the face of the deep. And the Spirit of God moved upon the face of the waters.*" *How does this take place?*

Let us go back *to Jeremiah 4:24.* "*I beheld <u>the mountains, and, lo, they trembled</u>, and <u>all the hills moved lightly</u>. 25 I beheld, and, lo, <u>there was no man, and all the birds of the heavens were fled</u>.*" The earth is formless; there are no inhabitants, no birds, and is now in darkness. Was the earth a frozen mass?

In verses 26–27, it is written, *26.* "*I beheld, and, lo, the fruitful place was a wilderness, and all the cities thereof were broken down at the presence of the Lord, and by his fierce anger.* No trees, no tender shoots, no leaves. *27.For thus hath the Lord said, the whole land shall be <u>desolate; yet will I not make a full end</u>.*" The only visible thing left of this first age is water possibly frozen on the face of the earth—the earth is void of all that was.

Verse *28;* "*For this shall the earth mourn, and <u>the heavens above be black</u>;* [no sunshine] *because I have spoken it, I have purposed it, and will not repent, neither will I turn back from it.* [No sun! No life] *29. The whole city shall flee for the noise of the horsemen and bowmen; they shall go into thickets, and climb up upon the rocks: every city shall be forsaken, and <u>not a man dwells therein</u>.*"

There are no men or women, no Ark, not even Noah! We now read of Satan: *Jeremiah 4:30.* "*What are you doing, O devastated one? Why dress yourself in scarlet and put on jewels of gold? Why shade your eyes with paint? You adorn yourself in vain. Your lovers despise you; they seek your life."* This was Satan, king of Tyre, king of fire, the devil, the serpent, and the antichrist. We have read of him in Isaiah 14:12–17, and Ezekiel 28:11–19. In verse *13, it says, "You have been in* <u>*Eden the garden of God*</u>*; every precious stone was thy covering."* This is an Account of Satan as he was placed in the first earth age and now is held under Michael's watchful eye until *Revelation 12:7. "And there was war in heaven: Michael and his angels fought against the dragon" 9. "And the great dragon was cast out, that old serpent, called the Devil, and Satan."*

Part 6
In This Second Age, We Are Born of Women with a Free Will

Could our souls and spirit have existed with God before flesh man was created in this second age? We are now born of woman and are in flesh bodies made from the dust of the earth: *Gen. 3:19. "By the sweat of your brow you will eat your food until you return to the ground, since from it you were taken; for dust you are and to dust you will return."* God gave us our spirit or soul: *Ecclesiastes. 12:7 "Then shall the dust return to the earth as it was: and the spirit shall return unto God who gave it."* We have an earthly body made of the dust of the earth and also given by God the breath of life our spiritual presence.

We should consider at this point! *1 Thessalonians 4:13. Brothers, we do not want you* <u>*to be ignorant about those who fall asleep,*</u> [die] *or to grieve like the rest of men, who have no hope. 14. We believe that Jesus died and rose again and so we believe that God will bring with Jesus those who have fallen asleep in him. 15. According to the Lord's own word, we tell you that we who are still alive, who are left till the coming of the Lord, will certainly not precede those who have fallen asleep.* [The spirit or soul is already gone] This confuses some preachers the earthy body has turned to dust and the spirit or soul has returned to the creator *[John 1:1. -- the Word was with God, and the Word was God. 2. He was with God in the beginning.* [Jesus] *3. Through him all things were made The graves are filled with just decay or dust.*

Read and ponder on our being angelic beings in the first age: *Jeremiah. 1:5 "Before I formed you in the belly I knew you and before you came forth out of the womb I sanctified you, and I ordained you a prophet unto the nations."* This verse gives us further proof of the first age, our first insight to our being in an age before our present time. Many astute scholars agree that we were in spiritual bodies having no flesh or gender. This can be concluded by the writings in KJV, *1 Corinthians 15:40: "There are also celestial bodies and bodies terrestrial: but the glory of the celestial is one, and the glory of the terrestrial is another."* In the NIV, it says, *"There are also heavenly bodies and there are earthly bodies; but the splendour of the heavenly bodies is one kind, and the splendour of the earthly bodies is another."* In verse *15:51. it is written, "Behold, I show you a mystery; we shall not all sleep, but we shall all be changed. 52. in a moment, in the twinkling of an eye, at the last trump: for the trumpet shall sound, and the dead shall be raised incorruptible, and we shall be changed."* We can read of our life as a spiritual body, and we will not marry when we are in spiritual bodies: *Luke 20:35. "And the resurrections from the dead, neither marry, nor are given in marriage."*

We have read about how Satan was put in charge of the first age and how his desire to be equal to God which brought about his destruction and the end of the first earth age. As we continue to study more scriptures, we find the words for pre-existence foreknew, predestined as written in the NIV, *Romans 8:29. For those God foreknew he also* <u>*predestined*</u> *to be conformed to the likeness of his Son, that he might be the firstborn among many brothers.*

Rom. 9:11. For the children being not yet born, neither having done any good or evil, that the purpose of God according to election might stand, not of works, but of him that calls; 12. It was said unto her, the elder shall serve the younger. 13. As it is written, Jacob have I loved, but Esau have I hated. [Why?]

Esau was the firstborn and had the birthright, but Satan, in his attempt to disrupt the seed line to Christ, influenced him to trade his birthright for a bowl of food. God foreknew he would trade it. Thus, Esau was hated before he was born of women in this second earth age.

In Ephesians, we read in *1:4. That he had chosen us in him before the foundation of the world, that we should be holy and without blame before him in love:5. Having* <u>*predestined*</u> *us unto the adoption of children by Jesus Christ to himself, according to the good pleasure of his will."* To help nail this down, let's look for ages in the Scriptures; this will take a little work.

Let's once again ask the Father's guidance to learn and unlock some truth by rightly dividing His Word.

1 Corinthians 2:6; states, *"Howbeit we speak wisdom among them that are perfect: yet not the wisdom of this* <u>*world,*</u> *nor of the princes of this world, that come to naught:* this is better understood in the NIV *We do, however, speak a message of wisdom among the*

mature, but not the wisdom of this <u>age</u> or of the rulers <u>of this age</u>, who are coming to nothing." The two words written in: first the KJV is <u>world</u>; in the NIV, the word is translated as <u>age</u>; they are both translated from the same word. In verse 7, it says, "But we speak the wisdom of God in a mystery, even the <u>hidden wisdom</u>, which God <u>ordained before the world</u> unto our glory." Ordained before the "WORLD" or the second Age? Let's do a word study.

<u>World</u>; *Strong's no. 165 Transliterated: aion Phonetic: ahee-ohn' Text: from the same as 104; properly, <u>an age</u> by extension, perpetuity (also past); by implication, the world; especially (Jewish) a Messianic period (present or future): —<u>age</u>, course, eternal, (for) ever (-more), [n-] ever, (beginning of the, while the) world (began, without end).*

Here, Strong's Concordance has given us so much information to meditate on. First, we see the words "<u>an age</u>," "<u>also past</u>," then the next "<u>specially (Jewish) a Messianic period</u>," and <u>present and future</u>, etc. This alone speaks out volumes to those who have eyes to see and ears to hear and realize that there is a first, second, and a third earth age written of in the Bible, the Word of God.

John 3:16. For God so loved the world that he gave his one and only Son, that whoever believes in him shall not perish but have eternal life. [in the third age].

John 14:19. Before long, the world will not see me anymore, but you will see me. Because I live, you also will live [by his work on the cross.] *:22. Then Judas* [not Judas Iscariot] *said, "But, Lord, why do you intend to show yourself to us and not to the world?"* [He just didn't get it.] *23. Jesus replied, "If anyone loves me, he will obey my teaching. My Father will love him, and we will come to him and make our home with him."*

John 17:1. These words spoke Jesus, and lifted up his eyes to heaven, and said, Father, the hour is come; glorify thy Son, that thy Son also may glorify thee.

He continues *in John 17:24: "Father, I will that they also, whom thou hast given me, be with me where I am; that they may behold my glory, which thou hast given me: for thou loved me <u>before the foundation of the world</u>."*

Note that if you read the study "God's Verbal Picture" found in chapter 3, you will find more proof of the first earth age. God verbally describes a huge creature that roamed the earth billions of years ago: (Job 40:15) "Behold now behemoth, <u>which I made with thee</u>; he eats grass as an ox."

Archaeologists have uncovered bones and the remains of various huge animals and giants and small winged creatures, small shells, but have never found any bones of the first-age spiritual bodies.

Chapter 3

God's Verbal Drawing

What is it? An elephant? A hippopotamus? A giraffe?

What is it? Does the inspired word hold a key? Can we rightly divide the word to glean a clear picture to this puzzle? We read in Job 40:15-19.

Behold now the behemoth, which I made with thee; he eats grass as an ox. Lo now, his strength is in his loins, and his force is in the navel of his belly. [We can begin to create a mental picture; [a huge oval powerful shaped body].

He moves his tail like a cedar: the sinews of his stones are wrapped together. [We now attach a long tail similar to a cedar tree to our mental picture]

His bones are as strong pieces of brass; his bones are like bars of iron. He is the chief of the ways of God: he that made him can make his sword to approach unto him. [The bones are big strong as steel but he is still under Gods control].

Let's take pen in hand and draw picture. We will start with a huge egg-shaped body with big round heavy legs. (Much like the body of an ox, elephant, or a hippopotamus and heavy legs like iron. But we must draw a tail like a Cedar tree; tall or long and coming to a point. Hum.)

In Verse: 20. we read: *"Surely the mountains bring him forth food, where all the beasts of the field play."* [Now this suggests a long neck a creature that can eat or get food from high places. We now can add along neck like a Giraffe to our image]

Verse 21–23 says, *"He lies under the shady trees, in the covert of the reed, and fens. The shady trees cover him with their shadow; the willows of the brook compass him about. Behold, he drinks up a river, and haste's not: he trusts that he can draw up Jordan into his mouth."* (A powerful huge animal, he has no fear.)

Finally the last clue: verse 24. *"He takes it with his eyes: his nose pierces through snares."* (Our creature has a neck like a giraffe a small head but a pointed snout that can pierce through snares. My mental picture is a huge body with barrel legs a long tail and neck and a pointed nose.)

I have only seen pictures, but in my mind, this has to be like a creature from the first age a Dinosaur!

Looks like a Dinosaur?

Let's briefly study the book of Job. The book of Job can be classified as a book of rhetorical questions.

Should at any point you feel overwhelmed by this study; please feel free to fast forward and read the Epilogue at the end of the chapter for help.

The subject in the book of Job starts with Job 1:1 and 6–7: You will note Satan was among them and soon takes over trying to redeem himself.

1. There was a man in the land of Uz, whose name was Job; and that man was perfect and upright, and one that feared God, and eschewed [shunned] evil.

6. Now there was a day when the sons of God came to present themselves before the Lord, and Satan came also among them. 7. And the Lord said unto *Satan, where have you come from? Then Satan answered the Lord, and said, from going to and fro in the earth, and from walking up and down in it.*

We have learned in a previous study the fall of Lucifer/ Satan and the destruction of the first earth age. The book of Job appears to be Satan's attempt to exonerate his actions using Job as a scapegoat.

We read of Satan's downfall in *Ezekiel 28:2: "In the pride of your heart you say, 'I am a god; I sit on the throne of a god in the heart of the seas.'"* God had made Satan *in Ezekiel 28:11: "You were the model of perfection, full of wisdom and perfect in beauty. 15. You were blameless in your ways from the day you were created till wickedness was found in you."* Then in this second earth age, he appears, in the planted garden of Eden to deceive Eve, and we learn that Satan's spirit is a very heavy influence on this second age: *2 Corinthians 4:4 "The god of this age has blinded the minds of* *unbelievers, so that they cannot see the light of the gospel of the <u>glory of</u>* <u>*Christ, who is the image of God.*</u>" You will notice that the first <u>god</u> <u>is not capitalized</u>; thus <u>Satan is present in this second age.</u> <u>The</u> <u>second God is capitalized.</u>

Satan will try to defend himself from his falling out of God's favour. We can glean from this as we study the scriptures found in: *Job 1:8. "And the Lord said unto Satan, have you considered my servant Job, that there is none like him in the earth, a perfect and an upright man, one that revere's God, and turns away and shuns evil? 9. 'Does Job fear God for nothing?' Satan replied. 10. 'Have you not put a hedge around him and his household and everything he has? You have blessed the work of his hands, so that his flocks and herds are spread throughout the land. 11. but stretch out your hand and strike everything he has, <u>and he will surely curse you</u> to your face.'* [This was Satan's attempt to make Job his scapegoat] *12. The LORD said to Satan, 'Very well, then, everything he has is in your hands, but on the man himself do not lay a finger.' Then Satan went out from the presence of the LORD."*

Satan has challenged God to strip Job of everything; God would accept the challenge, but Satan was not to harm even a hair on Job. <u>It is imperative that we understand Job had no idea</u> <u>of the deal between God and Satan as to what was to transpire in</u> <u>his family or his life.</u>

Through Job's wife, Satan tried to get Job to denounce God: *Job 2:9. "His wife said to him, 'Are you still holding on to your integrity? <u>Curse God and die!</u>'"* Now for the next thirty-six or more chapters, three of Job's friends later a fourth will chime in and try to break Job's love and trust in God.

We can parallel a similar deception when Satan deceived Eve in the Garden. How did Satan deceive Eve? We will learn the answer in "Apple or Truth." Adam was banned and became mortal; the tree of life was also in the Garden, but through this tree Jesus, God will give us a second chance of everlasting life.

The book of Job has also been considered by many as a very mystical book written as an allegory based on a place known as the Arabia Deserta located above the thirty parallel in a land known as Uz, inhabited by Job and his friends. The name of Job can be found in *Genesis 46:13: "And the sons of Issachar; Tola, and Phuvah, and Job, and Shimron."* We also find the name of one of his friends in *Genesis 36: "These are the names of Esau's sons; Eliphaz the son of Adah the wife of Esau."* In *Job 2:11, we also find Eliphaz the Temanite, Bildad the Shuhite, and Zophar the Naamathite."* In *Job chapter 32 we are introduced to Elihu the Buzite.*

The author of the book of Job ranges from Job or one of the friends mentioned or even Moses, whether Moses wrote of it from the position of experiencing it firsthand, which is very doubtful, or based partly on a real occurrence in the past and handed down then embellished or took place in the first earth age. Whoever wrote the book of Job did so with the inspiration of God maybe as a teaching tool.

The most mystical part comes when God asks rhetorical questions in: *Job 38:4: "Where were you when I laid the earth's foundation? Tell me, if you understand."* God continues to ask rhetorical questions in, for example, *39:27: "Does the eagle soar at your command and build his nest on high?"* Then he asks *in 40:15: Look at the behemoth, which I made along with you and which feeds on grass like an ox."* The behemoth as described in the Bible can only refer to the first-age Dinosaur! The words *"which I made along with you"* can only relate to the time when Satan is in an angelic body and the chief cherubim in charge of the first age.

Some theologians break the book of Job down as having five parts:

1. Historical facts as to location and to a discussion between God and Satan (Job 1–2)

2. Job's debate with three friends (3–31)

3. Job's discussion with Elihu, a Buzite (32–37)

4. The theological verses or God speaks (38–42)

5. The end and God's blessing (42:12)

Part 1

Working with this outline, we find a reference to a historical location in *Job 1:1: "There was a man in the land of Uz, whose name was Job; and that man was perfect and upright, and one that feared God, and eschewed evil."* Then in verse 1:6, there is a huge change that sets up the rest of the book—Satan is talking with God *in Job 1:6: "Now there was a day when the sons of God came to present themselves before the Lord, and Satan came also among them. 7. And the Lord said unto Satan, from where have you come? Then Satan answered the Lord, and said, from going to and fro in the earth, and from walking up and down in it."* If you have read thee chapter

"The Three Earth Ages," you would have read of how Satan was created perfect: *Ezek. 28:11*. *"You were the model of perfection, full of wisdom and perfect in beauty."* Satan was in charge of the first age until he wanted to take the place of God: *Ezek. 28:2*. *"Because your heart is lifted up, and thou hast said, 'I am a god, I sit in the seat of God.'"* This caused the total destruction of the first earth age.

We return to Satan talking to God. One can conclude that Satan was pleading for a second chance: *Job 1:8*. *"And the Lord said unto Satan, Have you considered my servant Job, that there is none like him in the earth, a perfect and an upright man, one that reveres God, and shuns evil?"*

Now Satan will try to discredit *Job 1:9*. *"Does Job revere God for nothing?"* In verse *:11*, Satan tells God, if you take away his possessions, Job will *"surely curse you to your face."*

This scenario is played a second time in but is more forthcoming: *Job 2:1. On another day the angels came to present themselves before the LORD, and Satan also came with them to present himself before him. 2. And the LORD said to Satan, Where have you come from? Satan answered the LORD, from roaming through the earth and going back and forth in it. 3. Then the LORD said to Satan, Have you considered my servant Job? There is no one on earth like him; he is blameless and upright, a man who fears God and shuns evil. And he still maintains his integrity, <u>though you incited me against him to ruin him without any reason</u>.*

God will now give Satan permission to try to destroy Job's love for Him: *Job 2:6. The LORD said to Satan, "Very well, then, he is in your hands; but you must spare his life." 7. So Satan went out from the presence of the LORD and afflicted Job with painful sores from the soles of his feet to the top of his head.*

Satan has assaulted Job; he will now influence Job's wife and then his friends to turn *on Job 2:9. His wife said to him, "Are you still holding on to your integrity? Curse God and die!"*

Part 2

We read of Job's agony in 3:1–2 and 26: *"After this, Job opened his mouth and cursed the day of his birth. 2. He said: "May the day of my birth perish, and the night it was said, 'A boy is born!' 26. I have no peace, no quietness; I have no rest, but only turmoil."* Through Job's wife, Satan had tried to get Job to denounce God and now for the next thirty six or more chapters, Job's friends try to discredit Job and hurl insults starting in;

Job 4:1. Then <u>Eliphaz</u> *the Temanite replied, "If someone ventures a word with you, will you be impatient? But who can keep from speaking?"* He continues to berate Job: *4:17. "Shall mortal man be more just than God? Shall a man be more pure than his maker? : 21. Does not their Excellency which is in them go away? They die, even without wisdom. Job15:7. Are you the first man that was born? Or were you made before the hills? 15:9. What do you know that we do not know? What insights do you have that we do not have?* Then <u>Zophar</u> the Naamathite started his berating in *Job11:4. You say to God, 'my beliefs are flawless and I am pure in your sight: 5. Oh, how I wish that God would speak, that he would open his lips against you.*

Then <u>Bildad</u> the Shuhite replied. *Job 25:4. How then can a man be righteous before God? How can one born of woman be pure?"*

Part 3

Now we move on to more chatter. It is now <u>Elihu</u> who accuses Job of sinning as he speaks to Job in *32:34*. *"Men of understanding declare, wise men who hear me say to me, 35. <u>Job speaks without knowledge; his words lack insight</u>.' 36. Oh, that Job might be tested to the utmost <u>for answering like a wicked man</u>! 37. <u>To his sin</u> he adds rebellion; scornfully he claps his hands among us and multiplies his words against God."* These are all falsehoods and have Satan's thumbprint. [This might well be the verses that angers God and he will end this test set in place by Satan] All through the twenty-eight chapters, Job has refused to speak out against God.

But Job had spoken out to his tormentor. *Job 21:34.* *"So how can you console me with your nonsense? Nothing is left of your answers but falsehood!"*

In the final berating of Job, Elihu *asks Job 37:15. "Do you know when God disposed them, and caused the light of his cloud to shine? 16. Do you know the balancing of the clouds, the wondrous works of him which is perfect in knowledge? 17. How your garments are warm, when he quiets the earth by the south wind? 18. Have you with him spread out the sky, which is strong, and as a molten looking glass? 19. Teach us what we shall say unto him; for we cannot order our speech by reason of darkness."*

But another condescending verse is: *37:24: "Men do therefore fear him: [God] he respects not any that are wise of heart."* This verse spoken by Elihu has all the negativity of Satan. Job has been righteous through the whole ordeal! But the next chapter is very confusing; God speaks out of the storm which was the Satan's attempt to have Job curse God. And he addresses his remarks to Job who is innocent. The only clear answer is that God is speaking through Job, but his remarks are truly aimed at the four berating friends and Satan. This knowledge will be authenticated by Job 40:15 when God says, *"Behold now the behemoth, which I made with thee."* This was in the first age and He was clearly speaking through Job to Satan.

Part 4

We now read of God's response; it will not take too much to understand that God is speaking to Job, but his remarks are actually speaking directly to the four accusers and Satan: *Job 38:1-2. "Then the LORD answered Job out of the storm." "Who is this that darkens my counsel with words without knowledge?* This statement is without a doubt aimed at the four and Satan. Clearly he is not speaking only to Job who has not denounced God. 40:3-5. Then Job answered the LORD: *"I am unworthy--how can I reply to you? I put my hand over my mouth. I spoke once, but I have no answer-- twice, but I will say no more."* [Job 9:3. *Though one wished to dispute with him, he could not answer him one time out of a thousand. 9:15. Though I were innocent, I could not answer him; I could only plead with my Judge for mercy.*]

Now we can find reference to Satan and the first earth age along with the Dinosaurs in 40:5: *"Look at the behemoth, which I made along with you and which feeds on grass like an ox."* We move ahead to 42:7: *"After the LORD had said these things to Job, he said to Eliphaz the Temanite, 'I am angry with you and your two friends, because you have not spoken of me what is right, as my servant Job has"*. By this verse Elihu was not friends with the older three men.

Part 5

To further prove that the condescending remarks were not directed to Job, we read of God's blessing in Job 42:12: *"The LORD blessed the latter part of Job's life more than the first."* We can now ponder, did this advent really take place, or was it written as a sermon from God? If we put our trust and faith in Him, we will overcome.

Epilogue to chapter Three.

To understand the Book of Job we must consider what the Apostles Peter wrote in *KJV 2 peter 3:9. The Lord is not slack concerning his promise, as some men count slackness; but is longsuffering to us-ward, not willing that any should perish (Key) but that all should come to repentance.* Stan has already been rejected and faces dire consequences for his action as chief Cherubim in the first age.

God in his realm allows Satan a hearing. Job chapter *1: 6. One day the angels came to present themselves before the LORD, and Satan also came with them.* God knew the reason Satan tagged along with the angels was to try to justify his attempt to be a god and thus his downfall. God in fairness asks: *1: 8. And the Lord said unto Satan, Have you considered my servant Job, that there is none like him in the earth, a perfect and an upright man, one that feareth* [reveres] God, *and escheweth* [shuns]*evil?*

Satan in his attempt to make Job a scapegoat to justify his downfall in the first earth age reply's in *1: 9. Then Satan answered the Lord, and said, does Job fear God for nought? 10. Have you not made a hedge about him, and about his house, and about all that he has on every side?* Have you not blessed the work of his hands, and his substance is increased in the land.

Satan is allowed to destroy everything Job has without Jobs knowledge, His response is noted in *1: 21. And said: Naked I came out of my mother's womb, and naked shall I depart: the Lord gave, and the Lord has taken away; blessed be the name of the Lord. 22. In all this Job sinned not, nor charged God foolishly.*

As we have read 2 peter 3:9. Above God in his infinite mercy will allow Satan to continue his plea for leniency? Satan in a second *attempt Job2:7. So Satan went out of the presence of the Lord, and smote Job with sore boils from the sole of his foot unto his crown. 8. And he gave him a potsherd to scrape himself with; and he sat down among the ashes.* Satan delights when Jobs wife appears*: 9. then said his wife to him; do you still retain your integrity? Curse God, and die. Job replied: 10. But he said unto her, you speak as one of the foolish women speaks. What? Shall we receive good at the hand of God, and shall we not receive evil?* In all this did not Job sin with his lips?

The book now introduces 3 friends who try to get Job who has no idea what is going on to say he sinned our blame God. For 34 chapters this continues. Then a younger person appears and for 4 chapters berates Job, Speaking falsehoods 35:1 we read:

Elihu spoke moreover, and said, 2. Do you think you this to be right, that you said, my righteousness is more than God's? Job had never claimed any more than I am innocent. Through all the storm of turmoil job had revered God. Finally God will speak in chapter 38 but Job will never know this whole scenario was orchestrated by Satan trying to justify his downfall in the first earth age.

God in chapter 42: starting in verse *7. And it was so, that after the Lord had spoken these words unto Job, the Lord said to Eliphaz the Temanite, My wrath is kindled against you, and against your two friends: for you have not spoken of me the thing that is right, as my servant Job had. 8. Therefore take unto you now seven bullocks and seven rams, and go to my servant Job, and offer up for yourselves a burnt offering; and my servant Job shall pray for you: for him will I accept: lest I deal with you after your folly, in that you have not spoken of me the thing which is right, like my servant Job.*

Then Job is rewarded: *12. So the Lord blessed the latter end of Job more than his beginning: for he had fourteen thousand sheep, and six thousand camels, and a thousand yoke of oxen, and a thousand she asses. : 13. He had also seven sons and three daughters.* Job will live another 140 years in peace.

Satan has not exonerated himself.

Chapter 4
Noah's Flood

Before we explore Noah's flood, here are a few recorded historical facts:

1. Up until 500 BC, the world was considered flat.

2. Egyptian history dates back to 3100 BC, 652 years before Noah's flood.

3. Chinese history dates back before the flood to 2356 BC, eight years before Noah's flood. The most reliable historic sources agree that Noah's flood was 2348 BC. (Time in BC counts backward: 4004–0). Jesus, born 3–4 BC, and began his ministry in AD 27.

4. The Shu-King historic records of China states that King Yao came to the throne in 2356 BC—this was eleven years before the start of Noah's flood—and ruled China for many years after the flood.

5. Egypt also has one of the oldest existing recorded civilizations in the world. Most

scholars believe that the Egyptian kingdom was first unified in about 3100 BC. In Egypt, the eleventh dynasty began to reign about 2375 BC over a great and powerful nation twenty-seven years before Noah's flood.

Do these historical facts discount the Bible or stand together? This study may help you decide how far the flood covered maybe God had set boundaries!

What you will read later in Genesis 10:1–7 should raise an interesting question. Why a subject change in verse 5. Verse 6 reverts to original subject? We will in this study look for the answer! It will shock some.

Gen. 7:23 <u>And every living substance was destroyed which was upon the face of the ground</u>, both man, and cattle, and the creeping things, and the fowl of the heaven; and they were destroyed from the earth and Noah only remained alive, and they that were with him in the ark.

This part of the verse *"And every living substance was destroyed,"* along with *"and they that were with him in the ark,"* will be examined along with other subjects connected to Noah's flood as we rightly divide the Word in this study:

Gen. 7:24. "And the waters prevailed upon the earth <u>an hundred and fifty days</u>." This verse also will become <u>very important to understand the truth about Noah's flood</u>

After the Noah's flood *Gen. 9:11. "--neither shall there anymore be a flood to destroy the earth."* In Exodus 10:4, *"Else, if you refuse to let my people go, behold, tomorrow will I bring the <u>locusts</u> into thy coast: 5. And they shall <u>cover the face of the earth</u>"* (earth Strong's no. 776). We need to do a word search to clarify the statement *"<u>cover</u>*

the face of the earth." As you read your Bible, you are subjected to the translators' and scribes' interpretation or translation of a Hebrew or Greek word. These words can be translated to support the popular thought or a deeper truth. Two questions: (1) Did the flood cover the whole earth? (2) Did the locusts cover the whole earth (Key)?

This will be one of the most important word studies as it will help you decide. Was the whole planet earth covered with the flood or with locusts, or was it only a localized area?

<u>Earth:</u> *Strong's ref. no. 776 Romanized 'erets Pronounced eh'-rets from an unused root probably meaning to be firm; the earth (<u>at large</u>, or, <u>partitively a land</u>): KJV—X common, <u>country</u>, earth, <u>field</u>, ground, land, X <u>nations</u>, way, + <u>wilderness</u>, world.*

As we can see, the word earth as used in Genesis 9:11 and Exodus 10:4–5 can be narrowed to an area such as at large or partially a land as a country down to a field, so a flood could have been as many scholars claim contained to a specific area as the Bible relates to Noah's flood.

Some scientists claim there are high water-level marks at different locations around the world! High water-level marks, this would mean the flood was only deep in that area and not covering the whole planet!

Some scientists and biblical scholars suggest that the flood could be eastward from the Tigris and Euphrates Valleys, in the mountain basin in Sinkiang. This basin is surrounded by taller mountains. Within this basin are several smaller mountains that could be fully submerged by a flood or well below the rim created by the surrounding mountains. The ark could have come to rest on one of these lower mountains.

As part of their evidence, they have detected and found a high watermark on the slopes of the higher mountains surrounding this mountain basin in Sinkiang, which form the rim of this basin, suggesting that at one time this basin was flooded or was a lake, leaving a well-marked shoreline high on the taller mountains. Many scholars believe that Noah's flood was in this valley surrounded by mountains or a similar area.

Other scholars argue that if this was the case, why didn't God just tell Noah to take his family and climb over the higher mountains to avoid the coming flood instead of spending time to build the ark? One answer was that he was giving the other people a chance to repent and be saved.

What these critics fail to realize is that Satan had attempted to taint the seed line to Christ. The flood was only a cleansing, not a destruction of the world or of an age. This leads us to ask why God caused Noah's flood. Was it a cleansing flood caused by God and His plan to save a tribe or race to be His chosen people?

We read in *Deut. 7:6 "For you are a holy people unto the Lord thy God: the Lord thy God hath chosen you to be a special people unto himself, above all people that are upon the face of the earth."* The chosen people will continue to keep the seed line pure until the birth of Christ our Saviour. Satan had made several attempts to taint or destroy this seed line. The final straw came when the giants or Nephilim appeared on earth and had children with some of the direct descendants of Adam and Eve or the Adamic race. They will become or known as the Israelites.

The reason for the flood: *Genesis 6:1 "And it came to pass, when men began to multiply on the face of the earth, and daughters were born unto them, 2. That the sons of God saw the daughters of men that they were fair; and they took them wives of all which they chose".* This included the daughters of Noah, the descendants of Adam and Eve. *"The sons of God"* or fallen angels, possibly they were Satan followers in the first age? We can read of them in the following:

Jude 1:6And the angels who kept not their first estate, but left their own habitation, he hath reserved in everlasting chains under darkness unto the judgment of the great day.

Genesis 6:3.And the Lord said: My spirit shall not always strive with man, for that he also is flesh: yet his days shall be an hundred and twenty years. 4. There were giants in the earth in those days; and also after that, when the sons of God came in unto the daughters of men, and they bear children to them, the same became mighty men which were of old, men of renown.[Had Satan orchestrated a plan to divert the purity of the seed line to Christ?] *5. And God saw that the wickedness of man was great in the earth, and that every imagination of the thoughts of his heart was only evil continually. 6. And it repented the Lord that he had made man on the earth, and it grieved him at his heart.*

Eve had thanked God for Cain! But she had been deceived by the serpent. Genesis 4:1 states, *"I have gotten a man from the Lord."* Genesis 6:7 says, *"And the Lord said, I will destroy man whom I have created from the face of the earth; both man, and beast, and the creeping thing, and the fowls of the air; for it saddens me that I have made them.* [God had totally destroyed the first age.] *8. But Noah found grace in the eyes of the Lord."* Thus, this flood is only a cleansing flood.

In the NIV, Genesis 6:4 says, *"The Nephilim were on the earth in those days—and also afterward—when the sons of God went to the daughters of men and had children by them. They were the heroes of old, men of renown."* Jude 1:6 states, *"And the angels who kept not their first estate, but left their own habitation, he hath reserved in everlasting chains under darkness unto the judgment of the great day."*

Genesis 6:14: "Make thee an ark of gopher wood." Noah built a huge ship so that his immediate family and animals will survive, as well as two of every flesh, birds that fly and find a leaf then a place to roost! The giants or Nephilim along with their wives and children perished, including part of the polluted Adamic race.

Let's take a look at 2 Peter and read of the other flood that completely destroyed the first earth age: *2 Pet. 3:5. "For this they willingly are ignorant of, that by the word of God the heavens were of old, and the earth standing out of the water and in the water: 6. whereby the world that <u>then was</u>, being overflowed with water, <u>per-ished</u>."* Important word study!

<u>Perished</u>. *Strong's ref. no. 622 Romanized apollumi Pronounced ap-ol'-loo-mee from GSN0575 and the base of GSN3639; <u>to destroy fully</u> (reflexively, to perish, or lose), literally or figuratively: KJV— destroy, die, lose, mar, perish.*

This was <u>not Noah's flood as there was nothing left</u>. Many scholars turn a blind eye to the word perished and its true implication "to destroy fully." Noah's flood could, as some suggest, have been only a small region of the earth where Noah and his relatives lived. In John, we read 8:44: *"You are of your father the devil, and the lusts of your father you will do. He was a murderer from the beginning, and abode not in the truth."* Cain, "a murderer," had killed Abel and gone to the land of Nod where he married a Gentile. Their descendants were to become the Kenites, a tribe or part of the Gentiles that could well have been part of the "bring two of every flesh." In this verse, Jesus is confirming that the Kenites survived Noah's flood! Word study is called for again. Who are the Kenites?

Strong's ref. no. *7017 Romanized Qeyniy Pronounced kaynee'or Qiyniy (1 Chr. 2:55) {kee-nee'}; patronymic from HSN7014;* <u>*a Kenite*</u> *or member of the tribe of Kajin: To dig deeper, KJV—Kenite. Strong's no. 7014 - Kajin,* <u>*the name of the first child,*</u> *also of a place in Palestine, and of an Oriental Tribe:—*<u>*Cain,*</u> *Kenite (-s).*

We have learned that Cain is the first murderer whose father was the devil or Satan. To really understand this truth, reading the chapter; "<u>Apple or the Truth</u>" will help in authenticating this.

We can also read of the first-age flood in *Psalm 104:6.* "*You covered it with the deep as with a garment: the waters stood above the mountains. 7. At your rebuke they fled; at the voice of your thunder they hasted away.*" Here we have read that the waters <u>hastened away</u> unlike Noah's flood where the waters receded slowly over a long period of 150- plus days and more. Noah remained in the ark as it had come to rest on a high point; the water was still receding in the valley. We need to research to rightly divide and find the deeper truth in His Word. Let's research the word hasted.

Strong's no. 2648 Transliterated: khaw-faz' Phonetic: khawfaz'Text: a primitive root; properly, to start up suddenly, i.e. (by implication) to <u>*hasten away,*</u> *to fear: - (make) haste (away), tremble.*

These floodwaters destroyed the <u>first earth age</u> and took only a short period of time to recede at God's command: In *Psalm 104:30. When you send your Spirit, they are created, and* <u>*you renew the face of the earth*</u> *Genesis 1:3 "And God said, Let there be light: and there was light. 6. And God said, Let there be a firmament in the midst of the waters, and let it divide the waters from the waters.*"

This created the start of the second earth age, not slowly subsiding as in Noah's flood of this second age.

To further clarify, we read in *Psalm 104:9*, *"Thou hast set a bound (boundary) that they may not pass over that they turn not <u>again to cover the earth</u>."* Again, no to cover the earth but have boundaries" this had to be the First earth age? Could these boundaries have been set in anticipation of Noah's flood? Was the flood of Noah's time centered in an area only mostly inhabited by the Adamic race only?

Let's consider what we have studied above and ask where could the dove get an olive leaf, not a waterlogged branch, if all had been destroyed? Wouldn't Noah have gathered seeds to replant? Did the second dove fly in a different direction? Or find a roost elsewhere?

Noah was told to take two of every flesh. Are we the other races, "the Gentiles," are we not flesh? The fallen angels, however, are not born of woman. They are like us in *Genesis 1:26: "And God said; Let us make man in our image, after our likeness."* These fallen angels resembled us. While the Israelites wandered the desert for forty years, they ate angel food or manna in the desert. Our Father created the earth to be inhabited in the first earth age (Isa. 45:18). He destroyed the world because of the rebellion, of Lucifer (Satan). This was the "Katabole" or the overthrow of the world, and one-third followed Satan of which we can read of in Revelations 12:4, thus confirming that there was a first age.

We in this second age will have the opportunity to choose right between wrong. *2 Peter 3:6: "Whereby the world that then was, being overflowed with water, perished."* Let's once more compare Noah's flood of his time in the second age. Noah's flood did not fully destroy the world but only cleansed it. Ponder this! *Jeremiah 4:23. I beheld the earth, and, lo, it was without form, and void; and the heavens, and they had no light. 24. I beheld the mountains, and, lo, they trembled, and all the hills moved lightly. 25. I beheld, and, lo, there was no man, and all the birds of the heavens were fled. 26. I beheld, and, lo, the fruitful place was a wilderness, and all the cities thereof were broken down at the presence of the Lord, and by his fierce anger.*

We read in *Genesis 1:2: "And the Spirit of God moved upon the face of the Waters."* The earth was covered with water; if everything had been destroyed by a shaking and water, how is it possible that the olive tree could grow so fast as to produce a tender branch that could produce a leaf?

According to the encyclopaedia, the earliest-known Egyptian pyramids are found at Saqqara, northwest of Memphis. The earliest among these is the Pyramid of Djoser (constructed 2630 BCE–2611 BCE), which was built during the third dynasty. Noah's flood was in 2438 BC, 192 years after the construction of the pyramids had started. A time count down to 0 then AD starts 0–2016. Yet we have read in verse *26, "I beheld, and, lo, the fruitful place was a wilderness, and all the <u>cities thereof were broken down</u>."* These earliest-known Egyptian pyramids were not destroyed by Noah's flood and are still standing today. Two different floods are recorded in the Bible for those who can rightly divide the Word of God.

Genesis 7:4: "And the ark rested in the seventh month, on the seventeenth day of the month, upon the mountains of Ararat." The specific mountain is not identified. *Genesis 7:20: "Fifteen cubits upward did the waters prevail; and the mountains were covered.*

This is roughly twenty-five to thirty-one feet—eight meters. If all the mountains on earth were covered, the waters would have to cover Mount Everest, which is nearly six miles high, and the land would be covered by water more than six miles deep. In that case, where could this water have run off to when the flood subsided? It would take time to freeze and form icebergs!

To recap, Noah's flood, as many scholars claim, could have occurred eastward from the Tigris and Euphrates Valleys, in the mountain basin in Sinkiang, within the basin of which are several smaller mountains that could be fully covered by a flood. A high watermark found in many places along the mountains that rim this basin mark a positive shoreline. Could Mount Everest be part of God's restoration in this second age in the first earth age? *Jeremiah 4:24: "I beheld the mountains, and, lo, they trembled, and all the hills moved lightly."*

The Bible has verses that are overlooked or not understood by many scholars and teachers. We will look into these verses and check a word in the original manuscripts then use Strong's work to get a deeper meaning. These scriptures are after the flood of Noah's time and after they had left the ark. Here we will find a mystery about Genesis 10:5 mentioned at the start of this study.

Genesis 10:1: "Now these are the generations of the sons of Noah, Shem, Ham, *and Japheth: and unto them were sons born after the flood."* These are the descendants of the Adamic race. The Adamic race continues to flourish in the next verses: 2, 3, and 4 (but not in verse 5) and then continue in verses 6, 7, giving the names of the Adamic race again: (10:2) *"The sons of Japheth; Gomer, and Magog, and Madai, and Javan, and Tubal, and Meshech, and Tiras. 3. And the sons of Gomer; Ashkenaz, and Riphath, and*

Togarmah. 4. And the sons of Javan; Elishah, and Tarshish, Kittim, and Dodanim." We are ready for the mystery of verse 10:5; it is going to be very interesting?

All the races on earth must now toil and must chose right from wrong. What mystery does verse 5 reveal? Will we read of others or different races or the Gentiles other than the Adamic race who might have survived Noah's flood, the survivors of Noah's flood recorded in KJV?

Genesis 10:5 "By these were the isles of the Gentiles divided in their lands; every one after his tongue, after their families, in their nations." Were these people on the ark with the eight Adamic people, or was Noah's flood only in one area or basin? NIV Genesis 10:5 states, *"From these the maritime peoples spread out into their territories by their clans within their nations, each with its own language."* Here in verse 10:5 tucked in between verses 4 and verses 6! Verse 5 mentions that the Gentiles is a heathen nation. Could this be the sixth-day mankind? Noah was told to take two of every flesh; is this verse lauding to the different races? Verses 6 and 7 continue the records of the descendants of Noah.

Let's now read and examine the literal translation of Genesis 10:5, which are comparable to the original manuscripts and also provides a Strong's reference numbers by which we can discern and rightly divide the word and glean the truth.

> *Genesis 10:5. |0428| By these |6504| were divided |0336| the boundaries of |1471| the nations |0776| in their lands, |0376| each |3956| by his tongue, |4940| by their families, |1471| in their nations.*

We will now do a word study of the word nations no. 1471 in the Strong's Hebrew Dictionary.

<u>Nation:</u> *Strong's ref. no. 1471, Romanized gowy Pronounced go'-ee rarely (shortened) goy {go'-ee}; apparently from the same root as HSN1465 (in the sense of massing); a foreign nation; <u>hence, a Gentile;</u> also (figuratively) a troop of animals, or a flight of locusts: KJV—Gentile, heathen, nation, people.*

A foreign nation—this must mean that other than the Adamic race or Noah and his descendants, these, thus, must be the sixth-day people created male and female as recorded in *Genesis 1:27: "So God created man in his own image, in the image of God he created him; male and female he created them."* These are the Gentiles or other races. Most religionists dismiss this possible truth and claim that God created the races by placing a mark on Cain. After he killed Abel, his skin color changed. If this were true, how did they survive Noah's flood? Other teachers will claim that the races were created after Noah's flood by a curse for the sin of his son Ham and Noah's wife that produce a son, Canaan. For a deeper study, read on <u>"Where Did All the Races come from?"</u>

We now return to the Old Testament to read of the rest of Noah's descendants, the Adamic race that survived the flood in verse 5. We have read of the Gentiles. *Genesis 10: 6 "And the sons of Ham;*

Cush, and Mizraim, and Phut, and Canaan. 7. And the sons of Cush; Seba, and Havilah, and Sabtah, and Raamah, and Sabtecha: and the sons of Raamah, Sheba, and Dedan."

In the New Testament, we read, 1 Pet. 3:20, KJV: *"Which sometime were disobedient, when once the longsuffering of God waited in the days of Noah, while the ark was a preparing, wherein few, that is, eight souls were saved by water."* The NIV says, *"Who disobeyed long ago when God waited patiently in the days of Noah while the ark was being built. In it only a few people, eight in all, were saved through water."* The eight souls mentioned saved by water as well as by being on the ark are the Adamic race. The reference to being saved by water could well be a reference to a type of baptism or validation that they were saved and their descendants would continue and become a chosen race to carry the seed line to the birth of Christ. We can read of God choosing the Adamic race in *Deuteronomy 7:6: "The Lord thy God hath chosen thee to be a special people unto himself, above <u>all people</u> that are upon the face of the earth."* Here again we can ask, did the other races survive the flood? Was it a localized flood?

The Gentiles will be saved through the baptism of the Holy Spirit following the work done on the cross by Jesus. If we backtrack, Jesus was able to walk through walls after the crucifixion.

When he was placed in the tomb during the three days, Jesus went to those who had died before his work on the cross and preach the Gospel to save others. We can read of this in *1 Peter 3:18: "For Christ also hath once suffered for sins, the just for the unjust, that he might bring us to God, being put to death in the flesh, but quickened by the spirit: 19. By which also he went and preached unto the Spirits in prison."* Ecclesiastes 12:7 also states, *"Then shall the dust return to the earth as it was: and the spirit shall return unto God who gave it."* We can read of this place where the spirits go after death in *Luke 16:26: "And beside all this, between us and you there is a great gulf fixed: so that they which would pass from hence to you cannot; neither can they pass to us, that would come from thence."*

Epilogue for chapter four.

I would suggest you read the whole chapter of John 8:1–59.

The Christian that rightly divides the Word to find the truth and believes that the disciple John accurately quoted Jesus and accept Jesus's words as clear and explicit as to true facts must come to the realization that the other races survived the flood by being on the ark or that the flood could have been <u>localized</u>.

Let me just highlight a few scriptures: (John 8:2) "And early in the morning he came again into the temple, and all the people came unto him; and he sat down, and taught them."

Jesus then in verse 8:12 spoke again unto them, saying, *"I am the light of the world: he that follows me shall not walk in darkness, but shall have the light of life."* Paul warned the believers that they might be deceived: *2 Cor. 11:14 "And no marvel; for Satan himself is transformed into an angel of light. His light leads to the lake of fire."*

Jesus then enters the treasury: *John 8:20 "These words spoke Jesus in the treasury, as he taught in the temple: and no man laid hands on him; for his hour was not yet come."* In the verse *John 8:31, "Then said Jesus to those Jews which believed on him, If you continue in my word, then are you my disciples indeed; 33. They answered him, we are Abraham's seed, and were never in bondage to any man: how can you say, you shall be made free?"*

Jesus had preached: *John 3:18 "He that believeth on him is not condemned: but he that believeth not is condemned already, because he hath not believed in the name of the only begotten Son of God. John 8:39."* They answered and said unto him, Abraham is our father. Jesus said unto them, if you were Abraham's children, you would do the works of Abraham."*

Now that we have this knowledge again, I suggest you read the whole chapter. Let's move on to the verse that confirms the survival of the other races by the words of Jesus: *John 8:44. "You belong to your father, the devil, and you want to carry out your father's desire.* [Satan had attempted to destroy the true seed line to Jesus many times.] *He was a murderer* (through his son Cain) *from the beginning, not holding to the truth, for there is no truth in him. When he lies, he speaks his native language, for he is a liar and the father of lies."* The seed line of Satan survived Noah's flood! *8:48 "Then answered the Jews, and said unto him, Say we not well that thou art a Samaritan, and hast a devil? NIV 48 states, "The Jews answered him: 'aren't we right in saying that you are a Samaritan and demon-possessed?'"* Their answer was to void Jesus's teaching.

The Apostle Paul also confirms that there were other survivors besides the eight in all, who were saved through water. He wrote in Acts 13:8, KJV, *"But Elymas the sorcerer* (for so is his name by interpretation) *withstood them, seeking to turn away the deputy from the faith. 9. Then Saul* (who also is called Paul*), filled with the Holy Ghost, set his eyes on him, 10. And said, O full of all subtlety and all mischief, you child of the devil,*(Key) *you enemy of all righteousness, will you not cease to pervert the right ways of the Lord?"*

In the NIV, verse 10 *"You are a child of the devil and an enemy of everything that is right! You are full of all kinds of deceit and trickery. Will you never stop perverting the right ways of the Lord?"*

In Revelation, Jesus instructs John to write seven letters to the churches in NIV, *Rev. 2:8: "To the angel of the church in Smyrna write: These are the words of him who is the First and the Last, who died and came to life again. 9. I know your afflictions and your poverty—yet you are rich! I know the slander of those who say they are Jews and are not, but are a synagogue of Satan."* Here we see that Satan's descendants who survived Noah's flood are trying to pollute the church We read this also in another letter in *Revelation 3:7: "To the angel of the church in Philadelphia write: These are the words of him who is holy and true,—9. I will make those who are of the synagogue of Satan, who claim to be Jews though they are not, but are liars."* Lies are Satan's trademark.

Revelation 12:9: "And the great dragon was cast out, that old serpent, called the Devil, and Satan, which deceives the whole world: he was cast out into the earth, and his angels were cast out with him."

We read of the surviving Kenite race or sons of Cain; some preachers claim that Cain married one of his sisters! This does not make sense as why would if there were daughters of Adam be out of the presence of God and <u>dwell in the land of Nod before or after Adam and Eve were expelled from the planted garden eastward of Eden</u>? And who raised them? The only logical answer is they were part of the sixth day creating *Genesis 1:27. So God created man in his own image, in the image of God he created him; male and female he created them.*

We can find part of the genealogy of Cain and his wife or the spread of the serpent's or Satan's seed line that started out in the Garden of Eden with Eve in *Genesis 4:16: "So Cain <u>went out from the LORD's presence</u> and lived in the land of Nod, east of Eden. 17. Cain lay with his wife, and she became pregnant and gave birth to Enoch. Cain was then building a city, and he named it after his son Enoch. 18. To Enoch was born Irad,—19. Lamech married two women,—23. Lamech said to his wives, 'Adah and Zillah, listen to me; wives of Lamech, hear my words. I have killed a man for wounding me, a young man for injuring me.' 24. If Cain is avenged seven times, then Lamech seventy-seven times."* Jesus confirmed Cain's seed line: Again we read *John 8:44 "You belong to your father, the devil, and you want to carry out your father's desire.* [Satan's attempt to destroy the true seed line to Jesus.] *He was a murderer* (through his son Cain) *from the beginning, not holding to the truth, for there is no truth in him. When he lies, he speaks his native language, for he is a liar and the father of lies"*. <u>The seed line of Satan, his seed line, survived Noah's flood</u>! Were all the races on the ark, or was the flood localized?

Amen.

Chapter 5

Understanding the inspired Word Of God

Before we start this study of creation I would like to present a scenario based solely on the preponderance of basic logic having rightly divided the Word and coming to the conclusion that the Bible verifies there are three earth ages recorded in the Bible.

We may make the assumption that God has no gender and the Angels were created in his image without gender and in Angelic spiritual bodies *1 Cor. 15:38 But God gives it a body as he has determined 40. There are also heavenly bodies and there are earthly bodies ;* they roamed the earth in the first earth age with Lucifer being the head guardian a form of a king; *Ezekiel 28:12. "Son of man, take up a lament concerning the king of Tyre and say to him: `this is what the Sovereign LORD says: "you were the model of perfection, full of wisdom and perfect in beauty. 13. You were in Eden, The Garden of God;* the whole earth was a garden. They were on earth with the Dinosaurs; *Job 40: 15. "Look at the behemoth, which I made along with you and which feeds on grass like an ox.*

In this second earth age God created the sixth day Man with a earthly body, He created them Male and Female *Gen. 1: 27. So God created man in his own image, in the image of God he created him; male and female he created them.* Wen God formed Adam he had both DNA of male and female.

[Here again you may want to Jump ahead to Chapter 6 and read the first page]

Then God formed Adam and placed him in the planted garden east of Eden <u>with no gender</u>; *Genesis 2:8. Now the LORD God had planted a garden in the east, in Eden; and there he put the man he had formed.* While Adam slept God took a rib or DNA and formed his help mate Eve; *Gen. 2:21. So the LORD God caused the man to fall into a deep sleep; and while he was sleeping, he took one of the man's ribs and closed up the place with flesh. 22. Then the LORD God made a woman from the rib he had taken out of the man, and he brought her to the man.* in the planted garden east of Eden.

<u>We can now start our study:</u>
<u>Understanding the inspired Word Of God</u>

In chapter 2 we studied and established that there are three earth ages revealed in the Word, the Bible, we can study the "beginnings." We will start with the literal version complete with numbers that can be used with a Lexicon to establish the original word in Hebrew or Greek.

Genesis 1:1. 7225 In the beginning 1254 created 0430 God 0853 -8064 the heavens 0853 and 0776 the earth 2. 0776 and the earth 1961 was 8414 without form 0922 and empty, 2822 and darkness 5921 on 6440| the surface of 8415 the deep 7307 and the Spirit of 0430 God 7363 moving gently 5921| on 6440 the surface of 4325 the waters.

The word "was" Strong's ref. no. 1961 *Romanized hayah Pronounced haw-yaw a primitive root [compare HSN1933]; to exist, i.e., be or become, come to pass (always emphatic, and not a mere copula or auxiliary). KJV—beacon, X altogether, be(-come), accomplished, committed, like), break, cause, come (to pass), do, faint, fall, +follow, happen, X have, last, pertain, quit (one-)self, require, X us.*

We can use this information to clearly translate the two verses as belonging to the "Beginning" of the first earth age: *Genesis 1:1. "In the beginning God created the heavens and the earth. 2. Now the earth became formless and empty, darkness was over the surface of the deep, and the Spirit of God was hovering over the waters."*

We can now relate to the "beginning" of the second earth age in *Genesis 1:3. "And God said, 'Let there be light,' and there was light."* Like any book, when we understand the beginning, we can understand the body and the ending. We can glean a brief summary by understanding the biblical verses written by Peter and the verses found in the book of Revelations.

First earth age and the end of it: *2 Peter 3:6: "Where by the world that then was, being overflowed with water, perished."* This was not Noah's flood as all perished; refer to "Noah's Flood."

Second earth age, *2 Peter 3:7: "But the heavens and the earth, which are now, by the same word, are kept in store, reserved unto fire against the day of judgment and perdition of ungodly men."* We are told in *Matthew 24:22, "And except those days should be shortened, there should no flesh be saved: but for the elect's sake those days shall be shortened."* The wicked are reserved for the Lake of Fire; *Revelation. 20:10. "And the devil that deceived them was cast into the lake of fire and brimstone, where the beast and the false prophet are, and shall be tormented day and night for ever and ever."* We must draw your attention to the words above: "was" and the words "which are now."

The coming of the third earth age is recorded *in Revelation 21:1: "And I saw a new heaven and a new earth: for the first heaven and the first earth were passed away; and there was no more sea.* Sea in this verse refers to people: *Revelation. 17:15 "The waters you saw,—are peoples."* Here we should do a word study of first.

Strong's no. *4413, Transliterated: protos Phonetic: pro'-tos Text: contracted superlative of 4253; foremost (in time, place, order or importance):—before, beginning, best, chief(-est), first (of all), former.*

The word the translator or the scribes used first instead of former could well be in error and cause confusion, misrepresentation, or a misunderstanding for some of the learned or taught scholars, but the deeper truth can be found by independent study or self-study and examination of the scriptures or the entire Word of God—His letter to us.

We can suggest that the scripture would be better translated: "And I saw a new heaven and a new earth: for the first [former] heaven and the first [former] earth were passed away."

But in their defense, we can say that the second earth age will not perish, but a change will occur as Jesus returns to put his enemies under his feet and *save the second age as written in Revelation 19:11. I saw heaven standing open and there before me was a white horse, whose rider is called Faithful and True. – With justice he judges and makes war. 19. Then I saw the beast and the kings of the earth and their armies gathered together to make war against the rider on the horse and his army. 20. But the beast was captured, and with him the false prophet who had performed the miraculous signs on his behalf. With these signs he had deluded those who had received the mark of the beast and worshiped his image. The two of them were thrown alive into the fiery lake of burning sulphur. 21. The rest of them were killed with the sword that came out of the mouth of the rider on the horse, and all the birds gorged themselves on their flesh.*

We must understand that this is not the end of the second age for we read in *20:1, "And I saw an angel come down from heaven, having the key of the bottomless pit and a great chain in his hand. 2. And he laid hold on the dragon, that old serpent, which is the Devil, and Satan, and bound him a thousand years."* Jesus took control and preached and cleansed the second age for a thousand years (millennium) then as written in Revelation *20:7: "And when the thousand years are expired, Satan shall be loosed out of his prison, 8. And shall go out to deceive the nations which are in the four quarters of the earth."* Some religious teachers and scholars will again fall for his lies as they did at Christ's first coming; all of us in this second age have free will and must choose!

Revelation 20:9. "And fire came down from God out of heaven, and devoured them. [Here we read of the final lake of fire.] *10. And the devil that deceived them was cast into the lake of fire and brimstone, where the beast and the false prophet are, and shall be tormented day and night for ever and ever."* In 2 Peter 3:7, it is stated, *"But the heavens and the earth, <u>which are now</u>, by the same word, are kept in store, reserved unto fire against the Day of Judgment and perdition of ungodly men."* This is the end of the second earth age as written by Peter: *Revelation 20:14. "And death and hell were cast into the lake of fire. This is the second death. 15. And whosoever was not found written in the book of life was cast into the lake of fire."*

Then God sends down a new heaven and a new earth age—*Revelation 21:1 "And I saw a new heaven and a new earth." The third age of everlasting is set in place.*

To understand the complexity of the Bible, we must follow a subject throughout God's Word to find the deeper truth, starting with the first earth age, "the beginning" to the third earth age.

This research or study will basically only cover three main subjects. When we realize or grasp the significance of these three subjects and how they are interwoven throughout His Word, the Scriptures will open up and possibly reveal a deeper truth, blossoming into a new insight of God's living Word presented in the Holy Bible. As in any book, if we don't comprehend the beginning of the book, we will have a hard time to understand the middle or the end. The original manuscripts (OM) have no numbered chapters, verses, or punctuation marks as our modern-day Bibles. These were added by interpreters, translators, and finally by scribes, sometimes masking a deeper truth. Before the invention of the printing press, copies were hand copied by scribes.

The three subjects we will concentrate on are as follows:

1. A brief look into the beginning.

2. The creation of the Races. The Gentiles

3. The forming of 'eth-'Ha' ' âdhâm, <u>the Adamic race</u> who will become the chosen race to carry forth the seed line to the birth of Jesus.

We will be researching Genesis 1–6 and a few supporting scriptures.

First Subject: "The Beginning"

Genesis 1:1. In the beginning, God created the heaven and the earth. This took place at a time we cannot comprehend. God had created the Earth to be inhabited as we read in *Isaiah 45:18: "For thus said the Lord that created the heavens; God himself that formed the earth and made it; he has established it, <u>he created it not in vain, he formed it to be inhabited</u>: I am the Lord; and there is none else."*

The main challenge translators of the original manuscripts (OM) have is they may translate a word that can have different meanings. Thus, not relating the word to the subject alters the true meaning. The next verse is a great example. The Hebrew word hyn or hayah; it is a verb. In English, it should properly translated be "to be, become, became or come to pass."

The translators/scribes must have been confused by this Hebrew word or had not tied the subject to the rest of the Bible. This word (hyn) has been translated from Hebrew to <u>was</u> instead of become or became.(Key) *Genesis 1:2: "And the earth was* [this should be translated as became] *without form and void."* This can be confirmed by Strong's #1961, as we will elaborate later.

We can also confirm this by reading what God inspired: *Isaiah 24:3 "The land shall be <u>utterly emptied, and utterly spoiled</u>: for the Lord has spoken this word."* He we have read the earth <u>became</u> utterly *Void* (not was). When we have this key and turn it; the floodgates of supporting scriptures come to light such as *Psalm 104:30: "You sent forth thy spirit, they are created: and you renewed* (Key) *the face of the earth.* This can only verify that there was a first earth age before our present second earth age. We read in *Isaiah 24:19: "The earth is utterly broken down, the earth is <u>clean dissolved</u>, and the earth is moved exceedingly."* The earth is made void. This was caused by Satan's downfall in the first earth age. He had wanted to replace God. Many accept this destruction as Noah's flood; a suggested reading is chapter "Noah's Flood." At this point, I would suggest the Bible can be compared to a jigsaw puzzle; the various scriptures written by several writers are the pieces of the puzzle by properly dividing the scriptures, and following a subject, we get the full picture or true understanding of the Word of God.

We will now read and confirm Satan's downfall and the reason God ended the first earth age and the reason for its total destruction.

Ezekiel 28:12. "Son of man, take up a lament concerning the king of Tyre [king of fire, Satan/Lucifer] and say to him: 'this is what the Sovereign LORD says: 'You were the model of perfection, full of wisdom and perfect in beauty. 13. You were in Eden, the garden of God [At this point of time or age, the whole earth was a garden covered by vegetation! Drilling for oil in the frozen tundra has brought up from the depths evidence of palm wood]; *every precious stone adorned you: ruby, topaz and emerald,—and beryl. Your settings and mountings were made of gold; on the day you were created they were prepared. 14. You are the anointed cherub that covers; and I have set you so: you were upon the holy mountain of God; you have walked up and down in the midst of the stones of fire."* The fiery stones reflect the brilliance of the Throne of God. We will now read why God destroyed the first earth age.

Jeremiah 4:23. I beheld the earth, and, lo, it was without form, and void; and the heavens, and they had no light. Ezekiel 28:15: "You were perfect in your ways from the day that you were created, till iniquity was found in you. [Satan wanted to take the place of God and take his place on the Throne; one-third of the people began to worship Satan.] *16. Through your widespread trade you were filled with violence, and you sinned."* God was disappointed in what he had created. In frustration, he laid void the earth.

Again we can read of this in *2 Peter 3:6: "By these waters also the world of that time was deluged and destroyed."* This cannot be Noah's flood! In this flood, the first earth age or *"of that time was deluged and destroyed."* We can now feel comfortable with; *Genesis 1:2: "And the earth (became) without form, and void; and darkness was upon the face of the deep, And the Spirit of God moved upon the face of the waters."* Earth had become void and uninhabitable. God had cleansed the earth. This was the end of the first earth age.

General Information

One of the most respected works on translating the Hebrew and Greek into English is credited to Dr. James Strong, LLD, STD. His translation can be traced by a number that corresponds to his exhaustive works. One of the most important words that you must understand is in verse 2 of *Genesis 1:2: "And the earth was"* should be became. In the OM, the word is hyn, transliterated as hayah, and assigned the number 1961.

Dr. Strong's Concordance ref. no. 1961 hayah Pronounced haw-yaw a primitive root [compare SN1933]; to exist, i.e. <u>be or become come to pass</u> (always emphatic, and not a mere copula or auxiliary): A verb. KJV— beacon, X altogether, be (-come), accomplished, committed, like), break, cause, <u>come (to pass)</u>, do, faint, fall, + follow, happen, X have, last, pertain, quit (one-) self, require, X use.

You can see that the translators or scribes of KJV misinterpreted the word hyh. It is a verb, and some translators have now changed the word was to "being". A few Bibles will send you to the center column or the bottom of the page and offer the truth "or became." In Genesis 2, the translators or scribes added a second *was* in italics—"and darkness was upon the face of the deep." The second *was* is generally added to the Word for clarity to the English translation (as a past indicative of be); for example, in the direct translation of the original manuscript (OM) "<u>and saw God good</u>," compare this to the rearranged words with the added words for clarity "And God saw it was good (they added it and was). As you can see, they had a very responsible job to do. Another example is "and the Tree of Life was in the middle of the planted garden" (Strong's ref. no. 9999); was added for clarity.

This concludes our examination into the subject of "in the beginning." This subject will reappear later as we examine the Word more closely, rightly dividing the Word. If you wish to read more of this subject at this time, refer to the chapter "The Three Earth Ages."

Second Subject
The Creation of the Second Earth Age

Special note: "God said."(Key) God will now create all things by the spoken word or command. (Later we will read instead of using the spoken word, God will actually form 'eth-'Ha' 'âdhâm The Man Adam).

We must now rightly divide and follow the main subject in the Word as we begin to read of this, the second earth age or our present age: *Ps. 104:7 "At your rebuke the waters fled— 30. When you send your Spirit, they are created, and you renew the face of the earth."* Here we can reinforce the word replenish that some translators used in KJV, *Genesis 1:28: "And God blessed them, and God said unto them, Be fruitful, and multiply, and replenish the earth, God renews the Earth again."*

Genesis 1:3: "And God said, Let there be light: and there was light." God once again looks favourably on the Earth and will create a habitable earth. He is the light.

Revelation 21:23: "And the city had no need of the sun, neither of the moon, to shine in it: for the glory of God did lighten it, and the Lamb is the light thereof." John 1:5: "And the light shines in darkness; and the darkness comprehended it not."

By His Word, He lifted the veil of darkness: *Gen. 1:4 "And God saw the light, that it was good: and God divided the light from the darkness."* [The Sun and Moon are positioned in verses 1:14–16.] *Gen. 1:5. "God called the light Day, and the darkness he called Night. And the evening and the morning were the first day".* The dawn of a new Era or the start of the second earth age. *2 Pet. 3:8. "But do not forget this one thing, dear friends:* <u>*With the Lord a day is like a*</u> <u>*thousand years, and a thousand years are like a day*</u>.

<u>This was the end of the first day in God's time, one thousand years of our time.</u>

Genesis 1:6. "And God <u>*said*</u>*, Let there be a firmament in the midst of the waters, and let it divide the waters from the waters. 7. And God made the firmament, and divided the waters which were under the firmament from the waters which were above the firmament: and it was so.* [The water that covered the Earth was divided by air and the waters above became mist or vapour, we now relate this to our clouds.] *8. And God called the firmament Heaven.* [This will be expanded in verses 14 and 20, also relates to verse 1:2—"the Spirit of God moved upon the face of the waters"], *and the evening and the morning were the second day.*

<u>This ended the second day in God's time, two thousand years</u> <u>of our time.</u>

Genesis 1:9. "And God <u>*said:*</u> *Let the waters under the Heaven be gathered together unto one place, and let the dry land appear: and it was so.* [God now once again brings up the land from the depths, forming plains, the foothills and the Mountains.] *10. And God called the dry land Earth; and the gathering together of the water s called the Seas: and God saw that it was good. 11. And God said let the earth bring forth grass, the herb yielding seed, and the fruit tree yielding fruit after* <u>*his kind*</u>*, whose seed is in itself, upon the earth: and it was so. 12. And the earth brought forth grass and herb yielding seed after* <u>*his kind*</u>*, and the tree yielding fruit, whose seed was in itself, after* <u>*his kind:*</u> *and God saw that it was good.* [God has set up the Earth with a carpet of grass and plant Life, the grass was like a thick green carpet covering the earth, <u>full of different colour</u>

species of flowers and trees. Note that the word "his kind" makes evident that things will not evolve or change. This is repeated ten times; there is no evolving.] *13. And the evening and the morning were the third day".*

This ended the third day in God's time, three thousand years of our time.

Genesis 1:14. "And God said, Let there be lights in the firmament of the heaven to divide the day from the night; and let them be for signs, and for seasons, and for days, and years: [The sun, moon, and stars have now been created. Note that there are now seasons.] *15. And let them be for lights in the firmament of the heaven to give light upon the earth: and it was so. 16. And God made two great lights; the greater light to rule the day, and the lesser light to rule the night: he made the stars also. 17. And God set them in the firmament of the heaven to give light upon the earth, 18. And to rule over the day and over the night, and to divide the light from the darkness: and God saw that it was good. 19. And the evening and the morning were the fourth day".*

This ended the fourth day in God's time, four thousand years of our time.

Genesis 1:20. "And God said: Let the waters bring forth abundantly the moving creature that hath life, and fowl that may fly above the earth in the open firmament of heaven. [Here God creates breathing creatures that swim and fly and of different species and colors.] *21. And God created great whales, and every living creature that moved, which the waters brought forth abundantly, after their kind, and every winged fowl after his kind: and God saw that it was good.* ["After their kind" voids the evolution theory.] *22. And God blessed them, saying, Be fruitful, and multiply, and fill the waters in the seas, and let fowl multiply in the earth. 23. And the evening and the morning were the fifth day"*.

This ended the fourth day in God's time, five thousand years of our time.

Genesis 1:24. "And God <u>said</u>, let the earth bring forth the living creature <u>after his kind</u>, cattle, and creeping thing, and beast of the earth after his kind: and it was so. 25. And God made the beast of the earth after <u>his kind</u> and cattle <u>after their kind</u>, and everything that crept upon the earth after his kind: and God saw that it was good". Again we must respect the wording "after their kind." The cattle here would be the free-roaming buffalo, elk, deer, moose, even bears, etc. They are not domesticated animals; they were created to roam at will. They will be hunted as food along with birds and fish, distinguishable by size, shape, species, and color—all breathing creatures "after their own kind."

God will now create an earthly man or mankind

Genesis 1:26. "And God said, [we must pay attention to "God said" or spoke the word to create] *Let us make man in our image, after our likeness:* [Here God has created 'âdâm—in the OM, the word has no article or particle, thus it means "man." It implies a creation with no gender (this will be cleared up) and let them have dominion over the fish of the sea, and over the fowl of the air, and over the cattle, <u>and over all the earth,</u> and over every creeping thing that crept upon the earth. *27. So God created man in his own image, in the image of God created he him; <u>male and female created</u>*

he them. [We must respect God is All in All or "I am" and has no gender. God split the DNA, and we have a male and female. This in the OM becomes 'eth-' âdâm, which is now mankind. They will be allowed to roam the entire surface of the earth to hunt, fish, and live off the land.] *28. And God blessed them* [all the races had been created and are blessed; we will later learn of a chosen race of people, the Adamic race]; and God said unto them, Be fruitful, and multiply, and replenish the earth [a reference to the first age] *and subdue it: and have dominion over the fish of the sea, and over the fowl of the air, and over every living thing that moved upon the earth"*. God has given the Gentile; male and female a life of peace to roam at will and live off the land. It is very important that we understand "they live off the land." They have the whole dominion of the earth. This will change in about 1,500-plus years.

For clarity, in the original manuscripts (OM), written in ancient Hebrew there are three different meanings for the word-translated as just man. However by the addition of the article and the particle and the addition of an h we will be able to discern the difference.

1. Mankind—no article or particle.

2. The mankind—with article but no particle.

3. The man Adam—with article and particle and the addition of an h.

However, they are all translated in the Strong's Concordance as the same: Strong's refer. #. 120. Romanized 'adam Pronounced aw-dawm' from HSN0119; ruddy i.e. a human being (an individual or the species, mankind, etc.): KJV—X another, + hypocrite, + common sort, X low, man, person.

Let's examine the original words used to describe both men and women in the original manuscripts.

1. The first man, Gen.1:26: 'âdâm has no article or particle. 'âdâm = Man, a "Gentile". *Genesis 1:26: "And God said, Let us make man in our image, after* our likeness: [This is the first time man is used God and the Angelic beings have no gender In Strong's, the word is possibly related to the number 2242. "Text: of Persian origin; Zethar, a eunuch of Xerxes: The word eunuch suggests not capable to reproduce." but the verse continues and a new word is introduced meaning more than one] and let <u>them</u> this can be tied to Strong's number is 853 Romanized 'eth Pronounced ayth [here we see the word eth: thus we get 'eth-'âdâm KJV--[as such unrepresented in English]. The words man and then the word them must have had the original translators scratching their head.

Back to *Genesis 1:26. And God said: Let us make man in our image, after our likeness: and let them have dominion over the fish of the sea, and over the fowl of the air, and over the cattle, and over all the earth, and over every creeping thing that creeps upon the earth.* Mankind or both male and Female have the whole world to roam and have dominion over every creature including the fish of the Sea.

2. Then in: *Genesis 1:27: "So God created man in his own image, in the image of God created he him; <u>male and female created he them</u>.* [The next verse should help dispel any confusion.] *28. And God blessed them, and God said unto them, Be fruitful, and multiply, <u>and replenish the earth</u>, and subdue it: and have dominion over the fish of the sea, and over the fowl of the air, and over every living thing that moves upon the earth* [again they are created and free to roam the dominion of the earth. Not just in a garden]" (Gen. 1:27–28).

At this point in our study we can seriously ponder or ask why the scholars or educators cannot accept the fact that God at this point has created all the races accept the Adamic race. They loosely suggest that the mark of Cain, Ham son's incest with his mother was the cause of changing of the colour of skin or creation of the races; or other speculative theories!

[Here again you may want to Jump ahead to Chapter 6 and read the first page]

3. Then a third man mentioned 'eth-'Ha' ' âdhâm with both the article and the particle while h is also added. 'eth-'Ha''âdhâm = the Man Adam, the "Adamic Race". *Genesis 2:7. And the Lord God formed man of the dust of the ground, and breathed into his nostrils the breath of life; and man became a living soul". There is now an h in âdhâm.* [In Genesis 17:4–5, God makes a covenant with Abram. He is chosen, and his name will contain an h; Abram will become Abraham, Sarai his wife will become Sarah.] We will later read of this man 'eth-'Ha''âdhâm, formed from the dust of the ground not created by the spoken word of God. This man is formed in Genesis 2:7. This person will start the Adamic race. His descendants will become a chosen people whose seed line we can follow through the scriptures up to the birth of Jesus Christ.

At this point, we can ask why some translators/scribes were unable to unlock certain truths. In *Matthew 13:17, Jesus said, "For verily I say unto you, That many prophets and righteous men have desired to see those things which you see, and have not seen them; and to hear those things which you hear, and have not heard them."*

Jesus often spoke in parables, even to his disciples: "Then answered Peter and said unto him, Declare unto us this parable" then in *Luke 8:9. "And his disciples asked him, saying, what might this parable be? 10. And he* [Jesus] *said, unto you* [his disciples] *it is given to know the mysteries of the kingdom of God: but to others in parables; that seeing they might not see and hearing <u>they might not understand</u>.*" does tradition and dogma still hide or confuse some of the modern scholars? Can the average preacher answer the question? Who did Cain marry in the land of Uz? Refer to chapter 6.

Back to Genesis 1:27–28: "So God created man in his own image, in the image of God created he him; male and female created he them. God has created a male, a female and all the races. [We will read more of the Gentiles as Cain seeks a wife in Genesis 4:16 and later as we read of Noah's flood in Genesis 10:5.] And God blessed them, and God said unto them, Be fruitful, and multiply, and replenish the earth. Some versions of the Bible translate the Hebrew to "and fill the earth." The words replenish and fill can be interchanged as evident in Strong's number. 4390, KJV: Accomplish, confirm, + consecrate, be at an end, be expired, be fenced, fill, fulfill, (be, become, X draw, give in, go) full (-ly, set, tale), [over] flow, fullness, furnish, gather (selves, together), presume, replenish, satisfy, set, space, take a [hand-] full, + have wholly.

If the word replenish is used, this can be a reference to the destruction of the <u>first age</u>. Here is a good example: To find the truth, we must use other scriptures to guide us as to the most plausible translation to find the deeper truth: KJV, *Psalm 104:30. "You sent forth thy spirit, they are created: and you <u>renewed</u> the face of the earth.* This would perpetuate God to create this 2nd earth age."

God created man or them 'eth-' âdâm with the article but no particle; they are Mankind or the "<u>Gentiles</u>" who live a life of peace to roam at will the whole dominion of the earth. This will change in about 1,500-plus years. In verse 28, it says, "<u>And God blessed them</u>." Them meaning male and female, Gentiles, all the races are blessed. [We will later learn of a chosen race of people—the Adamic race 'eth-'Ha''âdhâm] —and God said unto them, "Be fruitful, and multiply, and replenish the earth." We still must determine if the word should be translated as fill or fill again!

Genesis 1:29. "And God said, Behold, I have given you every herb bearing seed, which is upon the face of all the earth, and every tree, in the which is the fruit of a tree yielding seed; to you it shall be for meat. [Here again we learn they live off the land.] *30. And to every beast of the earth, and to every fowl of the air, and to everything that crept upon the earth, wherein there is life, I have given every green herb for meat: and it was so.*

The 'eth-' âdâm, or mankind, are the Gentiles (all the races); they are fruit pickers, fishermen, and hunters living off the land that God had created for them. We can call them the "sixth-day creation" or mankind"; they are male and female, the different races who roamed freely on earth without toil or strife. They are told "and replenish the earth"; the word replenish will have ring truth when we can accept that there was a first earth age and that it had been destroyed.

Before we end this sixth day, let us move forward to KJV, *Genesis 2:4. "These are the generations of the heavens and of the earth when they were created, in the day that the Lord God made the earth and the heavens, 5. And every plant of the field before it was in the earth, and every herb of the field before it grew: for the Lord God had not caused it to rain upon the earth, and <u>there was not a man to till the ground.</u>* "(Key)* The NIV *Gen. 2:4. "This is the account of the* *heavens and the earth when they were created.* [This is when the LORD God made the earth and the heavens or recreated it in the second earth age.] *:5. And no shrub of the field had yet appeared on the earth and no plant of the field had yet sprung up, for the LORD God had not sent rain on the earth and <u>there was no man to work the ground.</u>"* This statement "there was no man to work the ground is ignored by most scholars but is one of the main KEYS to understand the beginning. Why would they need a farmer when we have read that the sixth-day man lived off the land and sea? God had created male and female; they were fruit pickers, hunters, and fishermen. They had dominion of the whole earth to roam at will. Not a husbandman, farmer, or a rancher restricted to a small area or as we will learn of a man placed in a "planted garden east of Eden".

Back to *Genesis 1:31: "And God saw everything that he had made, and, behold, it was very good. And the evening and the morning were the sixth day."* By his spoken word, God has created the second earth age and is pleased with his creation. Note that in verse 28, they are blessed and God comments "very good."

This ended the sixth day in God's time, six thousand years of our time.

Why did the translators or scribes end their first chapter here at Genesis 1: 31? The subject is continued. There is one more day. <u>The original manuscripts have no chapters.</u> God has one more day or one thousand years of our time to fulfill. Was their motive to quell a discrimination against the people who would become God's chosen race of people who are to keep the seed line pure to the birth of Jesus? The subject is not exhausted! Instead, the subject of creation is continued.

In *Chapter 2:1 "Thus the heavens and the earth were finished, and all the host of them.* [This verse sums up the six days of creation; God has one day to rest and review his work.] *2. And on the seventh day, God ended his work which he had made; and he rested on the seventh day from all his work which he had made.* [The related subject continues.] *3. And God blessed the seventh day, and sanctified it: because that in it he had rested from all his work which God created and made.* The creation subject continues.

God now reviews his creation of the second earth age, which began in Genesis 1:3. But the subject of his creation continues *in Genesis 2:4. These are the generations of the heavens and of the earth when they were <u>created</u>, in the day that the Lord God made the earth and the heavens.* This is the second age.

The next verse when carefully read and understood is very critical and offers a prelude to a new upcoming subject, the forming of 'eth-'Ha' ' âdhâm, "the Man Adam." *Genesis 2:6. "And every plant of the field before it was in the earth, and every herb of the field before it grew: for the Lord God had not caused it to rain upon the earth* [the rest of this verse speaks volumes of what is to come], *<u>and there was not a man to till the ground.</u>"* [God had created fruit pickers, hunters, and fishermen, but no husbandman farmer or rancher or domesticated animals.] the creation subject continues in verse *:6: But there went up a mist from the earth, and watered the whole face of the ground.* <u>This ends the subject of creation and should be the end of Chapter 1. The end of the seventh day in God's time, seven thousand years of our time.</u>

<u>God's word will now begin a new subject on the eighth day of God's time.</u>

Seven days or seven thousand man's years has taken place. Our modern-day calendar supposedly begins on the eighth day at 4004 BC, and we subtract to 0 BC at which time we start AD 1. The start of the second earth age then could be 7,000 + 4004 BC = 11,004 BC. 11004 + now the year 2015 AD = 13,019 years of the second Age.

Special Note

The sixth-day creation of "the mankind," the "Gentiles," is clouded for many by *Genesis 3:20. And Adam called his wife's name Eve because she was the mother of all living.* But because of their sin, all will die! Confusing? Other translators offer that Adam named his wife Eve because she would become the mother of all the living. This translation makes more sense. After Cain kills Abel, Eve gives birth to her third Son Seth, and this seed line is kept pure and carried forth to the birth of Jesus. Eve is called the mother of all living because her descendent shall be blessed; "the mother of all living" is related to the work of her descendant Jesus. "In Christ shall all be made alive," those who, regardless of race, believe and accept Jesus as their saviour will achieve everlasting life and be part of "the Living" it is written in:*1 Cor. 15:22. For as in Adam all die, even so in Christ shall all be made alive.*

Although Adam will die, his seed line through Eve or by umbilical cord to umbilical cord will be kept pure by the chosen race. Then with the work of Jesus culminating at the cross, we are given the chance to be part of "the Living."

The previous verse written by the Apostle Paul also tends to confuse most scholars and students who miss the subject or do not rightly divide the Word, the subject being the Adamic race, the seed line from Adam to Jesus, the Saviour, not a statement or relating to the subject of creation or the sixth-day creation of "mankind."

Third Subject
The Forming of Adam and the
Planting of the Garden of Eden

At the conclusion of the subject "creation," in *Genesis 2:5, we read, "And there was <u>not a man to till the ground</u>. 6. but there went up a mist from the earth, and watered the whole face of the ground."* [Here again you may want to Jump ahead to Chapter 6 and read the first page]. <u>We now begin a new subject</u> which will take place in a confined area, <u>the planted Garden of Eden</u>. In *Ezekiel 28:13, it is written, "Thou hast been in <u>Eden the garden of God</u>;* this was the whole earth."

We now start a new subject; *Genesis 2:7. "And the Lord God formed man of the dust of the ground, and breathed into his nostrils the breath of life; and man became a living soul.* This man <u>is formed from the clay of the earth</u>, <u>not created by the spoken Word of God</u>. In the OM, we find that the article and particle are present and is the first mention of 'eth-'Ha'' âdhâm; there is <u>an h added</u> in âdhâm, properly translated "the man Adam." Christ would be called the second Adam.

At this point in our study, let's compare the words created and formed and realize that it can relate to two separate events. God created male and female but only formed Adam, then while Adam slept, his DNA or female genes were taken to form Eve.

Created: *Strong's no. 1254 Transliterated: bara' Phonetic: baw-raw' Text: a primitive root; (absolutely) to create; (qualified) to cut down (a wood), select, feed (as formative processes): - choose, create (creator), cut down, dispatch, o, make (fat)*

Formed: *Strong's no. 3335 Transliterated: yatsar Phonetic: yaw-tsar' Text: probably identical with 3334 (through the squeezing into shape); ([compare 3331]); to mold into a form; especially as a potter; figuratively, to determine (i.e. form a resolution): -X earthen, fashion, form, frame, make (-r), potter, purpose.* - Eve was made from a rib or curve (helix, DNA) from Adam.

Historians now start the reckoning of time as 4004 BC. Genesis 2: 8 "And the Lord God planted a garden eastward in Eden; and there He put the man [here again it is 'eth-'Ha"âdhâm or "the Man Adam," the founder of the Adamic race] whom He had formed".

God formed this man, not created.as was the sixth day, or "the mankind," the Gentiles, in Gen. 1: 27.they roamed the grasslands of the dominion of the earth; however, Gen 2:5 states that there was not a man to till the ground. This simple statement speaks volumes to those who have eyes to see and ears to hear; to others, it is insignificant or for some reason kept hidden as it could be a reason for discrimination, but God loves all the races, the Gentiles. After Adam and Eve are banished out of the planted garden east of Eden for their sin, Adam and Eve will roam the earth along with the Gentiles. The descendants of 'eth-'Ha"âdhâm and Eve, through their third son Seth, will become God's chosen Adamic race of people. Why? They had brought death and will bring salvation or life to all who accept Jesus as their saviour.

The Holy Bible, from Genesis 4:25, basically traces the seed line of the chosen Adamic race from Adam's second and Eve's third son Seth, Noah, Abraham, Jacob, David, to Jesus the Saviour of all mankind who accept him. This is accurately recorded in Luke 3:23–37. Mary, whose mother was a Levite, represents the priest Line. Mary's father Heli represented the king line of Judah. By the Holy Spirit, Mary gives birth to Jesus. Some scholars feel that this knowledge of <u>a chosen Adamic race</u> has caused the discrimination against the Jews!

Jeremiah 24:7. "And I will give them a heart to know me, that I am the Lord: and they shall be my people, and I will be their God: for they shall return unto me with their whole heart". We will later find in Deuteronomy chapter 7 that they are the chosen race.

The many Gentile races up to this point had lived in peace. 'Eth-'Ha'' âdhâm, the man Adam, would bring "the Sin" that will bring forth man's sinful nature and expose the serpent, Lucifer, or Satan's influence to this second earth age. *2 Corinthians 4:4. "The god of this age has blinded the minds of unbelievers, so that they cannot see the light of the gospel of the glory of Christ, who is the image of God"* Notice that god is not capitalized and is referring to Lucifer/Satan and at this age Christ and God are then capitalized. All the races on the earth must now toil and must choose right from wrong.

Will we read that all the races survived Noah's flood? We can briefly now read of the survivors of Noah's flood in *Genesis 10:1–4. "Now these are the generations of the sons of Noah, Shem,*

Ham, and Japheth and unto them were sons born after the flood. 2. The sons of Japheth; omer, and Magog, and Madai, and Javan, and Tubal, and Meshech, and Tiras. Verses 3 and 4 continue with the names of the sons who are the Adamic race.

The next verse tucked in the middle of Noah's surviving genealogy makes mention of the Gentiles, a heathen nation. Could this be the descendants of the sixth-day mankind? Noah was told to take two of every flesh. Is this verse alluding to the different races? *Genesis 19:5. "By these were the isles of the Gentiles divided in their lands; every one after his tongue, after their families, in their nations".* Let's do a word study of nations as used here:

Strong's Ref. # 1471 Romanized gowy Pronounced go'-ee -a foreign nation; hence, a Gentile; also (figuratively) a troop of animals, or a flight of locusts: KJV—Gentile, heathen, nation, people. Jesus spoke of a division in *Matthew 10:5. These twelve Jesus sent forth and commanded them, saying, "Go not into the way of the Gentiles, and into any city of the Samaritans enter ye not: 6. But go rather to the lost sheep of the house of Israel."*

Following the fifth verse of Genesis 10, the subject returns to Noah's genealogy or the Adamic race. Genesis 10:6. "And the sons of Ham: Cush, and Mizraim, and Phut, and Canaan. 7. And the sons of Cush; Seba, and Havilah, and Sabtah, and Raamah, and Sabtecha: and the sons of Raamah, Sheba, and Dedan. 8. And Cush begat Nimrod: he began to be a mighty one in the earth".

Some religionists claim that God created the races by placing a mark on Cain after he killed Abel, and his skin color was changed. While other teachers will claim that the races were created after Noah's flood by a curse for the sin of Ham which produced a son Canaan, what had Ham done for his downfall?

We read in *Genesis 9:22*. *"Ham, the father of Canaan, saw the nakedness of his father, and told his two brethren outside.* What is this nakedness of his Father? *23. And Shem and Japheth took a garment, and laid it upon both their shoulders, and went backward, and covered the nakedness of their father; and their faces were backward, and they saw not their father's nakedness.* Again what is this nakedness? *24. And Noah awoke from his wine, and knew what his younger son had done unto him. 25. And he said, Cursed be Canaan; a servant of servants shall he be unto his brethren"* What had Canaan done? Canaan was the fourth son of Ham, but why was he cursed? Many commentators get stuck on this and fail to let the Bible interoperate "nakedness" as used in these verses to reveal the truth. Lev. 18:8. *"The nakedness of thy father's wife shall thou not uncover: it is thy father's nakedness.* Once again, the nakedness of your father, God by his command, makes this now a sin? But why was Canaan cursed? What had Ham's son Canaan done?

Now the Answer

It is revealed in *Leviticus 20:11*. *"And the man that Lieth with his father's wife hath uncovered his father's nakedness: both of them shall surely be put to death; their blood shall be upon them".* Here we have found that the answer to the nakedness of your father is to have intercourse with his wife. Ham had seduced Noah's wife, his mother; and she conceived a male who is born and named Canaan. Noah curses Canaan for the transgression of his son

Ham with Noah's wife. In *Leviticus 18:8, God made incest a sin. Some preachers claim that the curse was the darkening of the skin or the creation of the races.* Let's do a word study—lieth.

Lieth. *Strong's Number: 7901 Transliterated: shakab Phonetic: shaw-kab' Text: a primitive root; to lie down (for rest, sexual connection, decease or any other purpose): -X at all, cast down, ([lover-]) lay (self) (down), (make to) lie (down, down to sleep, still with), lodge, ravish, take rest, sleep, stay.*

Nakedness Strong's Ref. # 6172 Romanized 'ervah Pronounced er-aw' from HSN6168; nudity, literally (especially the pudenda) or figuratively (disgrace, blemish): KJV--nakedness, shame, unclean(-ness).

In *Genesis 7:15, it is written, "And they went in unto Noah into the ark, two and two of all flesh, wherein is the breath of life."* God had instructed Noah to take two of every flesh. Would this not include the different races whose flesh may have a different color?

The false teachers also misrepresent *1 Peter 3:18: "For Christ also has once suffered for sins, — that he might bring us to God, — 20. — God waited in the days of Noah, while the ark was a preparing, wherein few, that is, eight souls were saved by water."* They use this verse to say all except eight of the Adamic race were destroyed. This is truth because Satan had tried to taint the seed line to Christ; the flood was for the purification and destruction of the rest of the Adamic race because Satan had tried to corrupt the seed line to Christ through the fallen angels! But we read Cain's descendants survived the flood. Jesus said in *John 8:44, "You are of your father the devil, and the lusts of your father you will do. He was a murderer from the beginning, and abode not in the truth, because there is no truth in him. When he speaks a lie, he speaks of his own: for he is a liar, and the father of it."* Through Satan's son Cain; Satan had made his first attempted to destroy the true seed line to Christ by killing Adams son Abel.

As written *in Genesis 6:2, "that the sons of God saw the daughters of men that they were fair; and they took them wives of all which they chose,"* including the Adamic women, the "sons of God"! Who were they? For those who understand the first earth age, they are fallen angels, the giants or Nephilim, the followers of Satan.

"Sons of God," *Strong's # 5303 Text: or nphil {nef-eel'}; a feller, i.e. a bully or tyrant: giant).* Genesis 6:4 states, *"There were giants in the earth in those days; and also after that* [David would slay one] *when the <u>sons of God</u> came in unto the daughters of men, and they bear children to them.* God destroys them with water. God had instructed Noah to take his immediate family, his sons and daughter in-laws—they still had the pure DNA from Adam—and to take two of the rest of God's creation of <u>every breathing flesh</u>. The Gentiles or races were also breathing flesh and if in the area would be taken aboard the ark.

We explored this in depth in the study "Noah's Flood."

We will now return to the scriptures with *Genesis 2:5: "And every plant of the field before it was in the earth, and every herb of the field before it grew: for the Lord God had not caused it to rain upon the earth* [the rest of this verse speaks volumes of what is to come] *and there was <u>not a man to till the ground</u>."* God had created fruit pickers, hunters, and fishermen, <u>but no husbandman</u>. We will be introduced to the word formed a third subject in which God will establish "the planted garden east of Eden," an exclusive area, and here God will place the man Adam or 'eth-'Ha"âdhâm. We have read of God's creation of the sixth-day 'eth-' âdâm. In

Genesis 1:26–27, mankind who had the whole earth as their domain including the seas.

Genesis 2:7. "And the Lord God formed man of the dust of the ground, and breathed into his nostrils the breath of life; and man became a living soul. 8. And the Lord God planted a garden eastward in Eden; and there He put the man whom He had formed. 9. And out of the ground made the Lord God to grow every tree that is pleasant to the sight, and good for food; [Fruits and nuts; then we now read of two different trees], *the tree of life also in the midst of the garden,* [Jesus] *and the tree of knowledge of good and evil* [or Satan]" These two trees produce no edible fruit; this has confused some scholars! Jesus said in *Matthew 7:16, "By their fruit you will recognize them.* The two trees in the middle of the planted garden represent right and wrong, Jesus and Satan. And he said, unto you it is given to know the mysteries of the kingdom of God: but to others in parables; [God uses trees or fruit to represent persons] *Luke 8:10 - that seeing they might not see, and hearing they might not understand".* The trees <u>were not apple trees with edible fruit</u>!

We will pick up the subject in *Genesis 2:15: "And the Lord God took the man and put him into the <u>Garden of Eden</u> to dress it and to keep it."* ["The Man, Adam" was to work or till the soil. He was not to have the freedom to roam the earth as was the sixth-day creation or mankind] *16 "And the Lord God commanded the man, saying, of every tree of the garden you may freely eat:* [Here again many lose sight of truth, two of the tress in the middle of the garden have no edible fruit.] *17. But of the tree of the knowledge of good and evil,* [Satan] *you should not eat of it: for in the day that you eat thereof you shall surely die.* [Again we must separate these two trees that have no edible fruit to eat. One tree has knowledge of good and evil; the good attracts Eve, but then the evil part surfaces] suggested reading: The chapter "Apple or Truth,".

Continuing *Genesis 2:18 "The LORD God said, 'It is not good for the man to be alone I will make a helper suitable for him.' 19. And out of the ground the Lord God formed every beast of the field, and every fowl of the air* [these creatures are formed from the clay and are to be the docile or domesticated animals found in the Garden of Eden, the man Adam now is a Farmer and a Rancher; vs.19. continues] *and brought them unto Adam to see what he would call them: and whatsoever Adam called every living creature, that was the name thereof. 20. And Adam gave names to all cattle and to the fowl of the air and to every beast of the field; but for Adam there was not found a helpmate for him* [Special note the domesticated livestock in this area are separate from the beast or animals mentioned in Gen 1:24.they are the Bears, Tigers, Moose etc. the mentioned field was only in the Garden of Eden; the sixth-day mankind roamed the forests and grassland. vs.20. continues.] *but for Adam, no suitable helper was found.* [We can assume from this that Adam felt the need to have conversation with another person when God was not present.] *21. "And the Lord God caused a deep sleep to fall upon Adam, and he slept: and he took one of his ribs, and closed up the flesh instead thereof".*

The rib was the curve or as we know it today the helix curve or DNA. "The Man Adam" was formed, with both male and the female gender or the true representative of God and the Angles. *22. "And the rib [DNA] which the Lord God had taken from man, made he a woman, and brought her unto the man. 23. And Adam said this is now bone of my bones, and flesh of my flesh: she shall be called Woman, because she was taken out of Man. 24. Therefore shall* *a man leave his father and his mother, and shall cleave unto his wife: and they shall be one flesh. 25. And they were both naked, the man and his wife, <u>and were not ashamed</u>".* They lived in the peaceful, sinless Garden of Eden, much like the sixth-day mankind on the rest of the dominion of the earth.

Genesis 3:1"Now the serpent was more subtle than any beast of the field [generally a field is a worked or tilled land as opposed to a meadow or grassland] *which the Lord God had made. And he said unto the woman* [we must keep in mind we are now reading about the confines or boundaries of the Garden of Eden and that the serpent, Lucifer, or Satan is represented by a tree*]; has God said, you shall not eat of every tree of the garden?* The good side of Satan attracts Eve and Satan now tempts Adam and Eve*! 2. And the woman said unto the serpent, we may eat of the fruit of the trees of the garden:* [Those producing nuts and fruits.] 3. But of the fruit of the tree [Satan] which is in the midst of the garden, God has said, you shall not eat of it, neither shall you touch it, lest you die." [Here the word eat confuses or allows the teaching of the apple; the serpent/Satan had said.*] 4. "You will not surely die,"* the *serpent said to the woman.* This is the first of many lies to come. This was the first attempt of Satan to taint or destroy the advent of the Adamic seed line to Christ. *5. "For God knows that in the day you eat thereof, then your eyes shall be opened, and you shall be as gods* [more lies], *knowing good and evil".*

"The man Adam,"'eth-'Ha'' âdhâm, and Eve live only in God's truth up to this point in the Garden of Eden and were told not to eat or touch the tree of good and evil. The sixth-day eth-' âdâm, "mankind," roamed freely on the rest of the earth with free will with no restrictions.

Genesis 3:6. "And when the woman saw that the tree was good for food [Satan's silver lying tongue sparked the lust of her eyes] *and that it* [Satan] *was pleasant to the eyes, and a tree to be desired to make one wise,* (one more lie) *she took of the fruit thereof, and did eat, and gave also unto her husband with her; and he did eat"* What did they eat from the tree that had no edible fruit? Or did they partake in some other devious way?

We will soon learn that Eve had been more than lied to. Blinded by his lies, this again will be Satan's first attempt to destroy the seed line that was to lead to the birth of Jesus. "The Man Adam" had now gone against God and thus brought "the Sin," which will cause death to the whole earth, including the sixth-day creation "mankind." To really understand in depth what actually happened in the Garden of Eden it will be revealed in the chapter, "Apple or the Truth"

Genesis 3:7. "And the eyes of them both were opened, and they knew that they were naked; [shame and "the Sin" had come to the second earth age]; *and they sewed fig leaves together, and made themselves aprons".* Not covers for their mouth; for they had not eaten an "apple" as falsely taught. What had really taken place? *8. "And they heard the voice of the Lord God walking in the garden in the cool of the day: and Adam and his wife hid themselves from the presence of the Lord God amongst the trees of the garden".* Up to this point, Adam had a one-on-one relationship with God. *9. "And the Lord God called unto Adam, and said unto him: Where are you? 10. And he said, I heard thy voice in the garden, and I was afraid, because I was naked; and I hid myself. 11. And he said: Who told thee that you were naked? Have you eaten of the tree, whereof I commanded that you should not eat?* [Eve had been <u>beguiled</u> by the serpent or Satan they had lost her innocence.] *12. And the man said, the woman whom thou gave to be with me, she gave me of the tree, and I did eat* [or partook]".

Here, Adam, who had probably stood by and had heard the lies of the Serpent/Satan and experienced the actions, also felt the shame. He tried to put the whole blame on Eve. *Gen.3:13. "And the Lord God said unto the woman: What is this that you have done? And the woman said: The serpent beguiled me and I did eat.* [or partook]The word beguiled is number 5377 in Hebrew. We will also at this point refer to the New Testament: *2 Corinthians 11:3. "But I fear, lest by any means, as the serpent beguiled Eve through his subtlety, so your minds should be corrupted from the simplicity that is in Christ.* The word beguiled is number 1818 in Greek. Eve had been beguiled by the Serpent/Satan's subtlety."

At this point, a word research might be helpful and answer what had taken place in the Garden. The word "Beguiled" in Hebrew: *Strong's ref. no. 5377 Romanized nasha' Pronounced naw-shaw' a primitive root; to lead astray, i.e., (ment) to delude, or (morally)* to seduce: *beguile, deceive, X greatly, X utterly.* In the New Testament: Beguiled in Greek, *Strong's ref. no. 1818 exapatao* to seduce wholly.

To understand that Eve had not eaten an apple but had been deceived or seduced by Satan, again, this is covered in more depth in the study in the chapter "Apple or Truth".

Genesis 3:14"And the Lord God said unto the serpent, because you have done this, you are cursed above all cattle, and above every beast of the field; upon your belly shall you go, and dust shall you eat all the days of thy life. 15. And I will put enmity between you and the woman, and between your seed and her seed [Satan's seed will produce his descendants; we read of them in Genesis 4:17–24. her seed line came out of the DNA of Adam and is the Adamic seed line to Jesus through Seth]; *it shall bruise your head* [a deadly blow, Satan will end up in the lake of fire.] *and you shall bruise his heel* This is related to the nailing of Christ to the cross, but Jesus resurrects.

The seed line through Adam and Eve will become God' chosen race and will be protected and can be traced through the scriptures all the way to the birth of Jesus. Satan will continually try to disrupt or interfere with this plan of God through the seed line of the chosen race to give us our Saviour.

Gen. 3:16. "Unto the woman he said, I will greatly multiply your sorrow and your conception; in sorrow you shall bring forth children; and your desire shall be to your husband, and he shall rule over you. 17. And unto Adam he said, because you have hearkened unto the voice of your wife, and have eaten of the tree, of which I commanded you, saying, You shall not eat of it: cursed is the ground for your sake; in sorrow shall you eat of it all the days of thy life; 18. Thorns also and thistles shall it bring forth to you; and you shall eat the herb of the field; 19. In the sweat of your face shall you eat bread, till you return unto the ground; for out of it were you taken: for dust you are, and unto dust shall you return". Ecclesiastes 12:7 says, *"And the dust returns to the ground it came from, and the spirit returns to God who gave it."*

Unlike the sixth-day mankind who was created by the word of God, Adam was formed from the dust or earth of the ground. But death and evil has entered this second age. "And Adam called his wife's name Eve; because she was the mother of all living" (Gen. 3:20). This will be through her third son Seth, culminating with the birth of Jesus. Eve will become the mother of all living by Jesus's sacrifice on the cross.

"Unto Adam also and to his wife did the Lord God make coats of skins and clothed them" (Gen. 3:20). Here again he made cloths for the body, not a covering for the mouth. God sacrificed possibly a lamb to clothe them. Jesus would be called the Lamb of God and would also shed his blood on the cross for those who accept His sacrifice.

"And the Lord God said, Behold, the man is become as one of us, to know good and evil: and now, lest he put forth his hand, and take also of the tree of life, and eat, and live forever" (Gen. 3:22). This tree is Jesus, but before Adam can partake of its fruit or forgiveness, he and Eve are banished from the planted Garden of Eden.

This will be granted to those who believe in Christ because of His sacrifice on the cross. Christ was the other tree in "The Garden." "Therefore the Lord God sent him forth from the garden of Eden, to till the ground from whence he was taken" (Gen. 3:23). Adam and Eve are banished from the Garden and will now bring farming to the grassland. "So he drove out the man; and he placed at the east of the garden of Eden Cherubims, and a flaming sword which turned every way, to keep the way of the tree of life" (Gen. 3:24).

The flaming flashing sword will blind man from seeing God's planted Garden of Eden. Adam's wife, Eve, had been seduced and is now carrying the serpent (Satan's) seed (pregnant). They are banished and now allowed to travel the dominion of earth with the sixth-day creation the rest of the Gentiles, the races known as "mankind."

Genesis 4:1. "And Adam knew Eve his wife; and she conceived, and bare Cain [sex had entered their lives; however, this first child will be the product of the serpent or Satan's seed, Satan's first attempt to disrupt the seed line to Christ]; *and said, I have gotten a man from the Lord".* Eve felt blessed; she was too hasty in thanking God. She also has the seed from Adam! The next verse <u>in the original Manuscripts</u> properly translated reads, "**And she continued to bear his brother Abel.**"

Genesis 4:2. "And she again [the word again in Strong's Concordance is number. 3254—to continue to do a thing] *bare his brother Abel.* [This second born was the seed of "the man Adam." Thus they were twins; one the son or seed of Satan, the other the son or seed of "The Man Adam."] *And Abel was a keeper of sheep, but Cain was a tiller of the ground.* Here Satan tries to fool God by making Cain the tiller of soil.

We are reminded of Cain's descendants as it is written *in John 8:44: "You belong to your father, the devil* [Satan] *and you want to carry out your father's desire. He was a murderer from the beginning, not holding to the truth, for there is no truth in him. When he lies, he speaks his native language, for he is a liar and the father of lies."*

For those who have trouble with them being twins, we will understand this more when we reach Genesis 4:17 when Cain kills his twin brother and is banished from the family of Adam and Eve." Cain travels to the land of Nod where he takes a wife; one of the sixth-day creations, a Gentile; and his seed line or his descendants is traced for a short period Gen. 4:17–24. They will be known as Kenites, *Strong's no. 7014/7017. Kajin, the name of the first child, also of a place in Palestine, and of an Oriental tribe: Cain, Kenite (-s).*

Genesis 4:3. "And in process of time it came to pass, that Cain brought of the fruit of the ground an offering unto the Lord. [Adam had been formed to till the land!] *4. And Abel, he also brought of the firstlings of his flock and of the fat thereof. And the Lord had respect unto Abel and to his offering: 5. But unto Cain and to his offering he had not respect. And Cain was very wroth, and his countenance fell.* [God knew the truth about Cain.] *6. Then the LORD said to Cain, 'Why are you angry? Why is your face downcast? 7. If you do what is right, will you not be accepted? But if you do not do what is right, sin is crouching at your door; it desires to have you, but you must master it.'* [God gives Cain a chance to change his ways from that of his Father Satan.] *8. Now Cain said to his brother Abel, 'Let's go out to the field.' And while they were in the field, Cain attacked his brother Abel and killed him".*

The Truth about Twins
Medical science and journals have recorded this.

1. Identical twins.

    One sperm donor, one egg, but it splits in the womb, fertilized at same time.

2. Fraternal twins.

    One sperm donor, two eggs released to the womb, fertilized at the same time.

3. Half-identical twins.

One sperm donor, two eggs released to the womb, fertilized at different times.

4. Twins of different fathers.

Known as heteropaternal superfecundation. Two separate sperm donors from two separate males, who could be of a different race or color. When two eggs are released to the womb, they can be fertilized at different times by separate donors. One twin can have <u>a light complexion</u> and the other <u>a dark complexion</u>; their DNA will also be different.

Genesis 4:1. ---*"Eve bare Cain* ---. *2. And she again* [continued] *bare his brother Abel"* Two separate eggs in Eve's womb, but fertilized at different times by sperm of the serpent/Satan and Adam, two different DNA. Eve has Heteropaternal Superfecundation twins Cain and Abel. This fact is proven by Jesus when in John we read further proof of the deception of the father of Cain, the spread of the serpent's seed as carried out of the Garden of Eden with Eve. John 8:44. "You belong to your father, the devil, and you want to carry out your father's desire. [Satan had attempted to destroy of the true seed line by killing Abel.] *He was a murderer* [through his son Cain] *from the beginning, not holding to the truth, for there is no truth in him. When he lies, he speaks his native language, for he is a liar and the father of lies* [Satan his seed line had survived Noah's flood!]"

Gen. 4:9. "And the Lord said unto Cain, Where is Abel your brother? And he said, I do not know: am I my brother's keeper?" [Cain tries to hide the truth:] *10. "And he said, what have you done?*

[Once again God gives Cain a second chance to tell the truth*]; the voice of thy brother's blood cries unto me from the ground.* [This is the third time God gives Cain a chance to tell the truth.]*11. And now you cursed from the earth, which has opened her mouth to receive thy brother's blood from your hand; 12. When you till the ground, it shall not henceforth yield unto you her strength; a fugitive and a vagabond shall you be in the earth.* [Cain's descendants will never be allowed to reap from the ground. Or become successful farmers.] *13. And Cain said unto the Lord, My punishment is greater than I can bear. 14. Behold, you have driven me out this day from the face of the earth; and from your face shall I be hid; and I shall be a fugitive and a vagabond in the earth; and it shall come to pass, that every one that finds me shall slay me. 15. And the Lord said unto him, therefore whosoever slays Cain, vengeance shall be taken on him sevenfold. And the Lord set a mark upon Cain, lest any finding him should kill him".* Here again the unlearned use of "set a mark upon Cain" as their bases for the creation of the other races and feeds the ugly head of racism. Adam was banished from the Garden, but still He and His family to be are under God' eye.

Gen. 4:16. "And Cain went out from the presence of the Lord, and dwelt in the land of Nod, on the east of Eden. 17. And Cain knew his wife; and she conceived, and bare Enoch and he built a city, and called the name of the city, after the name of his son, Enoch. The unlearned will promote that he found one of Adam and Eve's daughters, but he found that the sixth day created Gentile! They will be the start of the Kenite race. The serpent/Satan was the father of Cain. Cain in Hebrew is Kajin, *Strong's ref. no. 7014 Hebrew dictionary, transliterated: Qayin Pronounced kah'-yin the same as HSN7013 (with a play upon the affinity to*

HSN7069); Kajin, the name of the first child, (Cain) also of a place in Palestine, and of an Oriental tribe:—Cain. Kenite (-s). Strong's ref. no. 7017; a Kenite or member of the tribe of Kajin: KJV—Kenite.

Cain's seed line or descendants will be now briefly recorded. Cain has married one of the sixth-day daughters of "the Mankind," not a descendant of Adam. *Genesis 4:17. And Cain knew his wife; and she conceived, and bare Enoch: and he built a city, and called the name of the city, after the name of his son, Enoch. 18. And unto Enoch was born Irad: and Irad begat Mehujael: and Mehujael begat Methusael: and Methusael begat Lamech. 19. And Lamech took unto him two wives: the name of the one was Adah, and the name of the other Zillah. 20. And Adah bare Jabal: he was the father of such as dwell in tents, and of such as have cattle. 21. And his brother's name was Jubal: he was the father of all such as handle the harp and organ. 22. And Zillah, she also bare Tubalcain, an instructor of every artificer in brass and iron: and the sister of Tubalcain was Naamah. 23. And Lamech said unto his wives, Adah and Zillah, Hear my voice; — hearken unto my speech: for I have slain a man to my wounding and a young man to my hurt. 24. If Cain shall be avenged sevenfold, truly Lamech seventy and sevenfold".* This is the end of Cain's recorded seed line when he was in the land of Nod. His offspring or children will be referred to as the Kenites, part of the "Gentiles," not the "Adamic race." We now can start to trace the Adamic lineage to Jesus, which will be protected by the chosen people. God wants all his creation to survive; He will allow his Son Jesus to shed His blood to cover all the sins of the races and die on the cross with this promise *John 3:16. "For God so loved the world that he gave his one and only Son, that whoever believes in him shall not perish but have eternal life."* We are sinners! All we need to do is accept and repent and live for Christ.

Genesis 4:25 "And Adam knew his wife again; and she bare a son [Give birth], *and called his name Seth: For God, said she, hath appointed me another seed instead of Abel, whom Cain slew. 26. And to Seth, to him also there was born a son; and he called his name Enos: then began men to call upon the name of the Lord".* Why would the translators or scribes end the chapter here? Again the subject is continued in the following chapter.

Genesis 5:1. "This is the book of the generations of Adam. [Adam's seed line? This implies or confirms that there are other lines, such as the sixth-day creation and the Kenites.] *In the day that God created man, in the likeness of God made he him;* [He created "Mankind" then formed 'eth-'Ha"âdhâm "the man Adam" This verse connects both Adam and all God's people, all the races together. Adam is now allowed to roam the dominion of earth.]*2. "Male and female created he them; and blessed them, and called their name Adam, in the day when they were created".* [This was 'eth' âdâm or the mankind. Rightly dividing the Word, the next verse returns us to the Man Adam who was cast out of the Garden of Eden and was now mortal.]*3. "And Adam ['eth-'Ha' âdhâm] lived an hundred and thirty years, and fathered a son in his own likeness, after his image; and called his name Seth:* Adam's second son. We can now trace the seed line of Christ from Seth to Noah's Sons. *4. "After Seth was born, Adam lived 800 years and had other sons and daughters".* [Seth was Adam's second son, but Eve's third.] *5. "Altogether, Adam lived 930 years, and then he died. 6. When Seth had lived 105 years, he became the father of Enosh. 7. And after he became the father of Enosh, Seth lived 807 years and had other sons and daughters. 8. And all the days of Seth were nine hundred and twelve years: and he died".* [The names continue; we will skip ahead to verses.] *5:23. "And all the days of Enoch were three hundred sixty and five years: 24. And Enoch walked with God: and he was not; for God took him."* Here we have read that Enoch had not died but God took him.

Genesis 5:28. "And Lamech lived an hundred eighty and two years, and begat a son: 29. And he called his name Noah, saying, this same shall comfort us concerning our work and toil of our hands, because of the ground which the Lord hath cursed. [Noah will save the seed line to Christ. Satan will continue to attempt or destroy it.*] 30. After Noah was born, Lamech lived 595 years and had other sons and daughters. 31. Altogether, Lamech lived 777 years, and then he died. 32. After Noah was 500 years old, he became the father of Shem, Ham and Japheth".*

Shem was the eleventh in the Adamic seed line; Abraham would become the twentieth in the linage. Jacob was twenty-second in the lineage, and God changes Jacob's name to Israel. *Genesis 35:10. God said to him, "Your name is Jacob, but you will no longer be called Jacob; your name will be Israel.* God has changed his name to Israel. Judah, one of twelve sons of Jacob/Israel, was the twenty-third in the lineage to Christ; it was during this time Moses comes on the scene, and we read in *Exodus 19:5. "Now therefore, if you will obey my voice indeed, and keep my covenant, then you shall be a peculiar treasure unto me above <u>all people</u>: for all the earth is mine: 6. And you shall be unto me a kingdom of priests, and an holy nation."*

Deuteronomy 7:1 "When the Lord your God shall bring you into the land — to possess it, and you have cast out many nations before you".

Then in 7:6, it is written, *"For you are a holy people unto the Lord your God: the Lord your God has <u>chosen you to be a special people</u> unto himself, above all people that are upon the face of the earth."* These are the descendants of the Adamic race who are now chosen for their seed line will bring forth God's Son Jesus.

This was around 1491/1492 BC, the seed line of "this man Adam who will carry the seed line to our saviour Jesus. To continue to follow the seed line, we can pick this up in *Luke 3:36 with Seth and read backward to Heli. Mary was a first cousin to her husband Joseph.*

In *Genesis 6:1.It is written, "And it came to pass, when men began to multiply on the face of the earth, and daughters were born unto them* [all the races]. <u>*2. That the sons of God saw the daughters of men that they were fair; and they took them wives of all which they chose.*</u> [This included the daughters of Noah and his three sons Shem, Ham, and Japheth; the seed line would be kept pure through Shem's son Arphaxad.] *3. And the Lord said: My spirit shall not always strive with man, for that he also is flesh: yet his days shall be an hundred and twenty years. 4. There were giants* (NIV, Nephilim) *in the earth in those days; and also after that, when the sons of God came in unto the daughters of men,* (some would be the Adamic daughters) and they bare children to them, same became mighty men which were of old, men of renown. [Possibly the fallen angels from the first earth age; Satan's attempt to corrupt the seed line to Jesus.]"

Jude 6 states, "And the angels who kept not their first estate, but left their own habitation, he hath reserved in everlasting chains under darkness unto the judgment of the great day.

Genesis 6:5 declares, *"God saw that the wickedness of man was great in the earth, and that every imagination of the thoughts of his heart was only evil continually."* [Satan's evil spirit was allowed to roam the earth to tempt man's sinful nature. Man, now born of a woman has to choose between right and wrong; many today claim there is a safe "gray area" between wrong and really wrong. This is false teaching, possibly promoted by the Kenites.] *6. "And it grieved the Lord that he had made man on the earth, and it grieved him at his heart".* The LORD was grieved that he had made flesh man on the earth in this second age, and his heart was filled with pain. "The Man Adam" along with his wife Eve had brought shame and "the Sin" to the earth again, as we now have to face death.

God had totally destroyed the first age because of Satan and had witnessed that Satan's sinful nature was running rampant on the earth a second time and even some of the Adamic race were being compromised. *Genesis 6:7 "And the Lord said, I will destroy man whom I have created from the face of the earth; both man, and beast, and the creeping thing, and the fowls of the air; for it grieved me that I have made them. 8. But Noah found grace in the eyes of the Lord".* God chose to only cleanse the earth and the tainted seed line of Adam and maintain the seed line to our redeemer Jesus the Christ and Saviour.

1 Peter 3:20 declares, *"God waited in the days of Noah, while the ark was a preparing, wherein few, that is, eight souls were saved by water."* Noah and his three sons and together with their wives were the eight along with two of every flesh. Shem, one of Noah's sons, carries forth the seed line to Christ.

Jude 7. In a similar way, Sodom and Gomorrah and the surrounding towns gave themselves up to sexual immorality and perversion. They serve as an example of those who suffer the punishment of eternal fire. *Jude 11. Woe to them!* <u>*They have taken the way of Cain;*</u> *they have rushed for profit into Balaam's error; they have been destroyed in Korah's rebellion. 12. These men are blemishes at your love feasts, eating with you without the slightest qualm, shepherds who feed only themselves. They are clouds without rain, blown along by the wind; autumn trees, without fruit and uprooted—twice dead.* [Further proof of people surviving Noah's flood. Again we have read of man's sinful nature, which was unchecked.]

Noah is instructed to build an ark: *Gen. 6:14. So make yourself an ark of gopher wood; rooms shall you make in the ark, and shall coat it within and without with pitch.* Verse; *17. And, behold, I, even I, do bring a flood of waters upon the earth, to destroy all flesh, wherein is the breath of life,* <u>*from under heaven;*</u> *and everything that is in the earth shall die".* Where did the bird find the leaf? Was Noah's flood localizes?

Again the earth is cleansed, not destroyed. From under the heaven, was this an area or place where God was protecting his chosen people who revered Him? Read the next verse. Could this be an isolated region on earth? *18. But with you will I establish my covenant; and you shall come into the ark, you, and your sons, and their wives with you.* [These are the Adamic race that did not mix with the Nephilim, giants, or fallen angels.] *19. And of* <u>*every living thing of all flesh, two of every sort shall you bring into the ark,*</u> *to keep them alive with you; they shall be male and female"*

Every living thing of all flesh, two of every sort, this would be of every flesh regardless of color or race. (The dinosaur was extinct or of the first age.) This subject was covered in great detail in the study "The Three Earth Ages."

Now God gives further instructions of what Noah is to bring in pairs into the ark. *20. Of fowls after their kind, and of cattle after their kind, of every creeping thing of the earth after his kind, two of every sort shall come unto you, to keep them alive. 21. And take with you of all food that is eaten, and you shall gather it to thee; and it shall be for food for you, and for them. 22. Thus did Noah; according to all that God commanded him, so did he".* For more information and a deeper study on this subject, read the chatter "Noah's Flood."

Chapter 6
Who Did Cain Marry?

Before we answer this question let's examine and compare the newer translated NIV Holy Bible to the KJV to see if we are being led astray from truth.

NIV Acts 17: 26. <u>From one man</u> he made every nation of men that they should inhabit the whole earth; and he determined the times set for them and the exact places where they should live.

KJV Acts 17: 26. <u>And hath made of one blood</u> all nations of men for to dwell on all the face of the earth, and hath determined the times before appointed, and the bounds of their habitation;

The translators eyes were blinded to the truth because they could not rationalize where the different races came from? After the Scientists discovered there are many different types of blood instead of going back to the Bible for the answer to determine where the composite of the whole human body came from? Let's just look at what the Bible tells those whose Eyes and Ears that are fine tuned to God's answer:

NIV Ecclesiastic chapter 3: 20. All go to the same place; all come from dust, and to dust all return. Chapter 12: 6. Remember him--before the silver cord is severed, or the golden bowl is broken; before the pitcher is shattered at the spring, or the wheel broken at the well,

[We die]. *7. And the dust returns to the ground it came from, and the spirit returns to God who gave it.*

Now

KJV Ecclesiastic chapter 3: 20. All go unto one place; all are of the dust, and all turn to dust again. Chapter 12: 6. Or ever the silver cord be loosed, or the golden bowl be broken, or the pitcher be broken at the fountain, or the wheel broken at the cistern. [We die] *7. Then shall the dust return to the earth as it was: and the spirit shall return unto God who gave it.*

If you came here from the direction of a suggestion in a previous chapter I sincerely hope you found by the few verses presented above you found that there is a deeper truth than what some churches in good faith preach.

Did Noah's flood destroy the seed line of Cain? We can read Jesus's words in *John 8:42: "Jesus said to them, 'If God were your Father, you would love me, for I came from God and now am here. I have not come on my own; but he sent me. 43. Why is my language not clear to you? Because you are unable to hear what I say. 44. You belong to your father, the devil, and you want to carry out your father's desire. He was a murderer from the beginning, not holding to the truth, for there is no truth in him. When he lies, he speaks his native language, for he is a liar and the father of lies. 45. Yet because I tell the truth, you do not believe me!"*

First, we must understand that in the original manuscripts, Genesis was written in Hebrew, a Shemitic language. There are three different words for "man" in Hebrew, but all are translated as just "man" in the English KJV, NIV, and all modern Holy Bibles, which is misleading.

The translators did this, possibly out of concern and consequently to avoid racism that might come about when God promised a particular race. Genesis *12:2. "And I will make of thee a great nation, and I will bless thee, and make your name great; and you shall be a blessing: 3. And I will bless them that bless you, and curse him that curses you: and in you shall all families of the earth be blessed".* They become even more important as we read in the following:

Deuteronomy 7:6. "For you are a holy people unto the Lord your God: the Lord your God has chosen you to be a special people unto himself, above all people that are upon the face of the earth". God has claimed a chosen race, the direct descendants from Seth, Adam's second son whose seed line brings forth the Messiah the Lord Jesus Christ through him we all can be blessed.

In Genesis 1:26, God said, "Let us make man (the first 'âdâm =Man) *in our image, — God had created Man on the sixth day."* Then in the next verse, man is mentioned again) 27. *"So God created man in his own image, in the image of God created he <u>him</u>; <u>male and female created he them</u>".* From this verse we now see that he created both male and female <u>at the same time</u>, the sixth day creation <u>the Gentiles</u>; they are 'eth-' âdâm = the Mankind. (The word woman is not recognized until Genesis 2:22). They were fishermen and hunters and fruit pickers as we will understand as we read in *1:28. "And God blessed them, and God said unto them, Be fruitful, and multiply, and <u>replenish the earth</u>, and subdue it: and have dominion over the fish of the sea, and over the fowl of the air, and over every living thing that moves upon the earth, and have dominion over the fish of the sea, and over the fowl of the air. 29. And God said, Behold, I have given you every herb bearing seed, which is upon the face of all the earth, and every tree, in the which is the fruit* *of a tree yielding seed; to you it shall be for meat.* (Food*). 30. And to every beast of the earth, and to every fowl of the air, and to everything that creeps upon the earth, wherein there is life, I have given every green herb for meat: and it was so. 31. And God saw everything that he had made, and, behold, it was very good. And the evening and the morning were the sixth day."*

Then the Lord God rested on the seventh day.

On the eighth day, which would be Genesis 2, we read in verse 5. *"And every plant of the field before it was in the earth and every herb of the field* [note that this is the first time the word field is written or recognized in the Strong's Concordance. We therefore can assume it refers to the field or Garden to come] *before it grew: for the Lord God had not caused it to rain upon the earth, and* there was not a man to till the ground. *6. But there went up a mist from the earth, and watered the whole face of the ground. 7. And the Lord God formed* [the third 'eth-'Ha' *âdhâm* = the Man Adam] *man of the dust of the ground,* The Lord God had not created a man or woman to till the soil.*"* What we now call a husbandman or farmer.

The Lord God now forms Adam from the dust of the ground then causes Adam to slumber. While Adam is sleeping, God removes a rib or the curve or in modern technology the helix curve or DNA and forms Eve. I think a review of the word man will be helpful.

In the original manuscript (OM), there are three different meanings for the word man by the addition of the article and particle and the addition of an h.

First, Mankind — No article or particle. 'âdâm

Second, the Mankind — with article but no particle. 'eth-'âdâm

Third, the Man Adam — with article and particle and the addition of an h. The man named Adam is 'eth-'Ha"âdhâm

However, they are all translated in the Strong's Concordance no. 120, the same Strong's ref. no. 120. Romanized 'adam Pronounced awdawm' from HSN0119; ruddy i.e. a human being (an individual or the species, mankind, etc.): KJV--X another, + hypocrite, + common sort, X low, man (mean, of low degree), person.

We return to the written word in Genesis 4: We find that Cain has killed Abel and Cain is speaking to the Lord. NIV, *Genesis 4:14. "Today you are driving me from the land, and I will be hidden from your presence; I will be a restless wanderer on the earth, 16. So Cain went out from the LORD's presence and lived in the land of Nod, east of Eden."* We now read that Cain has taken a wife, in the land of Nod she would have been from one of the sixth day created races a Gentile that God created in Genesis 1:27. *Genesis 4:17. "Cain lay with his wife, and she became pregnant and gave birth to Enoch. Cain was then building a city, and he named it after his son Enoch".*

Although Cain's wife's name is not mentioned, we now realize she must be a descendant from the sixth-day creation. To use the Bible verses to help clarify this, let us look at the sixth-day creation or mankind 'eth-' âdâm, who roamed the whole earth and lived off grains, fruit, and fish and animals. They are told in *Genesis 1: 28. "And God blessed them, and God said unto them, Be fruitful, and multiply, and replenish the earth, and subdue it: and have dominion over the fish of the sea, and over the fowl of the air, and over every living thing that moves upon the earth. 29. And God said, Behold, I have given you every herb bearing seed, which is upon the face of all the earth, and every tree, in the which is the fruit of a tree yielding seed; to you it shall be for meat* (food)."

On the eighth day, God formed Adam ('eth-'Ha"âdhâm) and Eve; they were possibly vegetarians according to *Genesis 2:6.* *"And the Lord God commanded the man, saying: Of every tree of the garden thou may freely eat. 7. But of the tree of the knowledge of good and evil, thou shall not eat of it: for in the day that thou eat thereof thou shall surely die."* We will read that after they are expelled out of "the Garden" following Noah's flood, the Adamic race or the direct descendants of Adam and Eve and Adam's second son Seth, the Adamic race of people are given permission to eat meat as was the sixth day man/mankind the Gentiles were allowed.

Genesis 9:1 "And God blessed Noah and his sons, and said unto them: Be fruitful, and multiply, and replenish the earth. 2. And the fear of you and the dread of you shall be upon every beast of the earth, and upon every fowl of the air, upon all that moves upon the earth, and upon all the fishes of the sea; into your hand are they delivered. 3. Every moving thing that lives shall be meat (food) *for you; even as the green herb have I given you all things.* God gives special instruction." In the KJV verse 4. *"But flesh with the life thereof, which is the blood thereof, shall you not eat."*

This is not a reference to blood transfusions as some falsely preach. The NIV verse *4 states, "But you must not eat meat that has its lifeblood still in it.* From both versions they now can eat Meat if it is bled properly. Moses when they were in the desert was warned in." *Leviticus 11:26,* "the carcasses of every beast which divided the hoof, and is not cloven-footed, or chews the cud, are Unclean unto you:* The swine fits this description and was created to be a Scavenger and was to cleanse the earth." The entire eleventh chapter of Leviticus is considered a health chapter.

Chapter 7

The Garden of Eden and

Apple or the Truth

We can read *in Genesis 2:8, "And the Lord God planted a garden eastward in Eden."* Before continuing the subject of the Garden and what transpired there, we will start our study with a few verses from the Bible, *Jeremiah 10:12: "But God made the earth by his power; he founded the world by his wisdom and stretched out the heavens by his understanding.*

In the Gospel of John, we read *1:1. "In the beginning was the Word, and the Word was with God, and the Word was God. 2. The same was in the beginning with God. 3. All things were made by him; and without him was not anything made that was made."* At this point, let us look up the word <u>word</u>.

Strong's ref. no. 3056 Romanized logos—something said (including the thought); - by extension, a computation; specifically (with the article in John) the Divine Expression (i.e., Christ).

"Christ is the spokesperson or <u>revealer</u> of God; <u>all things were made by him</u> (John 1:14). And the Word was made flesh, and dwelt among us, and we beheld his glory, the glory as of the only begotten of the Father, full of grace and truth."

With this information, we can start at the beginning, Genesis 1:1: "In the beginning God created the heaven and the earth." We have learned now that by his Word or Jesus, a part of the trinity, everything was made; Jesus was God's spokesman: "And God said, Let there be light: and there was light" (1:3). Jesus was present and also in *Genesis 2:15, "And the Lord God took the man, and put him into the Garden of Eden to dress it and to keep it. 16. And the Lord God commanded the man, saying, of every tree of the garden thou may freely eat: 17. But of the tree of the knowledge of good and evil, you shall not eat of it: for in the day that you eat (or partake) thereof you shall surely die."* We will do further study on the word *eat* later.

We can now return to the subject "The planted Garden east of Eden" in *Genesis 2:9, And out of the ground made the Lord God to grow every tree that is pleasant to the Sight, and good for food; the tree of life also in the midst of the garden; and the tree of knowledge of good and evil—* These two trees had no edible fruit." The tree of Life can only relate to Jesus; the other tree had good and evil and represents Satan. Satan's MO using his good side attracted Eve; then his evil side took over. After Eve and Adam ate or partook of the tree of knowledge, we read in *Genesis 3:13, "And the Lord God said unto the woman, what is this that thou hast done? And the woman said, the serpent beguiled me, and I did eat.* Or she partook of his fruit of lies!"

With this knowledge, we can move forward and ask what type of trees? Apple? Or was it fig trees? After Eve had partaken of the fruit of the tree in: *Genesis 3:7 "and the eyes of them both were opened, and they knew that they were naked; and they sewed fig leaves together, and made themselves aprons."* With this information, we can assimilate or connect the following verses: *Jeremiah. 24:1. "The Lord showed me, and, behold, two baskets of figs were set before the temple of the Lord, 2. One basket had very good figs, and the other basket had very naughty figs"* and *Matthew 7:17. "Even so every <u>good tree</u> brings forth good fruit; but a <u>corrupt tree</u> brings forth evil fruit."* Jesus said in <u>Matthew 7:16, "You shall know them by their fruit."</u>

The two trees in the middle of the Garden, one being the tree of knowledge the other the tree of life, had no edible fruit, or could we define them as trees representing good and evil? One is Satan the other represents Jesus.

Apple Or the Truth!

<u>You must decide for yourself which is right.</u>

I sincerely would hope that you will not be offended by this introduction story based on the writings found in the Holy Bible. I wrote this introduction with the sole purpose to get the attention of some readers. For some, I hope it will set the scene paralleling the misunderstood truth regarding an apple as generally taught, from the inspired Word of God written in the Holy Bible.

The scene is a lush, fragrant, peaceful location on Earth:

The light cool breeze was gently drifting over the pure sparkling Crystal-clear blue flowing waters of the river and the pure slightly rippling body of water. The gentle ripples of water seemed to come ashore, tickling the golden sand of the beach.

Lazily soaking up the warm sun is our voluptuous, sweet, blue-eyed blonde, a truly lovely innocent young lady. All alone she lay there in the buff in perfect harmony with nature, under the ever so gently swaying palm trees. It was, after all, a private island, a truly garden paradise.

He was tall, dark eyed, but with flowing, glistening wavy black hair that ever so gently caressed his shoulders as he leisurely strolled along between the palm trees on the golden sand of this private secluded beach. Oh yes, he was wise and crafty in his ways—from years of experience. Yet in spite of his age, he was still very beautiful and untouched by his many years: This handsome devil soon had his way with her. His suave appearance and silver-tongued promises had beguiled her. She had lost her most precious possession—her precious innocence.

The Father arrives too late. When he finds out what has happened, he calls the man a snake. "My daughter is pregnant with your seed! I will put enmity between your seed and hers." Sound familiar? Our Father had planned that a son and daughter, Adam and Eve, would start the Adamic race. Thus, starting the seed line bringing forth a man child, who would give his life so others might live.

Up to now, I have only been paralleling a story or verse written in *Genesis 3:13, "And the Lord God said unto the woman, what is this that you have done? And the woman said, the serpent beguiled me, and I did eat."*

Both our lady in our story above and Eve had been beguiled! Had Eve eaten an "apple" as taught by well-meaning but misled teachers, or is there a deeper truth to be found in the inspired Word of God? The Holy Bible.

I sincerely hope I have not offended anyone but whetted your appetite to read the rest of this search for the deeper truth. "Apple or the Truth."

<u>Part 1</u>

May we ask for Wisdom from our Father to guide us in this research? Amen.

To begin our study, let us begin with *Genesis 1: 26. "And God said, Let us make man in our image, after our likeness: and let them have dominion over the fish of the sea, and over the fowl of the air, and over the cattle, and over all the earth, and over every creeping thing that creeps upon the earth. 27. So God created man in his own image, in the image of God created he him; male and female created he them. 28. And God blessed them, and God said unto them, be fruitful, and multiply, and replenish the earth, and subdue it: and have dominion over the fish of the sea, and over the fowl of the air, and over every living thing that moves upon the earth."* They, 'eth-' âdâm or "mankind," had the whole earth to roam and were hunters, fishermen, and fruit pickers living off the land.

We will proceed to *Genesis 2:5: "And every plant of the field before it was in the earth, and every herb of the field before it grew: for the Lord God had not caused it to rain upon the earth, and <u>there was not a man to till the ground</u>."* God had not created a husband-man or farmer! *6. But there went up a mist from the earth, and watered the whole face of the ground.* [Here again you may want to Jump back to Chapter 6 and read the first page]. *7. "And the*

Lord God *formed man of the dust of the ground*, *and breathed into his nostrils the breath of life; and man became a living soul. 8. And the Lord God planted a garden eastward in Eden; and there he put the man whom he had formed.*" This formed man is different from the created mankind, the fruit pickers, hunters, and the fishermen. This man 'eth-'Ha"âdhâm has no gender He is placed in a separate place on earth "the planted Garden "and is formed exactly as God. After preforming the tasks of a husbandman he has a one on one relationship with God. We then read while he slept his rib or curve or DNA is separated to form his helpmate Eve.

In the original manuscript, the spelling that appeared in the manuscript is different for the created mankind, which is 'eth-' âdâm. Whereas, the formed man that is placed in the garden to till the soil is 'eth-'Ha"âdhâm; there is a *Ha* added and an *h* to 'âdhâm. This 'eth-'Ha"âdhâm is "the man Adam" as opposed to the created male and female or "mankind."

Genesis 2:9. "And the LORD God made all kinds of trees grow out of the ground—trees that were pleasing to the eye and good for food. In the middle of the garden there was the tree of life (Jesus*) and the tree of the knowledge of good and evil* (the serpent/Satan)".

The astute reader understands that these two trees bear no edible fruit and are in the middle of the Garden of Eden. These two trees represented everlasting life while the other represents the knowledge of good and evil or the sinful nature or Satan.

God commanded Adam in *Genesis 2:17, "But of the tree of the knowledge of good and evil, you shall not eat of it: for in the day that you eat you shall surely die."* We will learn more about the word *eat.* These trees in the middle of the Garden have no fruit! One represents Satan, who will try to undo or destroy God's plan for the salvation of all mankind. As you work your way through this material, you will understand and learn more about Satan, how his evil spirit influences, nurtures, and develops in mankind his own "sinful nature."

The original manuscripts (OM) were translated from Hebrew to Greek and then into English. We can wonder why some translators or scribes were unable to unlock certain truths. In Matthew 13:13 and 17, Jesus said, *"This is why I speak to them in parables: 'Though seeing, they do not see; though hearing, they do not hear or understand.' 17. For verily I say unto you, That many prophets and righteous men have desired to see those things which you see, and have not seen them; and to hear those things which you hear, and have not heard them."*

Jesus often spoke in parables that even his disciples asked. *Luke 8:9. And his disciples asked him, saying, what might this parable mean? 10. And he* (Jesus) *said: Unto you* (his disciples*) it is given to know the mysteries of the kingdom of God: but to others in parables; that seeing they might not see, and hearing they might not understand.*

Romans 11;8 "According as it is written, God hath given them the spirit of slumber, eyes that they should not see, and ears that they should not hear; unto this day". Could this be a reflection on *Daniel 12:9? He replied, "Go your way, Daniel, because the words are closed up and sealed until the time of the end.* Most theologians agree we are living in the end times.

Jesus only had the Old Testament to teach from; with this being said, sometimes we must go back to the original OM and, using *Strong's Dictionary*, try to glean how the original word relates to the subject. Our main objective is to unlock the truth about Eve in the Garden of Eden. Did she eat an apple as taught to us in Sunday school from the tree of knowledge of good and evil? This tree had no edible fruit! It was the serpent, the devil or Satan (but depicted as a tree), who wanted Eve to sin. Jesus said in *Matthew 7:16*, *"By their fruit you will recognize them."*

Part 2

Genesis 3:1 "Now the serpent was craftier than any beast of the field which the Lord God had made. And he said unto the woman, has God said, you shall not eat of every tree of the garden? 2. And the woman said unto the serpent, We may eat of the fruit of the trees of the garden: 3. But of the fruit (this is not edible fruit) *of the tree which is in the midst of the garden, God has said, You shall not eat of it, neither shall you touch it, lest you die.* [There is no poison fruit!] *4. And the serpent said unto the woman, You shall not surely die:* [His lie continues.] *5. For God knows that in the day you eat thereof, then your eyes shall be opened, and you shall be as gods, knowing good and evil.* [This nails it down; there is no edible fruit.] *6. And when the woman saw that the tree was good for food* [food? for what?] *and that it was pleasant to the eyes* [was he a suave-looking person?] *and a tree to be desired to make one wise* [Satan's silver–lined tongue] *she took of the fruit thereof, and did eat, and gave also unto her husband with her; and he did eat".* In *Genesis 3:13*, *"and the Lord God said unto the woman, what is this that thou hast done? And the woman said, the serpent beguiled me, and I did eat."* First the good part of the tree attracted Eve, but then the evil side beguiled her.

There is no apple on this tree! Adam will also be held accountable for Eve's transgression as she falls for the lies and deception. As a student of his word, at this point <u>we should take time to try to find out what really transpired in "the Garden" by doing some word research</u> using Dr. Strong's works to analyze three keywords found in the scriptures above, enabling us to better understand the deeper meaning and truth of His Word. As we research the words *eat*, *touch*, and later the word *beguiled*, it will seem a little ambiguous at first; but as we work through this study, rightly dividing and quoting the Bible, the Word will bring forth the truth—it will become clear.

First the word *eat* in *Genesis 2:17: "But of the tree of the knowledge of good and evil, thou shall not eat of it: for in the day that you eat thereof you shall surely die."* Here the deeper reader or student understands the tree spoken of—Satan and his fruit is deception and lies of which they shall not eat or partake of. There is not an apple! There is a deeper study of the word *eat* at the end of this chapter. Now let's reread about the words: *eat, touch.* "But of the fruit of the tree which is in the midst of the garden, *Genesis 3:3. God hath said: <u>You shall not eat of it</u>, <u>neither shall you touch it</u>, lest you die".* Note that these two words are linked together and is a direct command from God. Now let's read about the word *beguiled. Gen. 3:13. "And the Lord God said unto the woman, what is this that you have done? And the woman said, the serpent <u>beguiled</u> me, and I did eat.* Eve had partaken of his lies and action.

By researching these three words—*eat, touch, beguiled*—in the *Strong's Concordance*, you will glean these three words that can have a different meaning, and the truth can be understood to dispel the myth as taught—Eve ate an "apple."

"*Eat*, Strong's Number: 398 Hebrew OT. Transliterated: 'akal Phonetic: aw-kal' Text: a primitive root; to eat (literally or figuratively): --X at all, burn up, consume, devour (-er, up), dine, eat (-er, up), feed (with), food, X freely, X in ... wise (-deed, plenty), (lay) meat, X quite."

Note that we get the best understanding of the way the word is used from. "But of the tree of the knowledge of good and evil, you shall not eat of it: for in the day that you eat (participate) you shall surely die" (Gen. 2:17). However, make note of the word *lay*. And when we dine we are participating; with this in mind, let's connect the other two words. Again if you need more clarification, please turn to the end of this chapter.

Touch. Strong's Number: 5060 Hebrew O.T. Transliterated: naga' Phonetic: naw-gah' Text: a primitive root; properly, to touch, i.e. lay the hand upon (for any purpose; euphem., to lie with a woman); by implication, to reach (figuratively, to arrive, acquire); violently, to strike (punish, defeat, destroy, etc.): --beat, (X be able to) bring (down), cast, come (nigh), draw near (nigh), get up, happen, join, near, plague, reach (up), smite, strike, touch.

In Hebrew, the word *naga* is "to touch" or "to lie with a woman. (Key)" Our first clue that Eve had not eaten an apple and suggests there is sexual behavior between Satan (the serpent) and Eve. The third and most revealing word we shall examine that will expose the real truth is *beguiled. Gen. 3:13* --"*The serpent beguiled me, and I did eat* [eat or did she partaken some other activity?]

"*Beguiled: Strong's Number: 5377 Hebrew OT. Transliterated: nasha' Phonetic: naw-shaw' Text: a primitive root; to lead astray, i.e. (mentally) to delude, or (morally) to seduce: --beguile, deceive, X greatly, X utterly." Here again this word has sexual meaning to seduce.*

For even more understanding and to help unlock and seal the truth, let us go to the New Testament to confirm and read of this event! In *2 Corinthians 11:1, "I hope you will put up with a little of my foolishness, but you are already doing that. 2. I am jealous for you with a godly jealousy. I promised you to one husband, to Christ, so that I might present you as a pure virgin to him."* God wanted a pure seed line to Christ, now here is why we came here to *11:3: "But I fear, lest by any means, <u>as the serpent (Satan) beguiled Eve through his subtlety</u>, so your minds should be corrupted from the simplicity that is in Christ."* Here again we find the word *beguiled*, but because it is used in the New Testament, we must research this word for its use in the Greek to English Dictionary.

The word *beguiled* in <u>Greek</u>; *Strong's Number: 1818 Transliterated: exapatao Phonetic: ex-ap-at-ah'-o Text: from 1537 and 538; <u>to seduce wholly</u>: beguile, deceive. - <u>seduced wholly</u>!*

So far we find no "apple" or indication and feel that the doors to a deeper truth are unlocking as to what really took place in the Garden. First John 3:12 states, *"<u>Not as Cain, who was of that wicked one</u>,* (Satan is the father of Cain.) *and slew his brother. And wherefore slew he him?* Because his own works were evil, and his brother's righteous." A little word like *of* speaks volumes of that wicked one here we have positive proof as to what happened in the Garden of Eden; the serpent or Satan had seduced Eve. <u>Satan was the father of Cain. Eve's first child was Cain "of that wicked one or Satan."</u> Satan, through Cain's descendants, will be known as the Kenites. Let's research the name Cain:

Cain: *Strong's No. 7014 Transliterated: Qayin Phonetic: kah'-yin Text: the same as 7013 (with a play upon the affinity to 7069);*

Kajin, the name of the first child, also of a place in Palestine, and of an Oriental tribe: Cain, Kenite(-s).

Cain, who was of that wicked one, the son of Satan.

The NIV *1 John 3:12 says, "Do not be like Cain, who belonged to the evil one and murdered his brother."* Clearly, Cain was the son of the serpent or Satan and not Adam's son. Eve had not eaten an apple but had been seduced by the evil one Satan.

Part 3

To continue our study on this subject, let us return to when Adam and Eve were in the planted Garden east of Eden: *Genesis 2:25. "And they were both naked, the man and his wife, and were not ashamed".* They were innocent and free of guilt or shame. No "sinful nature." Let's study what their life was like later in Genesis chapter three after the devil, the serpent or Satan, had his way with Eve. Satan had "beguiled her or seduced her" and Cain was the result we read in *Genesis 3:7: "And the eyes of them both were opened, and they knew that they were naked; and they sewed fig leaves together, and made themselves aprons."*

Aprons! They now feel shame; they covered their private parts with aprons. If they had eaten an apple, they would have covered their mouth ("apple" or truth?). Any parent who has read or heard the main warning sign of sexual abuse is shame, withdrawal, and guilt.

We can now understand verse *Gen.3:7. -- and they knew that they were naked,* which was after the beguiling or Satan's seduction of Eve. *9. "God called unto Adam, and said unto him, where are you? 10. And he said, I heard thy voice in the garden, and I was afraid, because I was naked; and I hid myself".* Adam was afraid or ashamed for what he had witnessed in the Garden.

God feels their pain. <u>Gen. 3:21. Unto Adam also and to his wife did the Lord God make coats of skins, and clothed them</u>. Had their private paradise, "the planted Garden east of Eden," warmed or changed, had it turned cold? No, they had been deceived by Satan and sinned.

In; *1 Timothy 2:14. "And Adam was not deceived, but the woman being deceived was in the <u>transgression</u>.* [Adam was present, listened to the lie, but did not partake in the sexual act but observed.] *15. notwithstanding she shall be saved in childbearing, if they continue in faith and charity and holiness with sobriety."* Take special notice of the word *childbearing*; it is a clue to the transgression of Eve (because Eve is part of Adam). "The sin" is now on mankind.

In *Romans 6:23, "For the wages of sin is death."* <u>Let's check the word transgression.</u>

Strong's Number: 3847 Transliterated: parabasis Phonetic: par-ab'- as-is Text from 3845 volation:—breaking, transgression. Strong's Number: 3845 transliterated: parabaino Phonetic: par-ab-ah'-ee-no Text: from 3844 and the base of 939; to go contrary to, i.e., violate a command: (by) transgress (-ion).

They had disobeyed God his; first command. (This was not part of the Ten Commandments).

Adam had stated; "Eve is now part of me" when God took the rib or DNA from him and formed Eve; this then is how Adam must share in her transgression or the breaking of the first command of God. [The first sin] And the man said, the woman whom you gave to be with me, she gave me of the tree, and I did eat. Adam had stood by listening to and accepted Satan's lies and had watched the seduction of Eve.

If you have come to the conclusion that Eve, like the lady in the opening story, was seduced by Satan, please read on; or if you still have doubts, please start from the beginning. You must decide the truth for yourself—was it an "apple" or seduction? Man's tradition of an apple or God's truth, as written to those who have eyes to see what the Bible truly reveals.

Part 4

Eve had been seduced; this will be Satan's first attempt to destroy the seed line to our Lord Jesus who would bring forth salvation; had the sixth-day creation sinned? This will become more evident as we understand and dig deeper into His Word. *Genesis 3:13. "And the Lord God said unto the woman, 'What is this that you have done?' And the woman said, the serpent beguiled me, and I did eat. 14. And the Lord God said unto the serpent, because you have done this, you are cursed above all cattle, and above every beast of the field; upon your belly shall you go, and dust shall you eat all the days of thy life: 15. And I will put enmity between you and the woman, and between your seed and her seed; it shall bruise your head, and you shall bruise his heel". The time will come.*

To clarify we must remember that Eve is formed from Adam's DNA, thus bruise his heel refers to the suffering of Jesus on the cross as they drove a nail through his feet

1 Cor. 15:45. The first man Adam was made a living soul; the last Adam (Jesus) *was made a quickening spirit.* Now "it shall bruise your head" refers to the final death of Satan in the lake of fire. We now look at the word *enmity.*

Enmity: Strong's no. 342. Transliterated: 'eybah, Phonetic: ay-baw'. Text: from 340; hostility: --enmity, hatred.

We can acquaint this to our present sinful nature.

To dig deeper and understand, we must go back *to Genesis 2:21. "And the Lord God caused a deep sleep to fall upon Adam, and he slept: and he took one of his ribs, and closed up the flesh instead thereof; 22. And the rib, which the Lord God had taken from man, made He a woman, and brought her unto the man."*

The word *rib* in Strong's no. 6763 when taken back to the Hebrew, then back to the prime root no. 6760 is "to curve."

Modern science has discovered the helix curve or DNA. We praise and thank the Lord for our gifts of learning, to understand his complex great work. While Adam was asleep, God took a rib or curve or what we with our modern science call the DNA and brought forth Eve. So now Eve has some of Adam's "seed" or DNA as part of her body! *Genesis 2:23. "And Adam said: this is now bone of my bones, and flesh of my flesh: she shall be called Woman, because she was taken out of Man."*

After Eve is seduced by Satan and carries his seed, we read in Genesis *4:1. "And Adam knew Eve his wife; and she conceived."* God will separate the two seed lines. Eve will have twins; if you plant a seed, you reap what you sow! We read in Genesis 4:8. Satan's son Cain will murder Adam's son Abel. (Twins)? This will be made clear in parts 6 and 7 of this writing)! 1 John 3:10 states, *"This is how we know who the children of God are and who the children of the devil* (Satan) are: Anyone who does not do what is right is not a child of God."

This can be better understood by reading the parable in the New Testament. *Matthew 13:36. "Then Jesus sent the multitude away, and went into the house: and his disciples came unto him, saying, declare unto us the parable of the tares of the field. 37. He answered and said unto them, <u>He that sowed the good seed</u> is the Son of man; 38. The field is the world; the good seed are the children of the kingdom; <u>but the tares are the children of the wicked one</u>; – This is Satan! As we read on. 39. The enemy that sowed them is the devil; the harvest is the end of the world; and the reapers are the angels".* When possible, Satan will continue to ruin God's plan to keep the seed line of Adam and Eve pure and thus bring forth our savior Jesus.

Part 5:
"Eve Is Carrying the Serpent's Seed and Adams"

Starting in *Genesis 4:1, "And Adam knew Eve his wife; and she conceived* [here Adam's seed is planted; Eve goes into labor] *and bare Cain, and said, I have gotten a man from the Lord."* It's a boy!

<u>The next verse is very important: Eve's gives birth to twins</u>

In Genesis 4:2, it is written, *"And she again bare his brother Abel.* <u>And Abel was a keeper of sheep, but Cain was a tiller of the ground.</u> A word study is needed to fully understand."

Again: Strong's Number: 3254 Transliterated: yacaph Phonetic: yaw-saf' Text: a primitive root; to add or augment (often adverbial, <u>to continue to do a thing</u>): -add, X again, X any more, X cease, X come more, + conceive again, continue, exceed, X further, X gather together, get more, give moreover, X henceforth, increase (more and more), join, X longer (bring, do, make, much, put), X (the, much, yet) more (and more), proceed (further), prolong, put, be [strong-] er, X yet, yield.

The word *bare* in the two verses above means "to give birth or to continue to give birth." The word *again* means to continue to birth or to give birth to twins. Did Jesus confirm this? Yes, in *John 8:44: "You are of your father the devil [Satan is the father of Cain] and the lusts of your father you will do. He was a murderer from the beginning, and abode not in the truth, because there is no truth in him." For he is a liar, and the father of it.*

Part 6

We have studied that Satan seduced Eve! Then God put enmity between the two seed lines. Eve had Adam's DNA thus his seed line to Christ! Again we read *in Genesis 4:1: "And Adam knew Eve his wife; and she conceived."* Now she also has Adam's seed; Eve began birthing and continued. Thus Cain and Abel were twins by two different fathers, Satan and Adam. Modern medical science has proven the birth of twins having two different fathers even to the degree of different skin color (Heteropaternal superfecundation).

The Truth about Twins

Medical science and Journals have recorded this.

1. Identical Twins. One sperm donor, One egg but it splits in the womb - fertilized at same time = Identical Twins.

2. Fraternal Twins. One sperm donor, Two eggs release to the womb - fertilized at same time = Fraternal Twins.

3. Half-Identical Twins. One sperm donor, Two eggs release to the womb - fertilized at different times = Half-Identical Twins.

4. Twins of different Fathers. Known as Heteropaternal Superfecundation. Two separate sperm donors. -- Two separate men even of different color or race. Two eggs release to the womb -- fertilized at different times by separate donors. One twin can be light complexion and the other dark complexion with different DNA.

In Genesis 4:1. it is written, *"And Adam knew Eve his wife; and she conceived, and bare Cain, and said, I have gotten a man from the Lord. 2. And she again bare his brother Abel."* Two separate eggs in Eve's womb, but fertilized at different times first by the sperm of the serpent or Satan and then by Adam, two different DNA. The result was Cain and Abel, and they were twins. We can speculate that God held Adam accountable because he participated or followed the actions of Satan's beguiling Eve. Satan had made his first attempt to taint the seed line to a savior, God, however, had planted two eggs in Eve's womb.

We can verify Satan as a father of Cain in the New Testament. *1 John 3:7. Little children, let no man deceive you: he who does what is right is righteous. 8. He who does what is sinful is <u>of the devil</u>; for the devil sinned from the beginning. For this purpose the Son of God was manifested,* [Jesus in a flesh body] *<u>that he might destroy the works of the devil</u>" :11. For this is the message that you heard from the beginning, that we should love one another. 12. <u>Not as Cain, who was of that wicked one,</u> and slew his brother. And wherefore slew he him? Because his own works were evil, and his brother's righteous".* Who is that wicked one? This is none other than Satan the serpent, the devil.

In the Gospel *of Matthew 13:38. The field is the world; the good seed are the children of the kingdom; but the tares are the children of the wicked one.* [This is not the field that Adam was formed to work or till.] *39. The enemy that sowed them is the devil; the harvest is the end of the world; and the reapers are the angels."*

In anger, <u>Cain murders</u> his twin brother Abel in a <u>field</u>! Adam and Eve were banished from the Garden of Eden <u>before</u> the birth of Cain or Abel in *Genesis 3:23. Therefore the Lord God sent him* (Adam) <u>forth from the Garden of Eden to till the ground from whence he was taken.</u> Special note! Adam was formed from the ground where the sixth-day fruit pickers, hunters, and fishermen roamed the earth, but there was no one to till the soil. God formed Adam and placed him in the Planted Garden East of Eden..

The serpent, the devil or Satan, through his son Cain had tried to interfere with the <u>true seed line</u> to our Christ. GOD said the blood cries out!. Cain is banished, not from Eden but the place where Adam and Eve now dwelt. Cain was cursed and sent away to the land of Nod where he marries and builds a <u>city</u>. This brings us to the question, where did his wife come from? The answer has to be a woman from the sixth-day creation and then Genesis 4:16, which records the genealogy of the serpent's seed through Cain as recorded in Genesis 4:17–24. This is well documented in the study "in order to understand the Bible, we must understand the Beginning." The wicked seed lives on; they are known as Kenites.

Kenites *Strong's ref. no. 7014 Romanized Qayin Pronounced kah'- yin the same as HSN7013 (with a play upon the affinity to HSN7069); Kajin, the name of the first child, (Cain).*

These {are} |7017| the Kenites. *Strong's ref. no. 7017, a Kenite or member of the tribe of Kajin: KJV—Kenite.*—Note the name of the first child.

Although Cain is the son of his father Satan, *John 8:39. "Abraham is our father,' they answered. 'If you were Abraham's children,' said Jesus, 'then you would do the things Abraham did. 40. As it is, you are determined to kill me, a man who has told you the truth that I heard from God. Abraham did not do such things. 41. You are doing the things <u>your own father does</u>.'* (They are Kenites, descendants of Satan, Cain.) *'We are not illegitimate children,' they protested. 'The only Father we have is God himself.' 42. Jesus said to them, 'If God were your Father, you would love me, for I came from God and now am here. I have not come on my own; but he sent me. 43. Why is my language not clear to you? Because you are unable to hear what I say. 44. <u>You belong to your father, the devil</u>* [This is Satan] *and you want to carry out your father's desire.* [This is Satan's son Cain.] *He was* *a murderer from the beginning, not holding to the truth, for there is no truth in him. When he lies, he speaks his native language, for he is a liar and the father of lies.45. Yet because I tell the truth, you do not believe me.*

For clarification: "he was a murderer" in the OM is "that one a Manslayer"; this is Cain. These verses identify and confirm Satan as the father of Cain; they both were liars—Satan for his lies in "the Garden of Eden" and Cain as the son who was the first murderer as written in *Genesis 4:9. Then the LORD said to Cain, "Where is your brother Abel?" "I don't know," he replied. "Am I my brother's keeper?"* God, however, knowing this in love gives Cain as he does all of us a chance to choose good or evil as recorded in Genesis. God gives Cain the opportunity to repent and turn away from his father Satan. *" "If you do what is right, will you not be accepted? But if you do not do what is right, sin is crouching at your door; it desires to have you.*

Now back to Adam, after the murder of his son Abel. In Genesis 4:25, dam's second child is born, Seth; and the genealogy of the seed line can be followed from Adam to Noah, Abraham, Jacob, Jesse, to David, as recorded in the Old Testament all the way to the New Testament, as recorded in Luke 3:21–37. Here, Mary's father Heli, who was of the tribe of Judah and her mother, who was a Levite, both descendants of Abraham. The seed line will blossom to its fullness, through Mary's virgin birth of our Lord and Savior Jesus the Christ.

Part 7

Let's address another question. Was Satan's seed line through Cain lost by Noah's flood? Cain went to find a wife in the land of Nod or from one of the descendants of the human race created on the sixth day, 'eth' âdâm mankind, or the Gentiles. Genesis 4:17. And Cain knew his wife; and she conceived, and bare Enoch: and he built a city, and called the name of the city, after the name of his son, Enoch. There geology is recorded or continued, 4:18- 24.

Suggested reading for an in-depth examination on this subject: "In order to understand the Bible we must understand the Beginning."

God commanded Noah to take "two" of every flesh! Are you dust or flesh? Or was the flood local to the area where the Giants or Nephilim (the fallen ones) who were trying to change or destroy the true seed line of Jesus! "There were giants (Nephilim in NIV version) in the earth in those days; and also after that, when the sons of God came in unto the daughters of men, and they bare children to them, the same became mighty men which were of old, men of renown (Gen. 6:4). Notice also after that "after the flood"?

They were intermarrying with mankind and also with the daughters of the Adamic line or the descendants of Adam—the Adamic race. Word study: the Giants or (NIV -Nephilim).

Strong's no. 5303 Transliterated: nphiyl Phonetic: nef-eel' Text: or nphil {nef-eel'}; from 5307; properly, a feller, i.e. a bully or tyrant: --giant. We can also read about these old men in the New Testament.

Jude verse 4: "For certain men whose condemnation was written about long ago have secretly slipped in among you. They are godless men, who change the grace of our God into a license for immorality and deny Jesus Christ our only sovereign and Lord." These could well be part of the one-third that followed Satan known as the fallen angels or religions that do not accept the Gospel.

To understand what happened to Cain's descendants during the flood, I suggest you read the chapter "Noah's Flood." Long after Noah's flood, we read of the Kenites.

Eve gave birth to her third son Seth, and the seed line is carried forward to Mary by both her parents. Eve is called the Mother of all Living; Mary shall be called blessed, relating to the work "in Christ shall all be made alive." We now can claim Jesus as our Savior by his work and sacrifice on the cross by which we can have everlasting true life. His blood as Abel's cries out. John 3:16, "For God so loved the world that he gave his only begotten Son, that whosoever believeth in him should not perish, but have everlasting life."

If this study has been of help, the credit belongs to the Father.

Epilogue

Should churches refrain from teaching the apple theory in Sunday school to the very young children? Young children need to develop their interest in literature; this is done with the aid of children books and fairy tales such as *Sleeping Beauty,* who was given a poisoned apple and was revived by a show of love, a kiss from a prince.

How much more meaningful would the story of Adam and Eve in the Garden of Eden become if it were taught there were trees for food but there were also two trees in the center of the garden! And the two trees bare no fruit but both were able to talk. One tree would have spoken of love and kindness, which represents good and Jesus. The other talking tree spoke lies, told bad stories, and did evil things. This tree was like a serpent, a very bad being, and was Satan or the devil. When Eve listened to this tree, the serpent bit or took advantage of her and made her belly swell; this brought forth the birth of Cain, a bad person.

Later as the child gains knowledge, they will understand that the venom of the serpent made Eve pregnant and brought forth Cain and his and our sinful nature.

Did Satan's seed line (Cain) survive Noah's flood? We read of the Kenites in the OT long after the flood. *Genesis 15:18. In the same day, the Lord made a covenant with Abram, saying, "Unto thy seed have I given this land, from the river of Egypt unto the great river, the river Euphrates."* The next verse mentions the following: *"19. The land of the Kenites."* Who are the Kenites? First Chronicles 2:55. "And the clans of scribes who lived at Jabez: the Tirathites, Shimeathites and Sucathites. These are the Kenites who came from Hammath, the father of the house of Recab." Let's dig deeper and find out who the Kenites are.

Cain is no. 7014 and no. 7017. *Strong's no. 7014 Transliterated: Qayin Kajin, the name of the first child, also of a place in Palestine, and of an Oriental tribe: — Cain, Kenite (-s). Strong's ref. no. 7017 from HSN7014; a Kenite or member of the tribe of Kajin: KJV--Kenite.*

We have read that the Kenites were the descendants of the firstborn of Eve and the father was the serpent or Satan; the child was called Cain who killed Abel, his twin brother fathered by Adam. Jesus confirmed that the Kenites survived Noah's flood in *John 8:44: "You belong to your father, the devil, this is Satan and you want to carry out your father's desire.* [This is Satan's son Cain.] *He was a murderer from the beginning, not holding to the truth, for there is no truth in him. When he lies, he speaks his native language, for he is a liar and the father of lies."*

For clarification: "He was a murderer" in the OM is "that one is a Manslayer"; this is Cain. John the Disciple whom Jesus loved wrote in *1 John 3:12: "Do not be like Cain, who belonged to the evil one and murdered his brother.* And why did he murder him? Because his own actions were evil and his brothers were righteous."

These verses identify and confirm both Satan as the father of Cain; they both were liars. Satan for lies in the planted Garden of Eden and Cain as the son who was the first murderer: *9. Then the LORD said to Cain, 'Where is your brother Abel?' 'I don't know,' he replied. 'Am I my brother's keeper?*

God, however, knowing this, in love gives Cain as he does to all of us a chance to choose good or evil as recorded in Genesis. God gives Cain the opportunity to repent and turn away from his father Satan.

The Word *Eat*

The smoking gun or key phrases KJV *Genesis 3:15. And I will put enmity between thee and the woman, and between thy seed and her seed;* [Satan had attempted to taint the seed line to Christ.] KJV *Genesis 4:1 And she again bare his brother Abel* [NIV Later she gave birth to his brother Abel.] They are twins.

Genesis 2:9. And out of the ground made the Lord God to grow every tree that is pleasant to the sight, and good for food; [edible fruit] [we now read of two other trees not bearing fruit] *the tree of life also in the midst of the garden, and the tree of knowledge of good and evil.* The tree of life is Jesus while the tree of knowledge of good and evil was the Serpent/Lucifer/Satan. No edible fruit on these trees.

After Eve and Adam ate or partook of the tree of knowledge (KJV, *Gen. 3:3. but of the fruit of the tree which is in the midst of the garden (the fruit of one is Life the fruit if the other is Evil) God hath said, Ye shall not eat of it, neither shall ye touch it, lest ye die. 4. And the serpent said unto the woman, Ye shall not surely die: 5. For God doth know that in the day ye eat thereof, then your eyes shall be opened,* (the verse 6. below validates her eyes are already open so the word eat is suspect to interpretation should it be partake?) *and you shall be as gods, knowing good and evil. Their eyes are open and now they see themselves a naked.*

There is no hint or implication of eating an apple: "*6. And when the woman saw* [her eyes were open] *that the tree was good for food,* [food for thought?] *and that it was pleasant to the eyes,* [her their eyes are open but no shame!] *and a tree to be desired to make one wise, she took of the fruit thereof, and did eat, and gave* *also unto her husband with her; <u>and he did eat</u>.* [Now their eyes or thoughts will be open to evil.] *7. Then the eyes of both of them were opened, and they realized they were naked; so they sewed fig leaves together and made coverings for themselves.* [They did not have a bad taste in their mouth but hid their private parts! They had not eaten an apple!]" *They had partaken in an activity!*

The Strong's number for *eat* in Genesis is *398, Romanized 'akal Pronounced aw-kal' a primitive root; to eat (literally or figuratively): KJV--X at all, burn up, <u>consume, devour</u> (-er, up), <u>dine</u>, eat (-er, up), feed (with), food, X freely, X in...wise (-deed, plenty), (<u>lay</u>) meat, X quite. <u>The word dine is to participate</u> in eating of food an action. The word lay is a position.*

If you came to this page for deeper clarification, there was much more that happened in the Garden for God to expel Adam and Eve than eating an apple.

Chapter 8

Paul, Our Sinful Nature, Rapture,

Christ's Second Coming

Apostle Paul's name at birth was Saul, born between AD 0 and AD 5 in Tarsus, a city in Cilicia, part of the Roman Empire (now part of Turkey). Paul was considered a Roman citizen. He was taken to Jerusalem by his parents who were Israelites; his father was a descendant of Benjamin, one of the twelve tribes. As a young boy, he studied Judaism under the great Hebrew teacher Gamaliel; thus his native tongue was Hebrew. He was believed to be a tent maker and learned Greek by working with Gentiles and wrote and spoke colloquial Greek, but because of poor eyesight, Luke and others who accompanied him wrote most of his dictated letters for him.

During his early adult years before conversion, Saul was an avid persecutor of the early Christian church: *Acts 9:1 "Meanwhile, Saul was still breathing out murderous threats against the Lord's disciples."* Paul confesses his persecution of early Christians in *Acts 22:19. And I said, Lord, they know that I imprisoned and beat in every synagogue them that believed on thee: 20. And when the blood of thy martyr Stephen was shed, I also was standing by, and consenting unto his death, and kept the raiment of them that slew him.*

Saul, a devoted believer in Judaism, was on his way to Damascus to disrupt the Christians; but on his way, he was converted to Christianity: *Acts 9:18.He got up and was baptized, 19. and after taking some food, he regained his strength. Saul spent several days with the disciples in Damascus. 20. At once he began to preach in the synagogues that Jesus is the Son of God. 21. All those who heard him were astonished and asked, 'Isn't he the man who raised havoc in Jerusalem among those who call on this name? And hasn't he come here to take them as prisoners to the chief priests?*

His name will now change from Saul to Paul as he begins his missionary journey to preach the Gospel of Jesus in many Christian and other churches throughout the lands: *Acts 13:9. Then Saul, (who also is called Paul,) filled with the Holy Ghost, set his eyes on him, 10. And said, O full of all subtlety and all mischief, thou child of the devil, thou enemy of all righteousness, wilt thou not cease to pervert the right ways of the Lord* [further proof of survivors of Noah's flood]? Peter validated Paul as an apostle in *2 Peter 3:15., "And account that the longsuffering of our Lord is salvation; even as our beloved brother Paul also according to the wisdom given unto him hath written unto you; 16. As also in all his epistles, speaking in them of these things; in which are some things hard to be understood, which they that are unlearned and unstable wrest, as they do also the other scriptures, unto their own destruction."*

Paul was not one of the original disciples of Jesus (Jesus was born in 3 or 4 BC, crucified AD 30; AD means "Anno Domini" or "in the year of our Lord"). Saul/Paul had no part in the writings of the four Gospels, but after a spiritual encounter with Jesus was baptized in AD 37, and after three years working in the church with Ananias was preaching the Gospel. He set out on his first missionary journey in AD 45: *Acts 9:15. The Lord said to Ananias, 'Go! This man* (Saul/ Paul) *is my chosen instrument <u>to carry my name before the Gentiles and their kings</u> and before the people of Israel. 16. I will show him how much he must suffer for my name.' 17. Then Ananias went to the house and entered it. Placing his hands on Saul, he said, 'Brother Saul, the Lord—Jesus, who appeared to you on the road as you were coming here—has sent me so that you may see again and be filled with the Holy Spirit.' 18. Immediately, something like scales fell from Saul's eyes, and he could see again. He got up and was baptized.*

Paul then traveled extensively, planting Christian churches wherever he went; he carried the responsibility for them in his heart and writing inspirational letters to them. He was inspired by God to pen or dictate at least thirteen letters that are included in the New Testament. Scholars have debated whether or not Hebrews was written by Paul; if Paul wrote Hebrews that would make his total contribution to the Bible fourteen books. Most of Paul's letters emphasize the lessons taught by Jesus and inspire in each of us the <u>power and wisdom</u> to <u>comfort and reward us</u>; Paul's epistles make Jesus more personal to our daily lives.

Paul (an Israelite of the Benjamin tribe but a Roman citizen) had Tertius write a letter for him to the church in Rome. *Romans. 10:10. For it is with your heart that you believe and are justified, and it is with your mouth that you confess and are saved. 11. As the Scripture says, 'Anyone who trusts in him* (Jesus) *will never be put to shame.' 12. For there is no difference between Jew and Gentile--the same Lord is Lord of all and richly blesses all who call on him.*

A Brief Bit of Information Regarding the Church

Jesus had said to Peter one of his disciples (Peter means "rock"), "On this rock I will build my church." The rock was not Peter or a physical stone; it was the truth. Peter had stated that Jesus is the Son of God *Matthew. 16:15. But what about you?" he asked. 'Who do you say I am?' 16. Simon Peter answered, 'You are the Christ, <u>the Son of the living God</u>.' 17. Jesus replied, 'Blessed are you, Simon son of Jonah, for this was not revealed to you by man, but by my Father in heaven. 18. And I tell you that you are Peter, and <u>on this rock I will build my church</u>, and the gates of Hades will not overcome it.*

<u>Jesus is "the Son of the living God." This is the truth, the rock on which his church is built on</u>! The church is not necessarily a building but the Gospel Paul was an apostle who learned the Gospel by a revelation from Jesus.

Gal. 1:11. "I want you to know, brothers that the gospel I preached is not something that man made up. 12. I did not receive it from any man, nor was I taught it; rather, I received it by revelation from Jesus Christ. 13. For you have heard of my previous way of life in Judaism, how intensely I persecuted the church of God and tried to destroy it".

We become in our hearts the true Church of Jesus when we accept his sacrifice on the cross and his cleansing blood he shed for us. It is written; we are in Church when two or more gather in his name. *Matthew 18:20. For where two or three come together in my name, there am I with them.* This could be on a park bench, but they are in church!

Paul and Peter Have a Falling-Out in Antioch

"When Peter came to Antioch, I opposed him to his face, because he was clearly in the wrong" *Matthew 18:20. Peter had given into the pressure of the Judaizers and was backsliding.* We read in *2:14, "How is it, then, that you force Gentiles to follow Jewish customs?* Peter was preaching you must be circumcised; this was nailed to the cross and done away with as well as all blood sacrifices of animals and circumcision of men. Now both men and women who accept Christ as Savior has a circumcision of the heart.

Paul preached in *1 Corinthians 7:19: Circumcision is nothing, and un-circumcision is nothing, but the keeping of the commandments of God.* After the shedding of Jesus's blood, circumcision and all blood rituals were nailed to the cross and we would receive *John 14:16. And I will pray the Father, and he shall give you another comforter, that he may abide with you forever. 14:26. But the Comforter, which is the Holy Ghost, whom the Father will send in my name, he shall teach you all things Romans. 2: 29. And circumcision is circumcision of the heart, by the Spirit, not by the written code. Such a man's praise is not from men, but from God.* We can read in *Romans 10:4. For Christ is the end of the law for righteousness to everyone that believeth.* This does not include the Ten Commandments.

Where did the Sin of the Flesh or Sinful Nature originate?

In many places in the original Greek writing the word sin has a prefix or the article "the" which would refer to the original sin of Adam and Eve "The Sin". When the translators or scribes penned the KJV of the Bible they failed to include the article "the", this sin brought to the forefront Satan' influence on flesh man and we now find words in the Bible that are used -- "evil desires", "when we were in the flesh", "fallen nature" and "sinful nature". All of these are directly related to what happened in "The planted Garden of Eden" when Eve was deceived or seduced by the serpent (Satan) and broke the first Command of God.

There is no mention found in the writings of the 39 plus inspired authors regarding sin or sinning of God' creation; the sixth Day 'eth-' âdâm mankind or male and female who roamed the entire earth in peace for 1500 years before God planted a Garden east of Eden and place Adam who was the all in all; formed in the likeness of God before he took the rib or curve or as we know it today the DNA and formed Adams help mate Eve. Suggest you read if you have not read "Apple or The truth"

Paul's teaching even today is misunderstood.

When Paul was on his second missionary journey he started a church in Thessalonica about 50 AD where he taught for three weeks but was forced to leave by the Judaizers. When Paul was in Corinth he got word that the Thessalonians were being influenced by Jews, who were trying to undue his teaching of Life through Christ. Paul writes the first of two letters the second only months later. Why?

Had they misunderstood his first letter and were waiting for the second coming of Christ. Today this false hope is preached as a Rapture theory or a snatching away of the church! Let us read the part of the first Letter that caused Paul to write a second letter of explanation.

"The subject- How they should live":

1 Thessalonians Chapters 4:1-4. Finally, brothers, we instructed you how to live in order to please God, as in fact you are living. Now we ask you and urge you in the Lord Jesus to do this more and more. For you know what instructions we gave you by the authority of the Lord Jesus. It is God's will that you should be sanctified: that you should avoid sexual immorality; that each of you should learn to control his own body in a way that is holy and honorable. We are to keep the sinful nature under check.

Chapter 4:11-12. Make it your ambition to lead a quiet life, to mind your own business and to work with your hands, just as we told you, So that your daily life may win the respect of outsiders and so that you will not be dependent on anybody. Verse 13 begins a new subject which could have been part of the reason for the urgency for Paul second letter.

Is Paul the Architect of the Rapture Theory?

Many of the present day Scholars and Preachers teach a snatching away theory or their rapture theory based mainly on what Paul in 51 A.D. wrote in 1Thessalonians but bypass the subject and start with; Ch.4:16-18.

The subject found in: *1 Thessalonians 4:13. But I would not have you to be ignorant, brethren, concerning them which are asleep, that you sorrow not, even as others which have no hope.* [Asleep or died.]

An early reference to the rapture can be found in a book published in Philadelphia, Pennsylvania, in 1788 but originally written in 1742-1744 in England, which taught the pre-tribulation rapture this was before the "Lacunza Writings" in 1812.

It is widely accepted the Rapture Theory is generally credited to John

Nelson Darby, a 19th-century theologian who had gone to Scotland after reading a Paper written by Margaret Macdonald. Some Theologian writers claim that while she was dangerously sick and thought she was dying, her mind in an altered state, began to experience considerable visionary activity. Others have written a young girl, Margaret McDonald living in Port Glasgow was in the Spirit and while talking in Tongues (or Babel) on an evening in 1830, between February 1st and April 14th, had a personal revelation about the end of the world and claimed it was related to the scriptures. The message she received during this prophetic vision convinced her that Christ was going to appear in two stages one to rapture the church and then return at the 7th trump.

Still others have written while events of this experience were still fresh in her mind, Margaret preserved a handwritten account of everything. The news of Margaret's revelation traveled fast and far. Edward Irving obtained a copy of Margaret's handwritten account and wrote of it in June 1830. A few weeks later John N. Darby journeyed to Scotland to visit Miss McDonald." He borrowed some of her prophetic ideas without giving her credit, modified them and passed them off as his own. In a book written by Darby "The Irrationalism of Infidelity" in 1835, he wrote that he had believed in the return of Christ was <u>after the tribulation period</u>, until he read of Margaret's revelation but now believe in the early rapture of the church! Thus the Rapture Theory began to be promoted by some scholars trying to claim there were hidden messages in the Word in hopes of bringing the people back to church. This filled their coffers!

If you ask a modern day Preacher why their church would be raptured? Their response would be to save our members from the great tribulation! However they start *with 1 Thessalonians 4:16. For the Lord himself shall descend from heaven with a shout, with the voice of the archangel, and with the trump of God: and the dead in Christ shall rise first:* Why would the dead need to be raptured?

The subject begun; *1 Thessalonians 4:13. Brothers, we do not want you <u>to be ignorant about those who fall asleep [or died]</u>, or to grieve like the rest of men, who have no hope.14. We believe that <u>Jesus died and rose again</u> and so we believe that God will bring with Jesus <u>those who have fallen asleep</u>* [died] *<u>in him</u>.* The graves have only decayed bodies the soul is already gone.

This subject will be further explored in Chapter 16. Is Jesus coming again?

Chapter 9
Where Did All the Races Come From?

First, let's examine some general information not accessible to most students. In the original manuscripts, there are three different Hebrew spellings or characters for "man." Dr. Strong's no. 120 and others do not bring this knowledge forward. As I am unable to type or print the original Hebrew font or alphabet as written in the original manuscripts, the difference spelling for man will be printed thusly,

> 'âdâm = Mankind
> 'eth-' âdâm = The Mankind
> 'eth-'Ha''âdhâm = The Man Adam

Let us begin with Genesis *1:24. "And God said, let the Earth bring forth the living creature after his kind, cattle, and creeping thing, and beast of the earth after his kind: and it was so. 25. And God made the beast of the earth after his kind and cattle after their kind, and everything that creeps upon the earth after his kind: and God saw that it was good." They are the same today and have the same markings and color.

Genesis *1:26. And God said, Let us make man* ['âdâm = Man] *in our image, after our likeness: and let them have dominion over the fish of the sea, and over the fowl of the air, and over the cattle, and over all the earth, and over every creeping thing that creeps upon the earth. 27. So God created man in his own image, in the image of God Created he him; male and female created he them.* [They are 'eth-' âdâm = the Mankind.]. Had God created men and women and every race, are they to be known as the Gentiles, just as he had created the different trees, colourful flowers, and birds, Animals and the many different fish of the seas. *28. And God blessed them, and God said unto them, be fruitful, and multiply, and replenish the earth, and subdue it: and have dominion over the fish of the sea, and over the fowl of the air, and over every living thing that moves upon the earth.* [This was the sixth day creation of all the gentiles or races] 29. Then God said, *"I give you every seed bearing plant on the face of the whole earth and every tree that has fruit with seed in it they will be yours for food.* Note that God blessed them;[this was not Adam and his formed helpmate Eve] they had the whole earth to roam, to hunt and fish and pick fruit.

Let's go one step further to see what other occupation is mentioned in the scriptures then we can tie all this together: *Genesis 2:5. And every plant of the field before it was in the earth, and every herb of the field before it grew: for the Lord God had not caused it to rain upon the earth, and there was not a man to till the ground. God had created hunters, fisherman, and fruit pickers, they live off the land they will be known as the Gentiles; but no husbandman or Farmer was found among them. 6. But there went up a mist from the earth, and watered the whole face of the ground.* God will now form 'eth-'Ha'âdhâm = The Man Adam. *7. And the Lord God formed man* ['eth-'Ha' âdâm] *of the dust of the ground, and breathed into his nostrils the breath of life; and man became a living soul. 8. And the Lord God planted a garden eastward in Eden; and there he put the man whom he had formed.*" Notice that God put this man he had formed in the garden <u>a separate place on the earth</u> to look after "the Garden of Eden," a husbandman (the start of the Adamic race). <u>The created mankind or all the other races</u> were to hunt and fish and live off the land. They had the rest of the earth to roam.

What might have confused the issue between the created man and the formed man was the fear of starting discrimination against the Adamic race that would become God's chosen people: *1 Cor. 15:45. And so it is written, The first man Adam was made a living soul; the last Adam was made a quickening spirit.*" Here Paul calls Adam the first man but Paul is comparing and speaking about the seed line that was from Adam to Christ. This is made clear when we understand *15: 47. The first man is of the earth, earthy: the second man is the Lord from heaven.*

The subject is not about the creation of the mankind; it is about connecting the seed line between Adam or the Adamic race and Jesus. Paul wrote in *Romans 5:19. For as <u>by one man's</u>* [the man Adam 'eth-'Ha''âdhâm] *disobedience many were made sinners, so by the obedience <u>of one</u> shall <u>many</u> be made righteous.* Who were the many? It has to be more than just a male and a female; it has to be referring to all the races created on the sixth day. Here, Paul relates to mankind those that were present in the world at large when "the sin" took place in the planted Garden of Eden.

When we consider the races that had been created on the sixth day, God rested on the seventh day, this would mean that mankind or all the races had been on earth for nearly 1,500 of our years with free will to choose right from wrong. This could well have been God's overall plan of salvation, forming Adam and placing him in the Garden of Eden so both the chosen race and the sixth-day races, "the mankind," or the gentiles could have a Saviour for our sinful nature. We must go one more step. Many of the preachers who teach or pick only one verse at a time are misled by not seeking out the subject such as Acts 17:26. Notice the difference in these two versions or translation of scripture.

Acts 17 26. And have made of <u>one blood</u> [we today know there are deferent types of blood so the word could be "And have been made of <u>one clay</u>"] *<u>all nations of men</u> for to dwell on all the face of the earth, and hath determined the times before appointed, and the bounds of their habitation.*

In the *NIV Acts 17:26, "From one man* [these translators change blood to one man instead of clay?] *he made every nation of men, that they should inhabit the whole earth; and he determined the times set for them and the exact places where they should live."* We can by these scriptures possibly link together the creation of the "all nation of men" or "every nation of men" whom had the whole earth to roam, and the forming of Adam who is placed in the Garden of Eden. It might help to do a word study.

A study of the word *nations: Number 1484 Transliterated: ethnos Phonetic: eth'-nos Text: probably from 1486; a race (as of the same habit), i.e. <u>a tribe</u>; specially, a foreign (non-Jewish) one (usually by implication, pagan): -- <u>Gentile</u>, heathen, nation, people.* Note that the word *nation* as used above can also be translated to non-Jewish, a separate tribe, the Gentiles or different races. The man Adam, 'eth'-'Ha"âdhâm formed and placed in the planted Garden; his seed line becomes known as the Jews. The chosen race and through them we have Jesus.

Abraham had a son *Gen. 21:3. and named him Isaac.* Isaac had a son whom he named Jacob; God changed Jacob's name to Israel Gen. 34:10. He would be the father of the twelve tribes. Ten of the tribes would cross over the Cacaos Mountains and intermarry with the rest of the world, [e.g., the tribe of Dan is thought to have migrated to Denmark]. Throughout the many centuries, mankind has intermarried with all races so many can claim to be descendants of the chosen people; and by accepting Jesus as our Saviour, we can all share eternal life.

Chapter 10
Did the Races Survive Noah's Flood?

The answer to this will take a little work but by rightly dividing the word, the truth can be found. Some preachers misinterpret or only look at one verse or only part of a scripture ("eight souls were saved by water"); this was Noah's flood and can lead to a misunderstanding.

In KJV, *1 Peter 3:20, it is written, "Which sometime were disobedient, when once the longsuffering of God waited in the days of Noah, while the ark was a preparing, wherein few, that is, eight souls were saved by water."* The eight souls were saved by water, not necessarily just their being on the ark. The "eight souls were saved by water" refers to a type of baptism or validation that they were saved and their descendants would continue to be the chosen race to carry the seed line to the birth of Christ. We can read of God choosing the Adamic race in *Deuteronomy 7:6: "For you are a holy people unto the Lord your God: the Lord your God <u>has chosen you to be a special people unto himself,</u> above <u>all people that are upon the face of the earth</u>."* The Gentiles or other races?

The Gentiles will be saved through the baptism of the Holy Spirit following the work done on the cross by Jesus. If we backtrack to *1 Peter 3:18. For Christ also hath once suffered for sins, the just for the unjust, that he might bring us to God, being put to death in the flesh, but quickened by the spirit: 19. By which also he* (Jesus) *went and preached unto the spirits in prison.*

After the crucifixion and during the period He was in the tomb, Jesus went to those "spirits in prison" who had died before his work on the cross and preached the Gospel, giving them who believed salvation.

In; 1 Peter *3:21 states, "The like figure whereunto even baptism does also now save us* (not the putting away of the filth of the flesh, but the answer of a good conscience toward God,) *by the resurrection of Jesus Christ."* To clarify, we can read this verse in the NIV, *3:21: "And this water symbolizes baptism that now saves you also—not the removal of dirt from the body but the pledge of a good conscience toward God."* It saves you by the resurrection of Jesus Christ.

Jesus validated that the other races survived Noah's flood in *John 8:44: "You are of your father the devil, and the lusts of your father you will do. He was a murderer from the beginning, and abode not in the truth, because there is no truth in him."* These are the descendants of Cain; you can read a brief genealogy account in Genesis 4:17–24.

We once again read in the OT: "Now these are the generations of the sons of Noah, <u>Shem</u>, Ham, and Japheth: These are the Adamic race with their wives, they are the 8 persons in total who were on the ark along with all other flesh, the Gentiles or the other races." Then *Genesis 10:1.Now these are the generations of the sons of Noah, Shem, Ham, and Japheth: and unto them were sons born <u>after the flood</u>. 2. The sons of Japheth; Gomer, and Magog, and Madai, and Javan, and Tubal, and. Meshech, and Tiras. 3. And the sons of Gomer; Ashkenaz, and Riphath, and Togarmah. 4. And the sons of*

Javan; Elishah, and Tarshish, Kittim, and Dodanim. [This raises a question: Why? This verse interrupts the flow of Noah's sons. Is this verse referring to the sixth-day creation after the flood or the Mankind, all the races, the Gentiles Gen. 1:27?] *10:5.By these were the isles of the Gentiles divided in their lands; every one after his tongue, after their families, in their nations."* Please note. The next verse reverts back to <u>Noah's descendants</u>: *Genesis 10:6, "And the sons of Ham; Cush, and Mizraim, and Phut, and Canaan. 7. And the sons of Cush; Seba, and Havilah, and Sabtah.*

Verse *10:21. <u>Noah's son Shem's</u> descendants are listed.* Noah was a descendent of the formed man Adam the Adamic race Gen. 2:7.

Were the Gentiles mentioned in Genesis 10:5 on the ark with the eight Adamic people, or was Noah's flood only in one area or basin?

Some scholars theorize that the races stemmed from when man was building the tower of Babel long after Noah's flood was based on Genesis 11:1–9 and the Bible teaching of this event. The building of this huge structure was approximately one hundred years after the flood, which would have taken many thousands of workers to construct. They promote that God scrambled their language that segregated the people. They then suggest this also separated the people into different tribes and they migrated to different parts of the earth! They continued through the sun and heat that the skin took on different colors, and due to intermarriage, people developed different facial shapes including more fat around the eyes leading to the shape of the eyes such as the Japanese and Chinese.

If this was true, then they were all descendants of the formed "the Man Adam, 'eth-'Ha''âdhâm," who was placed in the planted garden of Eden instead of the sixth-day creation or mankind created as male and female in Genesis 1:27, 'eth-' âdâm. Their theory begs the question, which tribe would become the chosen people or tribe that would keep the seed line pure to Jesus? What about DNA? If this theory that the races were a product of the Tower of Babel, it is not supported by facts found in encyclopaedia's. Ponder these facts!

1. Egyptian history dates back to 3100 BC, 652 years before

    Noah's flood was approximately 752 years before the Tower of Babel.

2. Chinese history dates back before this flood, 2356 BC, eight years before the flood. The most reliable historic sources agree that Noah's flood was 2348 BC. (Time in BC counts backward 4004–0). Jesus was born 3–4 BC and began his ministry in AD 27. The tower of Babel was approximately one hundred years after Noah's flood.

3. What you read in Genesis 10:1–7 should raise an interesting question! Verse 5 talks about Gentiles.

The Shu-King historic records of China dates that King Yao came to the throne in 2356 BC; this was eleven years before the start of Noah's flood and ruled China for many years after the flood.

Egypt also has one of the oldest existing recorded civilizations in the world. Most scholars believe that the Egyptian kingdom was first unified in about 3100 BC. In Egypt, the eleventh dynasty began to reign about 2375 BC over a great and powerful nation twenty-seven years before Noah's flood.

Chapter 11

History of the Bible and Moses

The Bible was the first book ever printed. God had written the Ten

Commandments on tablets of stone; we can we can assume that mankind must have had previous knowledge of writing. Even today, archaeologists uncover ancient tablets with markings. Some of the first were unearthed at Lachish and Tel-el-Amarna. As mankind moved forward, they began writing on animal skins and the inner bark of the linden tree. Moses is credited with and was told by the Lord to write the first five books in our Holy Bible between 1491–1451 BC. He wrote Genesis, Exodus, Leviticus, Numbers, Deuteronomy; and most scholars have accredited Moses as the author of the book of Job.

In the book of *Exodus 17:4, then the LORD said to Moses, "Write this on a scroll as something to be remembered and make sure that Joshua hea s it."* We also read *in Numbers 33:2, "At the Lord's command, Moses recorded the stages in their journey."* This is their journey by stages: Moses had writings from others and by direct inspiration from the Holy Spirit was able to write an accurate account of the years before his birth. His writings were known as the Pentateuch. Joshua wrote the end of Deuteronomy, which covered the death of Moses in chapter 34.

The skins or bark were later sewed together to form a scroll. Other scrolls were written by Joshua, Samuel, and many others. In 1 Samuel 10:25, Samuel explained to the people the regulations of the kingship. He wrote them down on a scroll and deposited it before the LORD. The Scrolls were lost and rediscovered in 550 BC (2 Kings 22:8; 2 Chron. 34:14): "While they were bringing out the money that had been taken into the temple of the LORD, Hilkiah the priest found the Book of the Law of the LORD that had been given through Moses." In Isaiah 30:8, it is written, *"Go now, write it on a tablet for them, and inscribe it on a scroll, that for the days to come it may be an everlasting witness."*

The Old Testament was written in Hebrew, Aramaic, or the Semitic languages with a few parts written in Chaldean. In the Early Hebrew Manuscripts (MS) (OM), there were no chapters, vowels, or punctuation marks, only consonants.

These Hebrew writings were known as the Tenach. The writings remained in the Semitic languages until 280–150 BC when they were translated by Jewish scholars and scribes into Greek at Alexandria, Egypt. This translation was known as the Septuagint; the manuscript's accuracy and reliability was confirmed by the discovery of the Dead Sea Scrolls, nine hundred in all, between 1947– 1956.

The Septuagint or Greek version of the Old Testament is believed to be written three hundred years before Christ. Then in the sixth to twelfth century, vowels were added and the manuscripts were called the Masorah or Masorectic text. The books were divided into chapters by Cardinal Hugo de St. Cher about AD 1250.

This Man Moses

The name "Moses" means "saved from the water," born an Israelite of parents who were descendants from the tribe of Levi. In Genesis 35:10, we read of Jacob (whose name was changed to Israel); Jacob will have twelve sons that will become the twelve tribes, off which much is written of in the bible.

Genesis 35:22 ------- "Jacob had twelve sons: 23. — Reuben the firstborn of Jacob, Simeon, Levi, Judah, Issachar and Zebulun. 24. — Joseph and Benjamin. 25. — Dan and Naphtali. 26. — Gad and Asher. These were the twelve sons of Jacob, The tribe of Levi was given the duty of the priesthood; the tribe of Judah would become the king line. Moses will be credited as the founder of the Jewish religion. His life can be divided up into three forty-year periods".

Moses's Life from Zero to Forty Years of Age

Moses was born in Goshen, Egypt, BC 1571, during the time when the Israelite people were treated as slaves, making bricks and all forms of demeaning labour to sustain and build the Egyptian empire. The Israelite male population had been growing at an alarming rate, causing concern to the Egyptians; they feared that there might be a rebellion; consequently, the king/pharaoh of Egypt decreed that all male newborn Israelite children be put to death. Geneses 1:16 provides, *"When you help the Hebrew women in childbirth —, if it is a boy, kill him; but if it is a girl, let her live."*

Moses's mother, a Levite, a Hebrew, after the birth of her son, concealed her infant for three months. Fearing for her son's life, she placed him in a pitch-covered papyrus basket and placed it in the reeds by the edge of a canal of the Nile River where the pharaoh's daughter was known to bathe. The princess, who history tells us, was a childless wife and came to bathe in the considered sacred river with her attendant slaves. Spotting the covered basket, the princess sent swimmers to retrieve the basket. When she uncovered the basket, the cries of the child moved her deeply, and she felt this as a gift from her gods.

One of her attendants suggested hiring an Israelite slave who had lost her child to nurse the baby; the chosen one was Moses's actual real mother, a descendant of the tribe of Levi. The princess later adopted the child, naming him Moses. Moses was accepted into the royal palace and raised as an Egyptian with his real mother silently teaching him the Jewish belief in one real God. As the adopted son of the princess, Moses was taught the wisdom of the Egyptians along with their lustful way of life and their many gods. The Egyptians had as many as seven hundred or more different gods.

Little is recorded in the Bible for the rest of his first forty years of his life. However, Moses's life as an Egyptian can be found in the recorded Egyptian history. His real mother's teaching of one God began to weigh on Moses's heart and spirit. Moses began to feel and witnessed the abuse his people, the Israelites, were forced to endure. One day after watching an Egyptian mistreating an Israelite, Moses, later thinking he was alone, struck this Egyptian, killing him and burying him in the sand. The Israelites rejected Moses for what he had done and were not ready to accept Moses as their leader, nor was Moses yet ready to serve or save his people. It was not long until his crime was discovered and because of his connection to the royalty through the princess adopting him as an infant, Moses was not punished but forced to abandon his status and leave the country.

Moses's Life at Forty to Eighty

His travels took him to Midian where he came to "the Well" (Exod. 2:15) and to the aid of some young maidens who were being mistreated by some Arabian sheepherders. One of these young maidens becomes his wife, and Moses begins several years working for her father Jethro who was considered an Arab; he treated Moses not much better than a slave even though they were blood related dating back to Abraham by way of his third set of children. Moses strengthened his belief in the Hebrew way and in God. God finally talks to Moses through a burning bush, and Moses is instructed to return to Egypt where he will free the Hebrews who will become God's chosen people (Deut. 7: 6) leading them to freedom and to the promised land given to Abraham east of the Jordan River and the Dead Sea all the way to the Mediterranean Sea, the land of Canaan or now partly known also as Palestine.

Moses's Last 80–120 Years

Moses's last years were spent wandering the desert, but because he had not followed God's instruction to the T, he was not allowed to enter the Promised Land, only view its vastness and beauty. Moses dies at age 120. But God had blessed him and secretly took his body. Through Moses, God also gave us the Ten Commandments.

The first five books of the OT—Genesis, Exodus, Leviticus, Numbers, and Deuteronomy—are credited to Moses as being written by him by stories handed down through the generations and the direct revelation and inspiration from God. The book of Job is accredited to have been inspired by God and written by Moses.

The King James Version dated AD 1611 contains sixty-six books—thirty-nine books written by thirty-one authors in the Old testament and twenty-seven books in the New Testament written by eight authors. These writings or books were gathered from three different continents—Africa, Asia, and Europe—written by thirty-nine authors over a period of 1,500 years, most of whom never had contact with one another. The older writings were copied or recopied several times as some of the materials used would start to deteriorate. There were many handwritten copied documents found; however, unless the words were found to totally agree in a minimum of ten different copies, they were considered not acceptable. Moses wrote 65 percent more of the Holy Bible than Paul.

In the New Testament, the Apostle Paul wrote two letters to Timothy from Rome: *1 Thimothy1:14 "The grace of our Lord was poured out on me abundantly, along with the faith and love that are in Christ Jesus. 15. Here is a trustworthy saying that deserves full acceptance: Christ Jesus came into the world to save sinners, of whom I am the worst. 16. But for that very reason I was shown mercy so that in me, the worst of sinners, Christ Jesus might display his unlimited patience as an example for those who would believe on him and receive eternal life*" (1 Tim. 1:14–16).

Then again Paul wrote to Timothy: "*All scripture is given by inspiration of God, and is profitable for doctrine, for reproof, for correction, for instruction in righteousness*" *(2 Tim. 3:16).* This verse confirms how Moses was able to write the first book, Genesis, and the first part of Exodus, relating back to "the beginning of creation" before his birth as recorded in Exodus 2:10; and during his life, Moses was inspired to write by God.

Why should we read the Bible for ourselves? In 1 Corinthians Paul wrote, *3:1. "Brothers, I could not address you as spiritual but as worldly—mere infants in Christ. 2. I gave you milk* [probably just a sermon] *not solid food, for you were not yet ready for it. Indeed, you are still not ready."* The deeper truth you will find as you read and rightly divided the Word.

If we look in the book of *Matthew 25:1. "at that time the kingdom of heaven will be like ten virgins who took their lamps and went out to meet the bridegroom. 2. Five of them were foolish and five were wise. The wise had found the truth by studying the Bible for themselves. 3. The foolish ones took their lamps but did not take any oil with them. They had not taken the time to really study the Word. 4. The wise, however, took oil in jars along with their lamps. They had read the Word and had a deeper understanding of the Word. 5. The bridegroom (Jesus) was a long time in coming, and they all became drowsy and fell asleep. 6. At midnight the cry rang out: 'Here's the bridegroom! Come out to meet him!' 7. Then all the virgins woke up and trimmed their lamps. [When you trim your lamp, you blow out the fire and cut off or trim the burnt part of the wick and add fuel.] 8. The foolish ones said to the wise, 'Give us some of your oil; our lamps are going out.' 9. 'No,' they replied, 'there may not be enough for both us and you. Instead, go to those who sell oil and buy some for yourselves.' 10. But while they were on their way to buy the oil, the bridegroom arrived. The virgins who were ready went in with him to the wedding banquet. And the door was shut. 11. Later the others also came. 'Sir! Sir!' they said. 'Open the door for us!' 12. But he replied, 'I tell you the truth, I don't know you.'"* We must study the Word to know Jesus and for Him to know us.

Today we only need to ask a question like, why are there still fish if we or they evolved maybe the scientist should look for Mermaids to find their missing link! If a single cell developed in the ocean and crawled up on the sand, there must have been a male and a female. Nowadays, the fish only outsmart fishermen sometimes but the atheist always. Einstein even gave credit to a higher power for his gift and knowledge.

Chapter 12

Rightly Dividing the Word

In; *2 Timothy 2:15 states, "Study to show thyself approved unto God, a workman who does not need to be ashamed, rightly dividing the word of truth."*

What is meant by rightly dividing the word? The original scrolls or manuscripts had no chapters; however, when men prepared and printed the Holy Bible, they inserted chapters. There may be two or more subjects interwoven throughout the chapter, and a subject can be carried over to a following chapter or even to different books or writings found in the book as a whole. A subject may be interrupted by a similar subject then the original subject will continue.

After examining Genesis 1:1–31, it would appear that the translators and writers ended the chapter before the subject matter of creation was completed, creating a break between chapter 1 and 2, which tends to mislead and interfere with the conclusion of the subject of creation and the start of a new subject. This tends to hide the question when Cain was banished to the land of Nod and has children (Gen. 3:17); where did his wife come from? Was the land of Nod the place where God had created mankind, male and female? Was this before He planted the Garden of Eden and formed Adam and then creating Eve from his DNA? There is mention of Eden, the Garden of God in the Bible; this had to represent the whole world as a garden. While drilling in the Artic, they have found palm wood below the ice.

Let's restart or look into the ending of the first chapter, picking it up: *"and to all the beasts of the earth and all the birds of the air and all the creatures that move on the ground—everything that has the breath of life in it—I give every green plant for food.' And it was so.* [In this verse, we read that God had given the breath of life to everything.] *31. God saw all that he had made, and it was very good. And there was evening, and there was morning, the sixth day"* *(Gen. 1:30–31).* This is where the scholars or scribes ended the first chapter, but the subject continues! There is one more day and then a summation of God's work up to Genesis 2:6. They now begin a new chapter.

Genesis 2:1. *"Thus the heavens and the earth were finished, and all the host of them. 2. And on the seventh day God ended his work which he had made; and he rested on the seventh day from all his work which he had made. 3. And God blessed the seventh day, and sanctified it: because that in it he had rested from all his work which God created and made.* Now starts the summation of Gods work up to this point. *4. These are the generations of the heavens and of the earth when they were created, in the day that the Lord God made the earth and the heavens, 5. And every plant of the field before it was in the earth, and every herb of the field before it grew: for the Lord God had not caused it to rain upon the earth, and there was not a man to till the ground. 6. But there went up a mist from the earth, and watered the whole face of the ground"*

Up to this point, the subject continues from *Genesis 1:3 "And God said, Let there be light: and there was light"* and continues to *Genesis 2:6 "But there went up a mist from the earth, and watered the whole face of the ground."*

By His word, God had created male and female in *Genesis 1:27: "Male and female created he them. — They were Hunters and fishermen and Fruit pickers."* Here is the important fact of the subject carried through to Genesis 2:5–6: <u>*"But there was no one to till the ground.*</u> [Here we read there was no husbandman or farmer/rancher.] *6. But there went up a mist from the earth, and watered the whole face of the ground."* Why would you need a gardener?

Now in Genesis 2:7–8, <u>we begin a completely new subject</u> and the subject changes to a small confined space, "the planted Garden of Eden": "And the Lord God formed man of the dust of the ground, and breathed into his nostrils the breath of life; and man became a living soul. [This Man is formed from, not created, a separate word in the Hebrew language and given the breath of life.] 8. And the Lord <u>God planted a garden</u> eastward in Eden; and <u>there he put the man</u> whom <u>he had formed</u>." This was a completely new event from the creation of mankind.

Let us backtrack and do a few word studies. First, the word *history* is not found in the OM, either in the OT or the NT. However, the words *generations* and *generation* are used. Using Strong's numbers, we find the following: Genesis 2:4. "These *are* the <u>generations</u> of the heavens and of the earth when they were created in the day that the Lord God made the earth and the heavens" The word *are* <u>was added for clarity</u>. Man's insertion of *"are"* to the Word <u>causes some of the confusion</u>. But <u>note</u> that with the *S* in *generations*, the original Hebrew word can be translated to or interpreted as "history."

The word *generations*. Notice the *S. Strong's ref. no. 8435 Romanized*

towldah Pronounced to-led-aw' or toldah {to-led-aw'}; from HSN3205; (plural only) descent, i.e. family; (figuratively) history: KJV—birth, generations.

Let's compare another scripture using the word *generation*, but note there is no *S.*

Jeremiah 7:29 says, "Cut off your hair, O Jerusalem, and cast it away, and take up a lamentation on high places; for the Lord has rejected and forsaken this generation that is under his wrath." Without the *S, the word* can be interpreted as an age.)

Generation, Strong's ref. no. 1755 Romanized dowr Pronounced dore or (shortened) dor from HSN1752; properly ,a revolution of time, i.e. an age or generation; also a dwelling:KJV—age, X evermore, generation, [n-] ever, posterity. [Note that there is no history.]

We now have since 1392 began the study of archaeology or man's looking into the past (history) ("history of archaeology," from *Wikipedia: The Free Encyclopedia*). "The Italian Renaissance historian Flavio Biondo (1392–1463) is recognized as one of the world's first archaeologists. [7] The first step forward towards archaeology as a science took place during the Age of enlightenment, also known as the Age of Reason, in Europe in the 17th and 18th centuries.[8]"

This is well after the 1611 translation of KJV. Using this information, the subject of creation in Genesis 1 should have been continued until the end of Genesis 2:6. "Thus the heavens and the earth were finished, and all the host of them *Genesis.2:2. And on the seventh day God ended his work which he had made; and he rested on the seventh day from all his work which he had made. 3. And God blessed the seventh day, and sanctified it: because that in it he had rested from all his work which God created and made.* [This was seven days for God but seven thousand years of our time.] 4. These are the generations of the heavens and of the earth when they were created, in the day that the Lord God made the earth and the heavens. [We read above with the *S* generations could be translated to history.] *5. And every plant of the field before it was in the earth, and every herb of the field before it grew: for the Lord God had not caused it to rain upon the earth, and there was not a man to till the ground.* This ties this verse to 1:11, 26, and 27 or creation of plant life and mankind. Up to this period, there were only hunters, fishermen, and fruit pickers. However, there was no husbandman or farmer/rancher. *6. But there went up a mist from the earth, and watered the whole face of the ground.* [Or Dew.]

We must understand the Mankind or the races created on the sixth day Genesis 11:26–27; they had freedom to roam the whole world and they had all the food they needed. This then raises the question why there was a mention of "there was no one to till the ground."

This concludes the subject of "Creation."

We now start a new subject.

God will establish "the planted Garden eastward of Eden" and "the forming or beginning of the seed line to Jesus the Christ."

It is important to note that 'eth-'âdâm or mankind was created in the subject of "creation" and was given the whole dominion of the earth to roam peacefully and freely.

Genesis 2:7 begins a new subject, and we will find that the location will change to "the planted Garden eastward of Eden." In this new subject, 'eth-'Ha''âdhâm, "the Man Adam, "is formed" from the dust of the earth and God gave him a name Adam and he will be restricted to the boundaries of "the Garden eastward of Eden."

Genesis 2:7 says, "And the Lord God formed man of the dust of the ground, and breathed into his nostrils the breath of life; and man became a living soul." Notice that the word *formed* is used, not *created!* This man in the original manuscripts has both the article and the particle with an added *h*—'eth-'Ha' 'âdhâm, "the Man Adam."This separates him from mankind.

Formed: *Strong's ref. no. 3335 Romanized yatsar Pronounced yaw-tsar' probably identical with HSN3334 (through the squeezing into shape); ([compare HSN3331]); to mold into a form; especially as a potter; frame, make (-r), potter, purpose.*

Gen: 2:8 "And the Lord God planted a garden eastward in Eden; and there he put the man whom he had formed. This formed man 'eth-'Ha''âdhâm is named Adam"

We must take note and rightly dividing the Word God planted a garden on earth or eastward Eden!

Gen. 2:20. And Adam gave names to all cattle—these are docile or domesticated animals; Adam was a husbandman restricted to the planted Garden *Gen. 2:9. And out of the ground (in the planted garden) made the Lord God to grow every tree that is pleasant to the sight, and good for food; the tree of life also in the midst of the garden, and the tree of knowledge of good and evil.* The tree of life represents Jesus, The tree of knowledge of good and evil represents the serpent or Satan. These trees have no edible fruit.

In the original manuscript, there are three different meanings to the word *man* by the addition of the article, particle, and an *h*: (1) man, (2) the mankind male and female, and (3) the man Adam. But the translators and lexicons <u>failed to recognize the article, particle, and the added *h*</u>, which has misled many theologians who do not have access to the original Hebrew manuscripts, which have the article, particle, and *h*, from rightly dividing the word.

They are all translated the same as just man: "a man, a human being, a person or mankind." The word *mankind* in the English dictionary means "all persons, this could be male or female or all the races." We explore the word in the original Hebrew manuscripts (OM):

1. The first one is 'âdâm which has no article or particle. 'âdâm = Man. Genesis 1:26 states, "And God said, Let us make man in our image, after our likeness: and let them have dominion over the fish of the sea, and over the fowl of the air, and over the cattle, and over all the earth, and over every creeping thing that creeps upon the earth." He was Created and allowed to roam the whole dominion of the earth.

2. The second one 'eth-' âdâm has the article but no particle and no h. 'eth-' âdâm = the mankind. Genesis 1:27 says, "So God created man in his own image, in the image of God created he him; male and female created he them. They are

Created and allowed to roam the whole Dominion of the Earth."

3. Then the third one, 'eth-'Ha''âdhâm, both the article and the particle. 'Eth-'Ha''âdhâm = This Man Adam. (Note that there is also an *h*.) Genesis 2:7 states, "And the Lord God formed man ('eth-'Ha' âdhâm = The Man Adam) of the dust of the ground, and breathed into his nostrils the breath of life; and man became a living soul. He was formed from dust and placed in the Garden eastward of Eden and his name is Adam. Adam's DNA was used to form Eve.

Chapter 13

What Is Judaism, Who Are the
Jews, Why Did They Reject Jesus?"

Judaism is the religion of the Jews.

1. The word *Judaism* originates from "the practices of Judea."

2. Judaism began when Abraham by God's instruction moved to the region of Canaan. Abraham as a boy was the first to realize that the idols of his people had no power; this led him to believe in <u>just one God</u>: *(Gen. 12:1) "The LORD had said to Abram, 'Leave your country, your people and your father's household and go to the land I will show you."* In *12:7, "the LORD appeared to Abram and said, '<u>To your offspring I will give this land</u>.' So he built an altar there to the LORD, who had appeared to him."*

3. Others may regard the true founder of Judaism to be Moses, who is traditionally considered because he is credited with writing the Torah, the first five books of our Holy Bible, including the life of Abraham and his family tree.

After about six years of warring among the twelve tribes, the Israelites claimed a vast area as a united kingdom under God. It became the land of Israel. Solomon built the first permanent temple in Jerusalem. One area was called Judah; the rest of the areas were named after the other eleven tribes.

When the twelve tribes divided, Jeroboam became the first king of the ten tribes known as the Northern Kingdom of Israel and named their new capital Samaria. Jeroboam set up two golden figures of Mnevis, the sacred calf, one at the southern and another at the northern boundaries of his kingdom, turning away from worship at the temple in Jerusalem that held the Holy of Holies or God's chosen place. Basically they turned away from God.

The tribe of Benjamin joined with the tribe of Judah, and they claimed the temple in Jerusalem as the center of worship; they were then called Jews. The ten tribes soon went into captivity and later were dispersed all over Europe and lost their identity.

Who are the Jews?

We must begin with Abraham and Sarah who had borne a son named Isaac; he had twins, Esau and Jacob. Esau sold his birthright for a bowl of stew to Jacob. Jacob was renamed by God "Israel." We read in Genesis 35:10, "God said to him, 'your name is Jacob, but you will no longer be called Jacob; your name will be Israel.' So he named him Israel." Israel fathers twelve sons; they become known as the twelve tribes or the "Israelites." Ten of the tribes separate and set up their own place of worship, they become known as the northern tribes. "And when he numbered them in Bezek, the children of Israel were three hundred thousand, and the men of Judah thirty thousand" (1 Sam. 11:8).

The tribe of Benjamin and Judah continued to use Jerusalem as their place of worship. We can read of a further division in *2 Samuel 20:1, "And there happened to be there a man of Belial, — a Benjamite: and he blew a trumpet, and said, we have no part in David, neither have we inheritance in the son of Jesse: every man to his tents, O Israel."* To clarify, Jesse was a descendant of the tribe of Judah; they become known as Jews. Jesse fathered David; this seed line brings forth Jesus our Savior. The NIV *1 Kings 12:6* states, *"When all Israel saw that the king refused to listen to them, they answered the king: 'What share do we have in David, what part in Jesse's son? To your tents, O Israel! Look after your own house, O David!' So the Israelites went home."* The House of David was the tribe of Judah and are later known exclusively as Jews.

The first time an Israelite is called a Jew is in *2 Kings 16:6: "At that time Rezin king of Syria recovered Elath to Syria, and drove the Jews from Elath: and the Syrians came to Elath, and dwelt there unto this day."*

Now a brief history of the Jews, during the time of Jesus. The Sanhedrin was the supreme council of the Jewish people in the time of Christ; it was a group of seventy-one, which was composed of chief priests, elders, scribes, lawyers, or those learned in the Jewish law. It became extinct in AD 425. The Sanhedrin was a Jewish judicial body formed by three different sects or religious parties:

1. The Essenes, the smallest group who believed that man should live in harmony with nature.

2. The Sadducees who were in denial of man's resurrection after death and believed there was afterlife.

3. The Pharisees who believed in an afterlife.

They all had the scrolls or our Old Testament (OT). But like the modern Christian churches, they only used scripture that would fit their dogma.

A new subject is "Why did some of the followers of Judaism, the Jews, reject Jesus?"

God had chosen them to be as follows: *"Then you shall be a peculiar treasure unto me above all people" (Exod. 19:5)*; *"Because he loved your forefathers and <u>chose their descendants</u>* (Israelites) *after them, he brought you out of Egypt by his Presence and his great strength" (Deut. 4:37)*; *"For you are a people holy to the LORD your God. The LORD your <u>God has chosen you</u>* (Israelites) *out <u>of all the peoples</u>* (Gentiles) *on the face of the earth to be his people, <u>his trea-sured possession</u>" (Deut. 7:6)*; and *"For you are a people holy to the LORD your God. Out of all the peoples on the face of the earth, the LORD has chosen you to be his treasured possession" (Deut. 14:2)*.

The concept of the Messiah has its foundation in our Jewish Bible, the Tanach, which teaches that all of <u>the following crite-ria **must** be fulfilled before any person can be acknowledged</u> as the Messiah: the Messiah must be from the tribe of Judah and a descendant of King David and King Solomon. Jesus's mother was the granddaughter of Heli, a descendant of the tribe of Judah. The Jews rejected Jesus because He failed, in their eyes, to do what they expected their Messiah to do—destroy evil and all their enemies and establish an eternal kingdom with Israel as the preeminent nation in the world. The prophecies in Isaiah and Psalm 22 describe a suffering Messiah who would be per-secuted and killed, but the Jews chose to focus instead on those prophecies that discuss His glorious victories, not His crucifixion. They turned a blind eye on prophecy.

In their Scrolls (OT), the prophet Isaiah wrote in *Isaiah 7:14, "Therefore the Lord himself shall give you a sign; Behold, a virgin shall conceive, and bear a son, and shall call his name Immanuel,"* Immanuel, which *means "God is with us."* The Jews had this in their scrolls, *"For to us a child is born, to us a son is given, and the government will be on his shoulders. And he will be called Wonderful Counselor, Mighty God, Everlasting Father, Prince of Peace" (Isaiah 9:6).* The Sanhedrin probably believed that the Messiah would be immortal and rule forever. *"Of the increase of his government and peace there will be <u>no end</u>. He will reign on David's throne and over his kingdom, establishing and upholding it with justice and righteousness from that time and <u>forever</u>. The zeal of the LORD Almighty will accomplish this. <u>No end</u>, and <u>forever</u>* here again (9:7).* The Sanhedrin would find fault with Jesus: But we have read His second coming would be not by birth but from descending.

When Jesus came to Jerusalem, He turned over the tables of the money changers in front of the temple and upset the economy. We read in *Mark 11:15. "And they come to Jerusalem: and Jesus went into the temple, and began to cast out them that sold and bought in the temple, and overthrew the tables of the moneychangers, and the seats of them that sold doves; 16. And would not suffer that any man should carry any vessel* (merchandise) *through the temple. 17. And he taught, saying unto them, Is it not written, My house shall be called of all nations the house of prayer? But ye have made it a den of thieves.* [This angered the priests and the Sanhedrin who were making a profit by selling sacrificial items.] *18. And the scribes and chief priests heard it, and sought how they might destroy him: for they feared him, because all the people were astonished at his doctrine. 19. And when even was come, he went out of the city."*

They are further angered when they heard the following:

1. Jesus claimed to be the Son of God—*John 14:9. "Jesus answered: 'Don't you know me, Philip, even after I have been among you such a long time? Anyone who has seen me has seen the Father. How can you say, "Show us the Father"?*

2. When they learned; *John 1:29 the next day, John saw Jesus coming toward him and said, "Look, the Lamb of God, who goats, and bulls to atone for their sins.* They believed that Jesus was a mere man, thus a violation of their sacred Jewish belief. In Judaism, no mortal can ever be divine and God and never die or take human form.

Paul would write in *1 Corinthians 1:22, "Jews demand miraculous signs and Greeks look for wisdom."* Jesus later preached in a synagogue: *Luke 4:16 "And he came to Nazareth, where he had been brought up: and, as his custom was, he went into the synagogue on the Sabbath day, and stood up for to read. 17. And there was delivered unto him the book (Scroll) of the prophet Esaias* [or Isaiah]. *And when he had opened the book, he found the place where it was written, 18. The Spirit of the Lord is upon me, because he hath anointed me to preach the gospel to the poor; he hath sent me to heal the broken hearted, to preach deliverance to the captives, and recovering of sight to the blind, to set at liberty them that are bruised, 19. To preach the acceptable year of the Lord. 20. And he closed the book, and he gave it again to the minister, and sat down. And the eyes of all them that were in the synagogue were fastened on him. 21. And he began to say unto them, this day is this scripture fulfilled in your ears"* They knew there was more to this verse! Jesus will, as we will read later, stop his reading mid-verse and sits down. They did not understand that this was the first part of a prophecy, his work, or first mission on earth.

Now here is the rest of the verse: *Isaiah 61:2 "And the day of vengeance of our God, to comfort all who mourn"* This last part of the verse represents or predicts the future after his crucifixion on the cross and when He comes the second time.

The Jews failed to grasp that this scripture had two subjects— the latter relating to his second comings. We can make this clearer by His (Jesus) first coming or subject, the acceptable year of the Lord or the Lord's favor and a new Covenant of everlasting life. Jesus would fulfill this on the cross and would save sinners from death caused by "the Sin" in the Garden of Eden. And He, Jesus, would become our Sabbath; every day we can now find rest in the Lord.

Mark 2:27. "And he said unto them, The Sabbath was made for man, and not man for the Sabbath [we must discern that Jesus is using the word *Sabbath* in reference to his birth]. *28. Therefore the Son of man is Lord also of the Sabbath."* T he Jews would several times accuse Jesus of breaking their Sabbath" *Sabbath* means "a day of rest." Jesus said in *Matthew 11:28 "Come to me, all you who are weary and burdened, and I will give you rest."*

The Apostle Paul wrote in *1 Corinthians 5:7. "Purge out therefore the old leaven that you may be a new lump, as you are unleavened. For even Christ our Passover is sacrificed for us: 8. therefore let us keep the feast, not with old leaven, neither with the leaven of malice and wickedness; but with the unleavened bread of sincerity and truth."* By understanding these verses, we can glean that <u>Jesus became our Sabbath</u> and with Him in our life every day of the week, we can find rest or our Sabbath day—"For even Christ our Passover." Paul wrote about Jesus in *Romans 11:27, "And this is my covenant with them when I take away their sins."* This is further explained in Hebrews 8:10, "This is the covenant I will make with the house of Israel after that time, declares the Lord. I will put my laws in their minds and write them on their hearts. I will be their God, and they will be my people. It is also written in *Hebrews 10:16,* *"This is the covenant I will make with them after that time, says the Lord. I will put my laws in their hearts, and I will write them on their minds."*

We read of the <u>first covenant</u> in *Galatians 4:24: "Which things are an allegory: for these are the two covenants; the one from the Mount Sinai, which gendered to bondage."* Moses brought down the Ten Commandments from Mount Sinai. <u>The second covenant was given by Jesus</u>; *Hebrews 10:16, "<u>this is my covenant</u>"* as read above. Are the laws or the commandments changed? No! But remembering and keeping Jesus in our life every day, we are more than fulfilling the fourth commandment.

The second coming of Jesus or the day of vengeance can be found on the last half of Isaiah 61:2: "His return will end, evil on earth, and lead to the death of Satan and his followers also to prepare the Earth for the great white throne judgment."

The Jews only had the writings of our OT; Jesus's birth was foretold many times, but they had chosen not to use their eyes to hear what was written in their Scrolls.

Isaiah 7:14. "*Therefore the Lord himself shall give you a sign; Behold, a virgin shall conceive, and bear a son, and shall call his name Immanuel.*" *Micah 5:2* "*But you, Bethlehem Ephrathah, though you are small among the clans of Judah, out of you will come for me one who will be ruler over Israel, whose origins are from of old, from ancient times*" Jesus's birthplace.

Zechariah 9:9. "*Rejoice greatly, O Daughter of Zion! Shout, Daughter of Jerusalem! See, your king comes to you, righteous and having salvation, gentle and riding on a donkey, on a colt, the foal of a donkey.*" Jesus entered Jerusalem on a Donkey" *12:10.* "*-- They will look on me, the one they have pierced*"—Jesus was pierced on the cross. *Malachi 3:1* "*Behold, I will send my messenger, and he shall prepare the way before me: and the Lord, whom ye seek, shall suddenly come to his temple, even the messenger of the covenant, whom ye delight in: behold, he shall come, said the Lord of hosts*". This would be John the Baptist. *3:5* "*So I will come near to you for judgment. I will be quick to testify against sorcerers, adulterers and perjurers, against those who defraud laborers of their wages, who oppress the widows and the fatherless, and deprive aliens of justice, but do not fear me,*" says the LORD Almighty. In the new testament, John 2:15 He turns their tables over".

Jesus taught from their scrolls. One of his last words on the cross was: *Matthew 27:46* "*Eloi, Eloi, lama sabachthani?*" — *Which means, "My God, my God, why have you forsaken me?*" Jesus was reminding and telling them to read their scrolls that predicted their actions this day down to the last detail Psalm 22:1–18. Here are only two verses: *Psalm 22:16.* "*Dogs have surrounded me; a band of evil men has encircled me, they have pierced my hands and my feet. [Jesus was nailed to the cross.] 18. They divide my garments among them and cast lots for my clothing."* This was written in their Scrolls more than one thousand years earlier. Many Jews, some who lost money or standing in their community could not accept Jesus as their Messiah and sought to kill Him. When Jesus overturned their tables near the Temple, John 2:15. Jesus wrote in *John 5:45,* *"But do not think I will accuse you before the Father. <u>Your accuser is</u>* <u>*Moses,*</u> *on whom your hopes are set."*

Moses gave them the Ten Commandments, but as we have learned, Jesus, for the believers who are baptized and repent, became our everyday Sabbath.

When two or more Christians are gathered in Jesus's name, they are attending His church regardless of the day of the week. Through this, the fourth commandment is still valid.

Back to *John 5:46. "If you believed Moses, you would believe me,* *for he wrote about me. 47. But since you do not believe what he wrote,* *how are you going to believe what I say?"*

The New Agers and others teach that there are many ways to have everlasting life, but here again their eyes cannot hear the Word. For it is written in *John 3:16, "For God so loved the world,* *that he gave his only begotten Son, that whosoever <u>believeth in him</u>* *should not perish, but have everlasting life."*

The origin of the naming of Jerusalem has been theorized by many. Here is one of them.

Before Joshua entered the Promised Land known as Canaan, the Canaanites named their god Shalem. The city we know as Jerusalem was first called "Urushalim" or "Urushalem." The prefix *uru* means "founded by" and the suffix *Salem* or *Shalem* was the Canaanite god of dusk.

Around 2500 BCE on Egyptian statues, the name Urushalim was first found. This evidence is confirmed by tablets found in Elba, Syria, dating back to 3000 BCE, on which the god Shalem was being honored in a city called Uruksalem.

Jerusalem more recently is often assumed to mean founded in peace or "city of peace," but there is no evidence for this interpretation in Hebrew.

Today, you are generally called a Jew if you live in a certain part of Jerusalem.

Chapter 14

Does the Holy Bible Teach
Discrimination or Racism?

There are many learned scholars of the Bible who would say rightly NO! Then there are many preachers of the Word who teach the Bible with their dogma story form, using the following false but in good faith; as an example: "Eve ate an apple" story, possibly validating their teaching to young children by using what the Apostle Paul wrote in *1 Corinthians 3:2: "I gave you milk, not solid food, for you were not yet ready for it."*

Do they preach this falsehood to hide the truth or avert racism? There might have been an apple tree in the Garden, but Eve partook of one of the two trees in the middle—the tree of good and evil that bore no edible fruit.

Those who read the Holy Bible cannot help but read of <u>God's Chosen People</u> or tribe beginning with *Genesis 6:18 "But Noah* [a descendant of Adam] *found grace in the eyes of the Lord"; Genesis 9:9 "And I, behold, I establish my covenant with you, and with your seed after you";* and *Deuteronomy 7:6.* <u>*"God hath chosen thee to be a special people unto himself,*</u> *above all people that are upon the face of the earth."*

Genesis 10:1. "Now these are the generations of the sons of Noah [who with their wives were on the ark] *Shem, Ham, and Japheth:* [*these are the Adamic race with their wives; they are eight persons in total*] *and unto them were sons born after the flood. 2. The sons of Japheth; Gomer, and Magog, and Madai, and Javan, and Tubal, and Meshech, and Tiras. 3. And the sons of Gomer; Ashkenaz, and Riphath, and Togarmah. 4. And the sons of Javan; Elishah, and Tarshish, Kittim, and Dodanim.* [In the next verse, we can possibly read of the survival of the sixth-day mankind, all the races, <u>the Gentiles.</u>] *5. By these were the isles of the Gentiles divided in their lands; every one <u>after his tongue,</u>* (tongue means language*) after their families, in their nations."* Were these people on the ark with the eight members of the Adamic race or was Noah's flood only in one area or basin? For a study, refer to index "Noah's Flood."

The descendants of "the Man Adam" to Noah and all the way to Abram are shown in *Genesis 15:18: "The Lord made a covenant with Abram,* (later called Abraham) *saying, Unto thy seed have I given this land, from the river of Egypt unto the great river, the river Euphrates."*

Gen. 17:21 "But my covenant will I establish with Isaac, which Sarah shall bear unto thee at this set time in the next year. This is Abraham's second-son birth by Sarah—Isaac. Isaac will have a son named <u>Jacob</u> (his name will be changed to Israel (Gen. 32:28). His descendants would become the tribe of the Israelites. Jacob had twelve sons; one was Levi, whose seed line brought forth Moses. Abraham's first son was by Hagar, Sarah's hand-maiden; his name was Ishmael. Most of his descendants become the Muslims.

Exodus 5:1. "And afterward, Moses and Aaron went in, and told Pharaoh, Thus said the Lord God of Israel, <u>Let my people go</u>, that they may hold a feast unto me in the wilderness". In Exodus 19:5, it is written, *"Then you shall be a peculiar treasure unto me above all people."*

Deuteronomy 4:37 states, *"Because he loved your forefathers and chose their descendants* [the Israelites] *after them, he brought you out of Egypt by his Presence and his great strength."* We now confirm that the seed line from Adam and Eve are the chosen people. *Deuteronomy 7:6. Then declares, "For you are a people holy to the LORD your God. The LORD your God has chosen you (Israelites) out of all the peoples (Gentiles) on the face of the earth to be his people, his treasured possession."* The Israelites or Jews will be persecuted by unbelievers.

Deuteronomy 34:27 says, *"And the Lord said unto Moses, Write thou these words: for after the tenor of these words I have made a covenant with thee <u>and with Israel</u>."* Moses blesses the tribe of Judah, descendants of the son of Jacob (Israel), their pure seed line to Jesus. KJV *Deut. 33:7. "And this is the blessing of Judah: and he said, Hear, Lord, the voice of Judah, and bring him unto his people: let his hands be sufficient for him; and be thou an help to him from his enemies".* The NIV *Deuteronomy 33:7 states, "And this he said about Judah: 'Hear, O LORD, the cry of Judah; bring him to his people. With his own hands he defends his cause. Oh, be his help against his foes!'"* God had a purpose for his chosen people; they were to keep a pure seed line from Adam to Mary whose mother was of the lineage of Levi (the priest line) and her grandfather Heli who was from the lineage of Judah representing the king line. The Holy Spirit causes Mary to become pregnant; our Savior is born and named Jesus. The chosen had a very difficult task to keep the seed line to Christ pure.

If all mankind were taught the truth found in his Word, racism could be set aside as the Bible traces one tribe to our Savior who will set all the races free by Christ's work on the cross. Adam and Eve had brought death not only to themselves but also to the sixth-day creation, the Gentiles, but then through Jesus's sacrifice on the cross, through Him, we can now receive the right to live in the third earth age forever without mankind's sinful nature; this will be an everlasting life of joy and peace.

Genesis 1:26 "And God said; Let us make man in our image, after our likeness: and let them have dominion over the fish of the sea, and over the fowl of the air, and over the cattle, and over all the earth, and over every creeping thing that creeps upon the earth. 27. So God created man in his own image, in the image of God created he him; male and female created he them [all the races, 'eth-' âdâm]. 28. And God blessed them [blessed all the races] and God said unto them, Be fruitful, and multiply, and replenish the earth, and subdue it: and have dominion over the fish of the sea, and over the fowl of the air, and over every living thing that moves upon the Whole earth". But sin comes into their life because of Eve and the man Adam 'eth-'Ha"âdhâm. *In Genesis 2:7, God had blessed his sixth day creation* (Gen. 1:26–27.). This now raises: Questions: (1) So what happened? (2) Why did God create the Garden of Eden?

[Here again you may want to backup to Chapter 6 and read the first page]

When Moses was inspired by God to write the book of Job, was he trying to send a profound message to us about an earlier period of time? Job 1:6. "Now there was a day when the sons of God came to present themselves before the Lord, and Satan came also among them. 7. And the Lord said unto Satan, from where have you come? Then Satan answered the Lord, and said: From going to and fro in the earth, and from walking up and down in it." This walking about could be referring to the first age, when God became disgusted with Satan. In this second age, Satan brought sin to the age. The spirit of Satan is still roaming the earth, going to and fro, tempting and misguiding. We are born in this second age with a free spirit to choose to follow our evil sinful nature or choose to live as a Christian.

KJV, Job 40:15 states, "*Behold now behemoth, which I made with thee; he eats grass as an ox.*" Here we see that Satan was present in the first earth age along with this creature, a dinosaur. You might want to refer to the index for "God's Verbal Picture."

We read in *Revelation 12:9*: *"And the great dragon was cast out, that old serpent, called the Devil, and Satan, which deceived the whole world: he was cast out into the earth, and his angels were cast out with him."* Satan now is held in heaven possibly since Jesus said *in Matthew 4:10. 'Away from me' Satan*. Again we can ask?

1. Had Satan earlier challenged God to let him return to earth, as the antichrist or false teacher/preacher with limited power to tempt mankind? He had once wanted to be the most high, above the Throne of God: exalt my throne above the stars of God: I will sit also upon the mount of the congregation, in the sides of the north: *14. I will ascend above the heights of the clouds; I will be like the most High.*"

2. Had God wanted to protect his sixth-day creation,
but wanted to accept Satan's challenge by creating
the Garden of Eden? God placed two special trees
in it that bore no fruit. One tree represented and
was the serpent/Satan, the other tree Jesus.

God formed "eth-'Ha' 'âdhâm, the Man Adam, a pure image
of himself, no gender but with the full spectrum of DNA who
lived in peace. This is supported by the scripture *Romans 5:9: "For
as by one man's [Adam] disobedience many were made sinners, so by
the obedience of one* [Jesus], *shall many be made righteous."* God
takes part of the DNA from Adam and forms Eve. They were
commanded to not partake of the tree of good and evil [Satan] in
the middle of the Garden of Eden.

Moses wrote in *Job 2:9, "Then said his wife unto him* [Job], *do
you still retain your integrity? Curse God, and die."* Was she also
tempted by Satan? In the book of Job, Satan had God strip Job
of everything including his children and all his vast possessions.

Had Satan in some way influenced God to take the female
DNA out of Adam and form Eve so he could tempt her? Death
was the outcome. Jesus came and by his work on the cross he
has given us everlasting life when we accept Him as our Savior
and repent.

"For God so loved the world, that he gave his only begotten
Son, that whosoever believeth in him should not perish, but have
everlasting life" (John 3:16).

Instead of causing discrimination, we should rejoice that God
formed Adam and placed him in the planted Garden of Eden
and the seed line ofAdam was carried to the birth of Jesus.. We
read in KJV, *1 Corinthians 15:45, "And so it is written, the first man*

Adam was made a living soul; the last Adam was made a quickening spirit." In the NIV, it is written: *"The first man Adam became a living being, the last Adam, a life-giving spirit."* Notice *"a living being"*; this will change as Adam would die. [Here again you may want to back track to Chapter 6 and read the first page] God had created male and female on the sixth day, all races, the Gentiles. Then He formed Adam; then while Adam slept, God took his DNA and formed Eve. Their offspring would become the Adamic race, later the chosen race, which was to maintain and protect the pure seed line until the birth of the second Adam or Jesus.

Many teachers cannot accept the creation of all the races in Genesis 1:27. This is due to the lack of not discerning or rightly dividing the word: (KJV, Gen. 3:20*) "And Adam called his wife's name Eve; because she was the mother of all living."* In the NIV, Genesis 3:20, *"Adam named his wife Eve, because she would become the mother of all the living."* Here again the word *become* has a deeper meaning; through the keeping of Adam and Eve's seed line to Jesus, by a chosen race the Adamic Race we can now have an everlasting living life.

Instead of causing discrimination, we should rejoice that God formed Adam. We read in *KJV 1 Corinthians.15:45, "And so it is written: The first man Adam was made a living soul; the last Adam was made a quickening spirit."* In the NIV is also written, *"So it is written: 'The first man Adam became a living being'; the last Adam, a life-giving spirit."* God had created male and female on the sixth day: all races, the Gentiles; He then formed Adam. Then while Adam slept, God took his DNA and formed Eve. Their offspring would become the Adamic race, later the chosen race which was to maintain and protect the pure seed line until the birth of the second Adam or Jesus.

Many students who read the NIV Acts 17: 26. From one <u>man</u> he made every nation of men that they should inhabit the whole earth; and he determined the times set for them and the exact places where they should live. Are led away from the truth! The word " man" should be clay or dust or the blood of the earth which would be water and dirt.

[Here again you may want to back tract to Chapter 6 and read the first page].

Chapter 15

Who Was or Is Jesus? Why Did He Come?

First: Jesus Was the Essence of God in a Mortal Earthly Body—Emanuel

John 6: 35. Then Jesus declared, "I am the bread of life. He who comes to me will never go hungry, and he who believes in me will never be thirsty.

John 14: 6. Jesus answered, "I am the way and the truth and the life. No one comes to the Father except through me.

After the sixth day creation of Mankind male and female God forms Man out of the dust of the earth in a complete one gender body and placed Adam in a planted Garden: *Genesis 2:8. And the Lord God planted a garden eastward in Eden; and there he put the man whom he had formed.* Adam had a one on one relationship with God but when Adams DNA is split to form Eve as help-mate. Eve sinned; they were expelled from the planted garden and lost their relationship with God. Now through Jesus we can find reconciliation with God.

His first coming was foretold in the Old Testament: *Micah 5:2. "But you, Bethlehem Ephrathah, though you be little among the thousands of Judah, yet out of you shall he come forth unto me that is to be ruler in Israel; whose goings forth have been from of old, from everlasting.*" From everlasting can be understood by reading NT, *John 1:1. "In the beginning was the Word, and the Word was with God, and the Word was God. 2. The same was in the beginning with God." John 1:14 says, "And the Word was made flesh, and dwelt among us."*

Isaiah 7:14: "Therefore the Lord himself will give you a sign: The virgin will be with child and will give birth to a son, and will call him Immanuel." Isaiah 9:6: "For unto us a child is born, unto us a son is given and the government shall be upon his shoulder: and his name shall be called Wonderful, Counselor, The mighty God, the everlasting Father, The Prince of Peace."

The crucifixion of Jesus is written in the Old Testament: *Psalm. 22:16. "For dogs have compassed me: the assembly of the wicked has enclosed me: they pierced my hands and my feet. 17. I may tell all my bones: they look and stare upon me. 18. They part my garments among them, and cast lots upon my vesture."* Also in: Isaiah 53:5. *"But he was wounded for our transgressions, he was bruised for our iniquities: — and with his stripes we are healed. — 7. He was oppressed, and he was afflicted, yet he opened not his mouth: he is brought as a lamb to the slaughter, 8.— for he was cut off out of the land of the living: 12. — and he bare the sin of many, and made intercession for the transgressors."*

We can now move on to the New Testament for his birth: *Matt. 1:23. "The virgin will be with child and will give birth to a son, and they will call him Immanuel"* which means, "God with us." *John 1:1: "In the beginning was the Word, and the Word was with God, and the Word was God." As you work your way through this chapter, you will find in 1:14: "The Word became flesh and made his dwelling among us."* God took a flesh body so he could set an example and to then shed his blood for our sins when we acknowledge Him—Jesus.

Mark 1:1, KJV: "The beginning of the gospel of Jesus Christ, the Son of God." Here at the very beginning, the first chapter of the book of Mark, we are told who Jesus was, "the Son of God."

Jesus was born of a woman using the egg of the woman and the overshadowing of the Holy Spirit of God. When Christ is added to his given name, the word *Christ* defines Jesus as the savior and the anointed one. In an earthly body, Jesus learned all the frailty of mankind, their passion, temptation, and his earthly body could be crucified.

The actual birth date of Jesus is uncertain; some say it was in the fall, September 29, 4 BC, which would make December 25 near the conception date? Today, some Jewish Christians who accept Christ as their Messiah believe that the birth of Christ was on day one of Nisan during lambing season. Jesus is considered the Lamb of God; they relate this back to Exodus 12:1–11 when the Passover lamb's blood was placed on the doorpost to save the inhabitants from death. This then relates to Jesus who on the cross became our Passover Lamb.

First Corinthians 5:7: *"For even Christ our Passover is sacrificed for us: In him we now find Rest a Sabbath."* Paul wrote in *Romans 1:3. "Concerning his Son Jesus Christ our Lord, which was made of the seed of David according to the flesh; 4. <u>And declared to be the Son of God</u> with power, according to the spirit of holiness, by the resurrection from the dead.* Matthew 11:28 says, *"Come unto me, all you that labor and are heavy laden, and I will give you rest".* Now in Christ every day is our Sabbath or rest."

Second: Why Did Jesus Come to This Age?

KJV, *1 John 3:8: "He that commits sin is of the devil; for the devil sinned from the beginning. For this purpose the Son of God was manifested, that he might destroy the works of the devil." NIV: "The reason the Son of God appeared was to destroy the devil's work."* Since "the first sin" recorded was committed by Eve in the Garden of Eden, being deceived by the serpent, the devil or Satan, her sin was breaking the first command from God. (Refer to "Apple or Truth" found in the index.) Mankind continued drifting away from the truth, and their sinful nature was running rampant on the earth; Moses was given the law, and by the sacrificing of animals and using their blood and burnt offerings, mankind was able to repent.

Jesus said in Matthew 5:17, *"Do not think that I have come to abolish the Law or the Prophets; I have not come to abolish them but to fulfill them."* Many students labor over what Jesus meant by this statement. This verse has two answers:

First. He embraced the law or Ten Commandments as evident when a Pharisee tried to trick him in *Matthew 22:36. "'Teacher, which is the greatest commandment in the Law?' 37. Jesus replied: 'Love the Lord your God with all your heart and with all your soul and with all your mind.' 38. This is the first and greatest commandment. 39. And the second is like it: 'Love your neighbor as yourself.'"* By this, he covered all Ten Commandments. The fourth commandment was at the time about the Sabbath or a day of rest, one day, and the seventh day. Now Jesus is our Sabbath so our day of rest is every day: (Cor. 5:7) "For even Christ our Passover" and (Matt. 11:28) "Come unto me, all of you that labor and are heavy laden and I will give you rest."

Second. Jesus was fulfilling the commandments as written in their Scrolls (our OT). Unrolling the Scroll, Jesus got up to preach in their synagogue. He read Isaiah 61 as recorded in the Gospel of *Luke 4:18. "'The Spirit of the Sovereign LORD is on me, because the LORD has anointed me to preach good news to the poor. He has sent me to bind up the broken-hearted, to proclaim freedom for the captives and release from darkness for the prisoners, 19. to proclaim the year of the Lord's favor.' 20. And he closed the book, and he gave it again to the minister, and sat down. And the eyes of all them that were in the synagogue were fastened on him.* [They knew there was more to the original verse!] *But instead of reading the rest of the verse he stated; 21. And he began by saying to them, 'Today this scripture is fulfilled in your hearing.'"* This was because he knew only part of the prophecy had been fulfilled; the second part was a prophecy that was to come in the future. Jesus was preaching from the Scrolls or OT. Isaiah 61:1 says, "*The Spirit of the Lord God is upon me; because the Lord hath anointed me to preach good tidings unto the meek; he hath sent me to bind up the brokenhearted, to proclaim liberty to the captives, and the opening of the prison to them that are bound; 2. To proclaim the acceptable year of the Lord.* [There is more to this verse, but Jesus stopped and rolled up the scroll. He was claiming that he was "here" thus fulfilling the first part of the scripture of the prophets: that a Messiah would come. Jesus knew the rest of the verse was to take place after his crucifixion; the verse continues.] *And the day of vengeance of our God; to comfort all that mourn;* this last part of the verse was to take place after his crucifixion." They would later expel him from the synagogue.

By Jewish custom, when the Mosaic Law given to Moses was broken, they could repent using the blood sacrifices of animals. *Hebrews 9:19. "For when Moses had spoken every precept to all the people according to the law, he took the blood of calves and of goats, 20. Saying, this is the blood of the testament which God hath enjoined unto you. 21. Moreover he sprinkled with blood — and sprinkled both the Scroll, and all the people, 22. all things are by the law purged with blood; and without shedding of blood is no remission* [of Sin]". Reference can be found in Exodus 24:1–8: "Males had also been marked by shedding of blood through circumcision." Genesis 17:10 states, "This is my covenant, which you shall keep, between me and you and your seed after you; every man child among you shall be circumcised." We will read that this is changed!

But when Jesus came to the temple, He found that the sacrifices had become corrupted; moneymaking was more important: *Matthew. 21:12. "And Jesus went into the temple of God, and cast out all them that sold and bought in the temple, and overthrew the tables of the moneychangers, and the seats of them that sold doves, 13. And said unto them: It is written. My house shall be called the house of prayer; but you have made it a den of thieves.* [This was one reason and also when Jesus said in *John 14:9, "Anyone who has seen me has seen the Father."* The corrupt priests and all in the synagogue sought to have Jesus killed.

By the shedding of Jesus's blood from beatings and the crown of thorns on the cross, Jesus covered our sins and did away with the Jewish Law or Mosaic Law of blood sacrifices. They were nailed to the cross and done away with, including circumcision.

Now, women, men, and children are Rom. 2:29 — and circumcision is circumcision of the heart, by the Spirit, not by the written code. We read in: Colossians 2:11 "Not with a circumcision done by the hands of men but with the circumcision done by Christ.

"For God so loved the world that he gave his one and only Son, that whoever believes in him shall not perish but have eternal life" (John 3:16). We now only need to accept Jesus as or Savior, repent in His name and by His shed blood our sins are blotted out of the book of life while hanging on the cross Jesus tried to remind the Jewish priests to study their scrolls *Matt. 27:46. "And about the ninth hour, Jesus cried with a loud voice, saying, Eli, Eli, lama sabachthani?"* That is to say, "My God, my God, why have you forsaken me?" Jesus was reminding them that in their scrolls, Psalm 22:1–18, it foretold of their very actions this day, even the prophesy that his hands and feet would be pierced and they would gamble for his robe.

Psalm 22:1. "My God, my God, why have you forsaken me? Why are you so far from saving me, so far from the words of my groaning?" Now we can read of the crucifixion that would take place over more than one thousand years hence. *22:7 "All who see me mock me; they hurl insults, shaking their heads". 14. "I am poured out like water, and all my bones are out of joint. My heart has turned to wax; it has melted away within me. 15. My strength is dried up like a potsherd, and my tongue sticks to the roof of my mouth; you lay me in the dust of death. 16. Dogs have surrounded me; a band of evil men has encircled me, they have pierced my hands and my feet. 17. I can count all my bones; people stare and gloat over me. 18. They divide my garments among them and cast lots for my clothing".*

The words Jesus spoke in Mark have a profound meaning. *Mark :27"And he said unto them, The Sabbath was made for man and not man for the Sabbath.* [by being born of Mary and the Spirit, Jesus will become our Sabbath; refer to 1 Corinthians 5:7 below]: [To clarify, Jesus became our Sabbath and came to earth for us but we did nothing for Him.] 28. Therefore the Son of man is Lord also of the Sabbath".

The Jews had several times accused Jesus of breaking their Sabbath, a day of rest. For the Christian, every day has become our Sabbath, and when two or more meet and share the Word, we are in Christ's Church observing the Sabbath regardless of the day of the week. NIV *1 Cor. 5:4 "When we are assembled in the name of our Lord Jesus his spirit, and the power of our Lord Jesus is present".* The next verse should clear this all up. 7: *"Get rid of the old yeast that you may be a new batch without yeast—as you really are. For Christ, our Passover Lamb has been sacrificed".* This Passover was "a Special Sabbath." *Sabbath* means "rest." In Matthew 11:28, it says, *"Come unto me, all you that labor and are heavy laden, and I will give you rest."* When is the Sabbath day of the week? To the Jew who has not accepted Christ, their Sabbath is still Saturday. Christians can observe the Sabbath every day including Saturday. When we accept Jesus the Christ as our savior, for the believer, Jesus became our new Sabbath, our rest. I repeat as written In the NIV, *1 Corinthians 5:3: "Even though I am not physically present, I am with you in spirit. — 4. When you are assembled in the name of our Lord Jesus and I am with you in spirit, and the power of our Lord Jesus is present, we are in Church."*

Hebrews 1:1"In the past God spoke to our forefathers through the prophets at many times and in various ways, 2. But in these last days *he has spoken to us by <u>his Son</u>, whom he appointed heir of all things, and through whom he made the universe. 3. The Son is the radiance of God's glory and the exact representation of his being, sustaining all things by his powerful word. After <u>he had provided purification for sins</u>, he sat down at the right hand of the Majesty in heaven.*

We now have the answer to who was Jesus. The scriptures clearly spell out who He was:

KJV Mark 1:1: The beginning of the Gospel of Jesus Christ, the Son of God.

NIV Mark 1:1: The beginning of the gospel about Jesus Christ, the Son of God.

Why did he come? KJV, *John 3:17 says, "For God sent not his Son into the world to condemn the world; but that the world through him might be saved."* NIV, *John 3:17 states, "For God did not send his Son into the world to condemn the world, but to save the world through him."*

We now have the brief picture of whom; <u>Jesus was and is His Gift— and his purpose.</u>

Chapter 16

Is Jesus Coming Again? Is There a Rapture First?

Some churches and evangelists preach that the rapture will occur or take place sometime in the near future. Jesus will come in the air on a cloud and catch up their believers from the earth and then return to heaven with their church members. They claim we are given a clear description of the Rapture in the Bible and quote *1 Thessalonians 4:16. "For the Lord himself shall descend from heaven with a shout, with the voice of the archangel, and with the trump of God: and the dead in Christ shall rise first:* [Why would the dead need to be raptured as the tribulation would have no effect on the dead?] *17. Then we which are alive and remain shall be caught up together with them in the <u>clouds</u>, to meet the Lord in the <u>air</u>: and so shall we ever be with the Lord."* They claim these scriptures will be fulfilled prior to the beginning of the tribulation period.

Paul spoke colonial Greek we will reference a scripture Hebrews 12:1. Wherefore seeing we also are compassed about with so great <u>a cloud of witnesses</u>, here the word cloud is used as a gathering.

The word "air" as used in the above scripture 17. Is: *Strong's Ref. # 109 Romanized aer Pronounced ah-ayr' from aemi (<u>to breathe unconsciously</u>, i.e. respire; by analogy, to blow); "air" (as naturally circumambient):* we read in *Genesis 2:7 and breathed into his nostrils* *the breath of life; and man became a living <u>soul</u>.*[the spiritual part of man]- thus the word air as used in vs. 17 –*_"<u>clouds, to meet the Lord in the air</u>"* could or should be interpreted as "<u>gather in the Spirit</u>" or a spiritual body Reference *1 Corinthians 15:51. Behold, I show you a mystery; we shall not all sleep, but we shall all be changed. :52. In a moment, in the twinkling of an eye, at the last trump: for the trumpet shall sound, and the dead shall be raised incorruptible, <u>and we shall be changed</u>.*

The rapture is not mentioned by Jesus in the Bible: (Matt. 16:27*)* <u>*"For the Son of man shall come in the glory of his Father with his angels*</u>*; and then he shall reward every man according to his works."* Would Jesus conduct an open or secret rapture opposing to what we read in *Acts 3:21? "He must remain in heaven until the time comes for God to restore everything, as he promised long ago through his holy prophets."* We are warned in *Colossians 2:8: "See to it that no one takes you captive through philosophy and empty deception, according to the tradition of men, according to the elementary principles of the world, rather than according to Christ."* Was Paul inspired to write the second letter to the Thessalonians to warn of false teachings? We can again ask, does the Bible support the teaching from some of the pulpits about a rapture?

Even in the newer translations of the Bible, we read in NIV, *Ezekiel 13:1–2: "And the word of the Lord came unto me 2. "<u>Son of man, prophesy against the prophets of Israel who are now prophesying</u>. Say to those <u>who prophesy out of their own imagination</u>."* Then in verse *13:20, "Therefore this is what the Sovereign LORD says: I am against your magic charms with which you ensnare people like birds and I will tear them from your arms; I will set free the people that you ensnare like birds."*

Now let's compare this verse as translated from the original manuscripts: (KVJ, Ezekiel 13:20*) "Wherefore this says the Lord God; Behold, I am against your pillows, wherewith you hunt the souls to make them fly, and I will tear them from your arms, and will let the souls go, even the souls that you hunt to make them fly."* In the newer translations, the word *fly* has been changed to "ensnare people like birds." Why? Was it to support the rapture theory? Jesus would rapture or fly us away? Sounds like the same false teaching that Eve ate an Apple?

Let's read some scriptures from the second letter written by Paul to the Thessalonians after he had received a letter from Timothy whom Paul had left behind to help and guide the new church filled with pagan converts and who were now backsliding and were becoming discouraged. Paul was now teaching the Gospel in Corinth and wrote the first letter to the church in Thessalonica. We will pick up on this: (NIV, 2 Thess. 2:1–5*) "Concerning the coming of our Lord Jesus Christ and our being gathered to him, we ask you, brothers, 2. not to become easily unsettled or alarmed by some prophecy, report or letter supposed to have come from us, saying that the day of the Lord has already come. 3. Don't let anyone deceive you in any way, for that day will not come until the rebellion occurs and the man of lawlessness is revealed, the man doomed to destruction. 4. He will oppose and will exalt himself over everything that is called God or is worshiped, so that he sets himself up in God's temple, proclaiming himself to be God things?"* Here, Paul is telling us that the antichrist will appear first capable of. 5. Don't you remember that when I was with you I used to tell you these great wonders* [the followers of the rapture theory will be deceived and follow him wrongly thinking he is the Christ putting their soul in jeopardy] *then Christ returns.*

Jesus warned in Matthew 24:13–15: *"But he who stands firm to the end will be saved. 4. And this gospel of the kingdom will be preached in the whole world as a testimony to all Nations, and then the end will come. 15. "So when you see standing in the holy place 'the abomination that causes desolation,'* (anti-christ) *spoken of through the prophet Daniel." "Let the reader understand— 21. For then there will be great distress, unequalled from the beginning of the world until now—and never to be equaled again. 22. If those days had not been cut short,* <u>*no one would survive, but for the sake of the elect those days will be shortened.*</u>*"* The elect or the believers are still here. *Rev 9:4. They were told not to harm the grass of the earth or any plant or tree, but only those people who did not have the seal of God on their foreheads. 5. They were not given power to kill them,* <u>*but only to torture them for five months*</u>*. And the agony they suffered was like that of the sting of a scorpion when it strikes a man".*

"So be on your guard; <u>*I have told you everything ahead of time*</u>*"* (Mark 13:23). Nowhere in any of the four Gospels did Jesus hint of the Rapture of a church or its followers or a secret coming. Jesus warned in *Matthew 24:4. Watch out that no one deceives you.* It was foretold in *Ezekiel 13:20 "Wherefore this says the Lord God; Behold, I am against your pillows, wherewith* <u>*you hunt the souls to make them fly*</u>).

<u>Epilogue</u>

Is the rapture theory confirmed by the Bible? No.

Jesus said in *Mark 13:23*, "*So be on your guard; I have told you everything ahead of time.*" In the book of *Revelation 1:1*, "*the Revelation of Jesus Christ, which God gave unto him, to show his servants things which must shortly come to pass; and he sent and signified it by his angel unto his servant John.*" Jesus relates to John in *Revelation 7:13–14*: "*Then one of the elders asked me, 'These in white robes—who are they, and where did they come from?' 14. I answered, 'Sir, you know.' And he said: '<u>These are they who have come out of the great tribulation</u>; they have washed their robes and made them white in the blood of the Lamb.'*" <u>*Who then had been raptured?*</u>

Revelation 9:1. "*And the fifth angel sounded his trumpet, and I saw a star fall from heaven unto the earth: and to him was given the key of the bottomless pit. 2. And he opened the bottomless pit; and there arose a smoke out of the pit, as the smoke of a great furnace; and the sun and the air were darkened by reason of the smoke of the pit. 3. And there came out of the smoke locusts upon the earth: and unto them was given power, as the scorpions of the earth have power. 4. And it was commanded them that they should not hurt the grass of the earth, neither any green thing, neither any tree; <u>but only those men which have not the seal of God in their foreheads</u>. 5. And to them it was given that they should not kill them, but that they should be tormented five months*".

If the trump sounded and there was a rapture of a church, who are "*the people <u>who would have the seal of God on their foreheads</u>*" those the Rapturist names as those left behind? They claim the trump will sound the church is raptured and quote *1 Thess. 4:16*.

"For the Lord himself shall descend from heaven with a shout, with the voice of the archangel, <u>and with the trump of God</u>: and the dead in Christ shall rise first." If the rapture takes place, but which trumpet is sounded? They quote *1 Corinthians 15:51. "Behold, I show you a mystery; we shall not all sleep, but we shall all be changed, 52. In a moment, in the twinkling of an eye, at the last trump: for the trumpet shall sound, and the dead shall be raised incorruptible, and we shall be changed."* The last trump is the seventh!

Revelation 9:13. "The sixth angel sounded <u>his trumpet</u>, — 14. — 'Release the four angels who are bound at the great river Euphrates.' 15. And the four angels who had been kept ready for this very hour and day and month and year were released to kill a third of mankind" This could be World War III and referring to the followers of the antichrist.

Then Jesus returns *in Revelation 11:15: The seventh angel sounded his trumpet, and there were loud voices in heaven, which said: The kingdom of the world has become the kingdom of our Lord and of his Christ, and he will reign for ever and ever.*

Let's read what Paul wrote in his second letter: *2 Thessalonians. 2:1. Concerning the coming of our Lord Jesus Christ and <u>our being gathered to him</u>, we ask you, brothers, 2. not to become easily unsettled or alarmed by some prophecy, report or letter supposed to have come from us, saying that the day of the Lord has already come."* They had believed in a false hope as they misunderstood "our being gathered to him" Today, many are led astray by a rapture theory they claim is hidden in 1 Thessalonians chapter 4 and teach only verses 16 and 17. Let's return to *2 Thessalonians 2:3. "<u>Don't let anyone deceive you in any way</u>, for that day will not come until the rebellion occurs and <u>the man of lawlessness is revealed</u>, the man doomed to destruction.*

This is Satan. *4. He will oppose and will exalt himself over everything that is called God or is worshiped, so that he sets himself up in God's temple, proclaiming himself to be God."* This is Satan's return; will those who believe in the Rapture be here to welcome him and be deceived by a false Rapture thinking he is Christ?

We read in Matthew 24:4. *"And Jesus answered and said unto them, Take heed that no man deceive you. 13. But he that shall endure unto the end, the same shall be saved."* Then we are warned in verse *23. At that time if anyone says to you, 'Look, here is the Christ!' or, 'There he is!' do not believe it."* 40. "Then shall two be in the field; the one shall be taken, and the other left. The believers in the words of Jesus will reject him as written in the Gospels.

Paul wrote *in 2 Thessalonians 2:5: "Don't you remember that when I was with you I used to tell you these things? :9. The coming of the lawless one will be in accordance with the work of Satan displayed in all kinds of counterfeit miracles, signs and wonders,* Those who have been taught the snatched away theory will possibly think they have been Raptured and begin to worship this impostor. Jesus never mentioned or even hinted of a secret snatching away or a rapture of the church. Let's read what Jesus said in *Mark 13:14: "When you see 'the abomination that causes desolation' standing where it (the impostor) does not belong—let the reader understand—then let those who are in Judea flee to the mountains."*

When the <u>seventh trumpet sounds</u>, now is <u>the true rapture or second coming</u>: *1 Corinthians 15:52 "In a flash, in the twinkling of an eye, at the last trumpet. For the trumpet will sound, the dead will be raised imperishable, and we will be changed. Where are the true Christians?" Matthew 24:13. "But he that shall endure unto the end, the same shall be saved. 14. And this gospel of the kingdom shall be preached in the entire world for a witness unto all nations; and then shall the end come."*

First Timothy 4:1 declares, *"Now the Spirit speaks expressly, that in the latter times some shall depart from the faith, giving heed to seducing spirits and doctrines of devils."* Could this be the "rapture theory"?

KJV *Revelation 22:12 "And, behold, I come quickly; and my reward is with me, to give every man according as his work shall be. 13 I am Alpha and Omega, the beginning and the end, the first and the last. 14. Blessed are they that do his commandments that they may have right to the tree of life, and may enter in through the gates into the city."*

Likewise, the NIV *of Revelation 22:12 "Behold, I am coming soon! My reward is with me, and I will give to everyone according to what he has done. 13. I am the Alpha and the Omega, the First and the Last, the Beginning and the End. 14. 'Blessed are those who wash their robes, that they may have the right to the tree of life and may go through the gates into the city.'"*

How great it would be if we could be snatched away but Jesus in *Luke 22:36. He said to them, "But now if you have a purse, take it, and also a bag; and if you don't have a sword, sell your cloak and buy one.* The Sword was the weapon of the time. This subject will be picked up again in the final Chapter 22.

To expose the false teaching of Revelation 3:10 if there was a rapture the Greek word "ek" would not have been used.

Chapter 17

What Is Born Again or From Above and Baptism?

An age-old question, but before we look for the answer, a better question would be, when does life begin? We read in *Genesis 1:30, "And to every beast of the earth, and to every fowl of the air, and to everything that creeps upon the earth, wherein there is life, I have given every green herb for meat: and it was so."* Let's do a word study *life*:

Strong's ref. no. 5315 Romanized nephesh Pronounced neh'-Fesh from HSN5314; properly, <u>a breathing creature</u>, i.e. animal of (abstractly) vitality; used very widely in a literal ,accommodated or figurative sense (bodily or mental).

Here we have learned that mankind, the sixth-day "mankind" male and female, 'eth-' âdâm, had the breath of life. *Genesis 2:7And then the Lord God formed man of the dust of the ground, and breathed into his nostrils the breath of life; and man became a living soul."* The man Adam" 'eth-'Ha' 'âdhâm was formed from the earth and his life began when he received the breath of life from god.

Does the Bible confirm or allude to when life begins; we are now born of women? The answer is a resounding yes. In the NT, St. Luke, who was a physician, the writer for one of the four gospels, in his Gospel 1:41 writes, Mary, who had just received the gift of the Holy Spirit and had conceived and now carried the embryo that was to be born Jesus, rushes over to her cousin Elizabeth's home who was also pregnant but six months along. [Now here is the answer to our question: Luke, a physician, writes in] *Luke 1:41: "And it came to pass, that, when Elisabeth heard the salutation of Mary, the babe leaped in her womb; and Elisabeth was filled with the Holy Ghost".*

The baby who would become known as John the Baptist in Elizabeth's womb recognized the soul in Mary's womb. This confirms that life begins at conception! We now become a living soul at conception. Unlike the creation of the sixth-day mankind 'eth-' âdâm and the formed Adam 'eth-'Ha' ' âdhâm. Mary will be giving the necessary breath and other nutrients through the umbilical cord. We only need to breathe on our own after the birthing process, but as we have read, we became a living soul in the womb.

We can now turn our attention to baptism as a guideline. Infants up to one year of age should be dedicated to God, and godparents should be selected, privately or through a church to offer guidance.

Children two to five should be taught at home or taken to a Holy Bible teaching Sunday school to start their journey and hopefully create a thirst for the Word.

Once the taught children reach the age of accountability between five and eight years of age or older, they should be given the opportunity to attend a church and experience at their chosen time when to be baptized by total submersion. Proverbs 22:6 states, *"Train a child in the way he should go, and when he is old he will not turn from it."* Any Christian can baptize or witness the acceptance of a believer in Jesus as their Lord and savior in a private pool, lake, or in any church with the proper facilities.

How great it would be if all nine-year-olds and early teenagers had the chance to attend a summer Bible camp and fellowship with other young Christians. Starting in the later teens, through early adulthood to maturity, we should take a lesson that every mother experiences with an infant. They start with milk and progress to pabulum and strained food and finally to chewable food. The Apostle Paul wrote in *1 Corinthians 3:1: "Brothers, I could not address you as spiritual but as worldly—mere infants in Christ. 2. I gave you milk, not solid food, for you were not yet ready for it. Indeed, you are still not ready."*

As adults, as we read through the Holy Bible we must try to find the subject of the chapter (sometimes there might be more than one subject), and once we do, reread the verses to find the deeper meaning or the solid food of each subject and try to connect it to other scriptures written by thirty-nine authors under the guidance of God.

Here are some thoughts and views:

1. The christening of a newborn baby is usually done to name Godparents to ensure that the baby will be brought up in a Christian environment.

2. Both children and adults in some churches declare their acceptance of Jesus Christ as their savior with the sprinkling of water on their foreheads (a religious declaration of faith).

3. Total immersion in water was (including Jesus) first done by John the Baptist in repentance to God.

Since the crucifixion of Jesus, when adults and children have reached the age of accountability, they should be baptized by total submersion. They will now acknowledge not only repentance, but also the last three stages of Jesus's life: <u>His death</u>, His <u>burial</u>, His <u>resurrection</u> by their public acceptance of Jesus as their Lord and Savior. As they emerge out of the water, they are given the gift of the Holy Spirit and are blessed; the Holy Spirit will guide them as they pursue truth and happiness.

4. We are born again of water and born of the Spirit. We have read that the flesh gives birth to flesh, but the spirit gives birth to spirit; they have been reborn from above.

Before we study the third chapter of the gospel of John as it relates to being born again or born from above, let's take a brief look at history.

The Sanhedrin was the supreme council of the Jewish people in the time of Christ and earlier. They were a group of seventy-one, which was composed of chief priests, elders, scribes, lawyers, or those learned in the Jewish law.

The Sanhedrin was a judicial body and constituted a supreme court. It became extinct AD 425; at the time, there were three different sects or religious parties among the Jews. They were the Essenes, the smallest sect; the Sadducees who were in denial of man's resurrection after death; and the Pharisees who believed in an afterlife. Nicodemus, a Pharisee, was a ruler of the Jews and a teacher of Israel.

The Gospel of *John 3:1. "Now there was a man of the Pharisees named Nicodemus, a member of the Jewish ruling council. 2. He came to Jesus at night and said, 'Rabbi* [Nicodemus, a teacher of the Jewish law, acknowledged Jesus as a rabbi] we know you are a teacher who has come from God. For no one could perform the miraculous signs you are doing if God were not with him.' 3. In reply Jesus declared, *'I tell you the truth, no one can see the kingdom of God unless he is born again.'* 4. 'How can a man be born when he is old?' Nicodemus asked. 'Surely he cannot enter a second time into his mother's womb to be born!' [Here we can understand the confusion; Nicodemus was only relating to the earthly body or after the amniotic sac is broken and the woman gives birth to earthly body.] 5. *Jesus answered, 'I tell you the truth, no one can enter the kingdom of God unless he is born of water and the Spirit or reborn from above.'"*

This may be confusing. *"You must be born of water"*—this is the validation of the soul. After our demise, Ecclesiastes 12:7 states, *"Then shall the dust return to the earth as it was: and the spirit shall return unto God who gave it."* The flesh body decays and returns to dust, but a validated soul returns to God, but what of the invalidated souls? Luke gives us an insight to where the good and bad dwell. *Luke 16:26 "And besides all this, between us and you a great chasm has been fixed, so that those who want to go from here to you cannot, nor can anyone cross over from there to us".*

After death, in the Apocrypha we read: starting in: *2 Esdras 7:78. For about death, the teaching is: When the final sentence goes forth from the Most High that a man is to die "when the soul departs from the body to return again to him who gave it, first of all it prays to the glory of the Most High; if it was one of those who scorned and did not observe the way of the Most High, and of those who have despised the law, and of those who hate those who fear God, such spirits shall not enter dwellings but wander about."*

Then in *2 Esdras7:101. We read of those who followed the law: They have freedom for seven days, to see on the seven days the things you have been told, and afterward they will be gathered in their dwellings.*

Back to*: John 3: 6 "Flesh gives birth to flesh, but the Spirit gives birth to spirit" This should clear up any confusion. Jesus continues in 7. "You should not be surprised at my saying, 'You must be born again. 8. The wind blows wherever it pleases. You hear its sound, but you cannot tell where it comes from or where it is going. So it is with everyone born of the Spirit.' 9. 'How can this be?' Nicodemus asked.* [He was still confused.] *10. 'You are Israel's teacher,' said Jesus* [Nicodemus was learned in the law of the Jews*] 'and do you not understand these things?'"* How many modern day preachers are unable to see the deeper truth but they still fill a need to energies' the populous - feed them milk as a baby and hopefully they will move to soft food to chewable meat.

Nicodemus's learning was limited to the Scrolls, but he missed the deeper teaching in *Ezekiel 25. "Then will I sprinkle clean water upon you, and you shall be clean: from all your filthiness, and from all your idols, will I cleanse you.* [God performs the first baptism, note the word *sprinkle.*] *26. A new heart also will I give you, and a new spirit will I put within you: and I will take away the stony heart out of your flesh, and I will give you a heart of flesh. 27. And I will put my spirit within you, and cause you to walk in my statutes, and you shall keep my judgments, and do them."*

John 3:11: "I tell you the truth, we speak of what we know, and we testify to what we have seen, but still you people do not accept our testimony."

As a Pharisee, Nicodemus believed in an afterlife but had not understood what was in the Scrolls of the time written by Ezekiel. Jesus also related to the work of John the Baptist when He said, "Our testimony, this would reflect on John the Baptist who baptized Jesus before he began his ministry." Today, baptism should be by submerging underwater to symbolize the work of the cross: (1) His death, (2) His burial, and (3) the resurrection of Jesus. This symbolizes our rebirth in Him by coming up out of the water. This confirms our belief in Christ.

First Corinthians 15:52 states, *"In a moment, in the twinkling of an eye, at the last trump: for the trumpet shall sound, and the dead shall be raised incorruptible, and we shall be changed."*

Back to *John 3:12–15. "I have spoken to you of earthly things and you do not believe; how then will you believe if I speak of heavenly things? [Again, meaningless!] 13. No one has ever gone into heaven except the one who came from heaven—the Son of Man [Jesus]. 14. Just as Moses lifted up the snake in the desert, so the Son of Man must be lifted up, 15. That everyone who believes in him may have eternal life."*

This is the baptism or born of the Holy Spirit and later a spiritual body. Christ was referring to *John 3:3 "we must be born again."*

16. For God so loved the world that he gave his one and only Son, that whoever believes in him shall not perish but have1 eternal life. [This could only be after Jesus was crucified on the cross.]*17. For God did not send his Son into the world to condemn the world, but to save the world through him.*

The reason God after his creation in verse Genesis 1:27.[God had created the Races or mankind 'eth-' âdâm, he then formed 'eth-'Ha' 'âdhâm "the Man Adam" and placed him in the planted Garden area where the first sin took place]. Adams first son is killed by the serpent's seed or Cain. God will watch over the seed line from Adam and Eve from their second son Seth to Mary. Their race had become "His Chosen People or race," and their seed line will bring forth the Savior Jesus the Christ in whom we all can once again have everlasting life.

With the Holy Spirit of God, Mary, who was a descendant of the chosen seed line, brings forth the baby Jesus. You can read more on this subject in "Does the Bible Teach Discrimination?"

Final Thought

John 2:18. Whoever believes in him is not condemned, but whomever does not believe stands condemned already because he has not believed in the name of God's one and only Son.

Chapter 18

Which Church Is Best? Is Tithing
Required by Christians?

"And when he had found him, he brought him unto Antioch. And it came to pass, that a whole year they assembled themselves with the church, and taught much people. And the disciples were called Christians first in Antioch" (Acts 11:26). First time the word *Christian* is mentioned in the Bible.

When Jesus asked in; Matthew 16:15. NIV, *"But what about you? Who do you say I am?"16. "Simon Peter answered, 'You are the Christ, the Son of the living God.' 17. Jesus replied, 'Blessed are you, Simon son of Jonah, for this was not revealed to you by man, but by my Father in heaven.* [Jesus now makes a statement.] *18. And I tell you that you are Peter, and on this rock* (here rock means truth) *I will build my church, and the gates of Hades will not overcome it.'"*

The Greek word *church,* using Strong's reference number.

1577, a calling out, i.e. (concretely) a popular meeting, especially a religious congregation (Jewish synagogue, or Christian community of members on earth or saints in heaven or both), as translated in KJV— assembly, church.

The word *Jewish synagogue* is a building where Jews assembled and was separate from the Temple of God.

"For where two or three are gathered together in my name, there am I in the midst of them" (Matt. 18:20). This verse confirms we can be in church sitting on a log in the wilderness, when two or more have a discussion about the Bible of Christ.

When we accept Jesus as the Son of God and accept Him as our Savior, we become part of his Church. Not of wood, stone, brick or concrete, but in our Spirit. *"And I tell you on this rock* [or this truth] *I will build my church."* If we assemble or gather outdoors or in a building, in a large or small group, to share the written Word to find and understand the deeper truth and give thanks for his blessings, this is the real church; and by this, we give to God his tithe not in money but love from our heart.

I have visited numerous very old and simply breathtaking churches in Sweden, several in Europe including Greece, the Vatican, and Israel; but they were only buildings. Both my parents immigrated from Sweden, but when I walked through the Bung Gate into the old city of Jerusalem, I felt like I had come home. The second time, I felt that a spiritual experience was my baptism in the Jordan River.

In our modern-day church, the speaker, priest or pastor should also relate to the <u>power of Jesus's sacrifice</u> and His accomplished work on the cross, and he should baptize by total immersion when possible. The sermon should be word for word, direct from the Bible, first determining the subject and reading the related verses. The preacher may then help the people understand the teaching, making reference to other scriptures that support the subject of the teaching. There should be a huge wooden empty cross to remind us that the Lord has risen and sent us the Comforter or Holy Spirit to guide us.

Paul wrote a warning to those who put the buildings ahead of God: *Romans 1:21 "For although they knew God, they neither glorified him as God nor gave thanks to him, but their thinking became futile and their foolish hearts were darkened. 22. Although they claimed to be wise, they became fools 23. And exchanged the glory of the immortal God for images made to look like mortal man and birds and animals and reptiles. 24. Therefore God gave them over in the sinful desires of their hearts to sexual impurity for the degrading of their bodies with one another. 25. they exchanged the truth of God for a lie, and worshiped and served created things rather than the Creator—who is forever praised".*

In Matthew it is *written 21:12, "And Jesus went into the temple of God, and cast out all them that sold and bought in the temple, and overthrew the tables of the moneychangers, and the seats of them that sold doves, 13. And (Jesus) said unto them: It is written, My house shall be called the house of prayer; but ye have made it a den of thieves."* Then we read of how Judas had betrayed Jesus and gone to the priest in *Matthew 27:3. "When Judas, who had betrayed him, saw that Jesus was condemned, he was seized with remorse and returned the thirty silver coins to the chief priests and the elders. 4. 'I have sinned,' he said, 'for I have betrayed innocent blood.' 'What is that to us?' they replied. 'That's your responsibility.' 5. So Judas threw the money into the temple and left. Then he went away and hanged himself."* This brings to mind the financial or the subject of tithing or 10 percent.

In Revelation chapters 2 and 3, Jesus reviews seven churches and only praises two out of the seven.

Did Jesus Support Tithing?

In *Mathew 19: 21, we read of a rich young man who wanted to have eternal life and Jesus said, "Give away all wealth to the poor and follow me.*[not to the Synagogue or church]" *Mark 12:41. "And Jesus sat over against the treasury, and beheld how the people cast money into the treasury: and many that were rich cast in much. 42. And there came a certain poor widow, and she threw in two mites, which make a farthing. 43. And he called unto him his disciples, and said unto them, Verily I say unto you, that this poor widow hath cast more in, than all they which have cast into the treasury."* The widow gave from her heart.

Jesus said *in Matthew 22:19. Show me the coin used for paying the tax.' They brought him a denarius, 20. And he asked them: Whose portrait is this? And whose inscription? 21. Caesar's,' they replied. Then he said to them, "Give to Caesar what is Caesar's, and to God what is God's.* What does God want? He only wants our obedience and our love.

After Christ had finished his work, he ended up on the cross, His crucifixion being ordered by the chief priests in John 19:6: "When the chief priests therefore and officers saw him, they cried out, saying, crucify him, — and crucify him." Jesus had interrupted their financial or gathering of tithes when he overturned the money tables in *Matthew 21:12. "And Jesus went into the temple of God, and cast out all them that sold and bought in the temple, and overthrew the tables of the Moneychangers and the seats of them that sold doves, 13. And said unto them: It is written: My house shall be called the house of prayer; but ye have made it a den of thieves.* The temple continues to be detestable in the eyes of the Lord, and the temple is destroyed and the people are taken into captivity twenty-seven years later. The entire collected Tithe that had been turned to gold was plundered. God had wanted their Love.

When Jesus sent out his appointed seventy-two teachers, he instructed them in *Luke 10:4. Carry neither purse, nor scrip, nor shoes: and salute no man by the way.* In *Luke 22:35, "and he said unto them, when I sent you without purse, and scrip, and shoes, lacked you anything? And they said: Nothing."* Jesus was telling his disciples not to take a begging bag or purse to collect tithe or money, the good news is free, and is to be preached for free; this was probably one of the reasons the priests wanted to have him crucified.

Paul went about his ministries by working and paying his own way; however, he did raise money for the needy. In 2 Corinthians 9:7, NIV, it is written, *"Each man should give what he has decided in his heart to give, not reluctantly or under compulsion, for God loves a cheerful giver."* Notice that there is no amount.

Should a Christian be bound by a tithe? Jesus never sanctified tithe giving, but if you find a church you are comfortable with and they supply your needs, you should financially be responsible for all costs and its upkeep. The bottom line is God wants your love and has no need for your money. <u>The best way to show your love for God is by reading and studying his letter to you</u>—the Holy Bible.

Some modern day preacher's both on and off the TV networks use as a scare tactic, to relieve even poor pensioners of their meager income. They say 10 percent of your pensions is to go to them then you pay your bills, quoting, *"Malachi 3:8. Will a man rob God? Yet you rob me. But you ask, 'How do we rob you?' In tithes and offerings"*. Here we must understand that if we read all of Malachi, we will find out that it is speaking of what the Levites and the priests were offering! They were robbing God. *Malachi 1:13. "When you bring injured, crippled or diseased animals and offer them as sacrifices, should I accept them from your hands?"* says the LORD. The Levites and priests are the ones robbing God in these scriptures. When the temple was destroyed and they all went into captivity, there were no more tithes or burnt offering. Today, God wants our love. Today, widows and seniors are supported by taxes paid to the government.

In early times, men honored God by the physical act of circumcision then supporting the tribe of Leviticus through tithes. They had no allotment in land but were in charge of the temple to act as mediator over disputes, uphold the law, attend to the sick, the well-being of widows, and those in need what we call welfare today.

Today, we have what is termed the separation of church and state. The state or government now provides help or welfare for the people supported by income and state or provincial taxes. The roll of the modern-day church is supposed to provide spiritual guidance for this; a reward should be given.

Just give all your love and trust to God, not in money or in repeated words such as repetitious prayers. Study his word to find truth. Just give your innermost being and he will be with you. If he is with you, you will never want.

If you feel you need help to guide you spiritually or to understand his word by all means seek out a church with a preacher who reads from the bible, identifying the subject and when you leave, you have knowledge of the Word, not fed man made dogma or just have a warm fuzzy feeling. This type of church earns the right to your financial support.

Chapter 19
What Foods Are We to Eat or Reject?

This subject starts with the health ordinances or statutes that were given to the Israelites in the desert, long before modern-day technology such as refrigeration, running hot water, and modern cooking devices like stoves, microwaves, etc.

KJV, *Mark 7:18 "And he said unto them: Are you so without understanding also? Do you not perceive, that whatsoever thing from without entering into the man, it cannot defile him; 19. Because it enters not into his heart, but into the belly, and goes out into the draught, purging all meats?"* The NIV adds to verse, *7:19. "For it doesn't go into his heart but into his stomach, and then out of his body".* (In saying this, Jesus declared all foods "clean.").

KJV, *Romans 14:14. 'I know, and am persuaded by the Lord Jesus, that there is nothing unclean of itself: but to him that esteems anything to be unclean, to him it is unclean".* Now the NIV: *"As one who is in the Lord Jesus, I am fully convinced that no food is unclean in itself. But if anyone regards something as unclean, then for him it is unclean."*

We will now turn or attention to 1 Timothy to see if the health or food laws were changed as taught by some. First Timothy chapter 1:1 says, *"Now the Spirit spoke expressly, that in the latter times some shall depart from the faith* [this is very important—"abandon the faith," they are atheist*], giving heed to seducing spirits, and doctrines of devils; 2. Speaking lies in hypocrisy; having their conscience seared with a hot iron; It is critical that we understand false teachers will be teaching and preaching falsehoods. 3. Forbidding marrying, and commanding to <u>abstain from meats</u>* [this part of the scripture along with what follows is not understood or misrepresented by many preachers the verse continues*] *"which God hath <u>created to be received</u> with thanksgiving of them which believe and know the truth."* If the preacher skips verse 3 and only read verse 4, then we can see the error. *"For every creature of God is good, and nothing to be refused, if it be received with thanksgiving."* The key is the words "created to be received", these are foods God spoke of *in Leviticus 5: "For it is sanctified by the word of God and prayer."* Please read on for the clarification.

The faithful are to eat certain foods created by God and avoid others. They are to be eaten and to be received with thanks given to God.

God gave the Israelites food laws in the book of Leviticus as they were wandering in the desert. They basically stated you should not eat scavengers as they were created to cleanse the earth.

Swine and vultures will eat anything even decayed, diseased dead flesh as will bottom feeders of the waters. Swine have no sweat glands to eliminate poisons, and scientists have warned you must cook pork well done to kill the bacteria. Today through proper food and refrigeration, they claim that pork can be cooked with a very slight pink color.

God's health food laws are recorded: Leviticus 11:1. *"The LORD said to Moses and Aaron, 2. "Say to the Israelites: 'Of all the animals that live on land, these are the ones you may eat: 3. You may eat any animal that has a split hoof completely divided and that chews the cud"* In the NIV, Deuteronomy 14:8 says, *"The pig is also unclean; although it has a split hoof."* Scientists claim that in cooking them properly, the health risk is very low. But I still would not eat a vulture.

Deuteronomy14:21"You shall not eat of anything that dies of itself: thou shall give it unto the stranger that is in thy gates, that he may eat it; or you may sell it to an alien: for you art a holy people unto the Lord thy God. Thou shall not seethe a kid in his mother's milk. In the NIV, it also states, *"Do not eat anything you find already dead. You may give it to an alien living in any of your towns, and he may eat it, or you may sell it to a foreigner. But you are a people holy to the LORD your God. Do not cook a young goat in its mother's milk."* By these verses, God inspired health laws <u>were not addressed to the Gentiles</u>! In one seminar I attended, we were told a single slice of ham or a slice of bacon will prevent us from entering heaven and we are not to have any wine! But I hold fast to *John 3:16: "For God so loved the world that he gave his one and only Son, that whoever believes in him shall not perish but have eternal life shall not perish but have eternal life."*

I now offer this verse to you again in the verse above, we just read "<u>that whoever believes in him</u>", KJV *Mark 7:14 Again Jesus called the crowd to him and said, "Hearken unto me every one of you, and understand: 15. Nothing outside a man can make him unclean that entering into him can defile him: but the things which come out of him, those are they that defile the man.16. <u>If any man has ears to hear,let him hear.</u>17. And when he was entered into the house from the people, his disciples asked him concerning the parable.18. And he* *said unto them, Are you so without understanding also? Do you not perceive, that whatsoever thing from without enters into the man, it cannot defile him:* Can we assume what we read in the Gospel goes into our brain but food goes into the belly and is excreated later? *19. Because it enters not into his heart, <u>but into the belly,</u> and goes out into the draught, <u>purging all meats?</u>* The NIV adds, *"In saying this, Jesus declared all foods 'clean.'"* In KJV verses *20. "And he said, that which cometh out of the man, that defiles the man. 21. For from within, out of the heart of men, proceed evil thoughts, adulteries, fornications, murders, 22. Thefts, covetousness, wickedness, deceit, lasciviousness, an evil eye, blasphemy, pride, foolishness."* I still would not eat an vulture but maybe a mouse!

I would suggest the health laws are for our protection; eating uncooked or uncured pork could cause sickness, but not a sin! This is clearly set out; it is a sin to break one of the Ten Commandments. The 4th is covered by accepting Christ and his shedding blood, every day with Jesus in our heart/mind is a day of rest or the Sabbath. Matthew11:28. "Come to me, all you who are weary and burdened, and I will give you rest. 29. Take my yoke upon you and learn from me, for I am gentle and humble in heart, and you will find rest for your souls. John 3:16. "For God so loved the world that he gave his one and only Son, that whoever believes in him shall not perish but have eternal life.

One other health law I would like to address is also written in Leviticus 17:11, KJV: *"For the life of the flesh is in the blood."* In the NIV, it is written, *"For the life of a creature is in the blood." 12. Therefore I said unto the children of Israel, No soul of you shall eat blood, neither shall any stranger that living among you eat blood.* Some religions confuse the health laws with modern-day blood transfusion: They dismiss or overlook the subject. We read of this in *Leviticus 17:13: "And whatsoever man there be of the children of Israel, or of the strangers that lives among you, <u>that hunts and catches any beast or fowl that may be eaten</u>; <u>he shall pour out the blood thereof,</u> and cover it with dust. 14. For it is the life of all flesh; the blood of it is for the life thereof: therefore I said unto the children of Israel, <u>You shall eat the blood of no manner of flesh: for the life of all flesh</u> is the blood thereof: whosoever eats it shall be cut off."* If the blood is left in the meat, it will very rapidly spoil and is unfit to eat.

The health laws were not given to condemn you or make you a sinner, but rather to avoid ailments or medical complications, eating peanuts or dairy can cause death in some individuals. Eating shrimp, catfish and even pork to some cultures has very little effect on some of the races health wise. The health Laws were given to the Israelites while they roamed the Desert for 40 years. In *1 Timothy 5:23. -- but use a little wine for thy stomach's sake and your often infirmities.* We are warned in: *Proverbs 20: 1. Wine is a mocker, strong drink is raging: and whosoever is deceived thereby is not wise.*

A strong drink can be a gallon of wine, 12 bottles of beer! The point is a little in moderation in food or drink unless you have an allergy would not be a sin as some preachers claim.

Chapter 20
The Real Easter Story

Is the word Easter in the Bible? Yes, in *KJV Acts 12:4: "And when he had apprehended him,* (Peter) *he put him in prison, and delivered him to four quaternions of soldiers to keep him; intending after Easter to bring him forth to the people."*

The word in the original manuscripts in Hebrew is Pecach, in Greek Pascha which is properly translated "Passover," not Easter. Strong's ref. no. 3957 Romanized pascha pronounced pas'-khah of Aramaic origin [compare HSN6453]; the Passover (the meal, the day, the festival or the special sacrifices connected with it): KJV—Easter, Passover. The KJV translators had misrepresented the Greek word.

The NIV corrects this error in *Acts 12:4: "After arresting him,* [Peter] *he put him in prison, handing him over to be guarded by four squads of four soldiers each. Herod intended to bring him out for public trial after the Passover."*

The word *Easter* comes from the word *Ishtar* and is associated with the "pagan god of fertility," thus we have the Easter egg and "quick like a bunny" in our vocabulary.

The early apostate church leaders reasoned some pagan customs should be accommodated. Was this influence the reason the translators of the KJV used the word Easter <u>rather than Passover</u>?

The Easter tradition including eggs supposedly laid by the rabbit are then associated with the crucifixion on a Friday and the resurrection of Christ on Easter Sunday. These common accepted dogmas of some churches as to Jesus's final days are very misleading to the real truth.

The truth can be found by examining the scriptures; the truth will be revealed that Christ was crucified on Wednesday at 9:00 a.m., died 3:00 p.m., and placed in the tomb before 6:00 p.m. on Wednesday. The fifteenth of Nisan or the Passover began Wednesday, 6:00 p.m. This would be the start of Thursday A special Sabbath. The Jewish day was from 6:00 p.m. or sunset to the following sunset.

Matthew 27:57. "When the even [evening] was come, there came a rich man of Arimathaea, named Joseph, who also himself was Jesus' disciple: 58. He went to Pilate, and begged the body of Jesus. Then Pilate commanded the body to be delivered. 59. And when Joseph had taken the body, he wrapped it in a clean linen cloth, 60. And laid it in his own new tomb, which he had hewn out in the rock: and he rolled a great stone to the door of the sepulcher, and departed. 61. And there was Mary Magdalene, and the other Mary, sitting over against the sepulcher".

We continue *Matthew 27:62. Now the next day that followed the day of the preparation,* (Passover) *the chief priests and Pharisees came together unto Pilate: 63. Saying, Sir, we remember that the deceiver* (Jesus) *said, while he was yet alive, after three days I will rise again. :64. Command therefore that the sepulcher be made sure until the third day, lest his disciples come by night, and steal him away, and say unto the people, He is risen from the dead: so the last error shall be worse than the first".* The NIV of Matthew 27:64 goes as follows: "So give the order for the tomb to be made secure until the third day. Otherwise, his disciples may come and steal the body and tell the people that he has been raised from the dead. This last deception will be worse than the first."

Jesus was crucified on the fourteenth day of Nisan at 9:00 a.m. our time. To get three days and three nights in the tomb, we start sunset Tuesday at 6:00 p.m. the start of Wednesday, the fourteenth day of Nisan, the preparation day. *"Now the first day of the feast of unleavened bread the disciples came to Jesus, saying unto him, Where wilt thou that we prepare for thee to eat the Passover?"* (The Last Supper meal was eaten the day before the Passover.) (Matt. 26:17).

Matthew 26:20. "Now when the even was come, he sat down with the twelve: 21. And as they did eat, he said, Verily I say unto you, that one of you shall betray me" Some scholars claim that Jesus knew that he was about to die and that the Jews would not have him crucified on the special Sabbath Passover, so Jesus celebrated the Feast of Unleavened Bread the day before.

At the time of Jesus, a day for the Jewish people begins at sunset or 6:00 p.m. our time; the day ended at sunset the following day. Our modern day is from 12:00 p.m. or midnight till the following day at midnight. They reckoned twelve hours of night and twelve hours of daylight. Tuesday at sunset 6:00 p.m. our time started the night (a period of twelve hours of nighttime) or their start of Wednesday the fourteenth day of Nisan, the preparation day. Jesus is arrested and is before Pilate the sixth hour (of the night period): John 19:14. "And it was the preparation of the Passover, and about the sixth hour: and he said unto the Jews, Behold your King!". This would have been 12:00 a.m. or midnight our time.

The trial of Jesus takes place during the night, and Jesus is crucified the third hour (of the daytime period) or our time 9:00 a.m. Jesus dies the ninth hour (of the daytime period) 3:00 p.m. our time and placed in the tomb around the eleventh hour (of the daytime period) or approximately Wednesday before 6:00 p.m. our time. The day of the Passover began at sunset Wednesday 6:00 p.m. the fifteenth day of Nisan. Christ was put in the tomb before sunset on Wednesday the fourteenth day of the Jewish month of Nisan near 6:00 p.m. The fifteenth day, Thursday, 6:00 p.m. would account for one night and one day. The sixteenth day, Friday, 6:00 p.m. would account for the second day. The seventeenth day, Saturday, 6:00 p.m. would account for the third night and day. Thus, Jesus arose sometime between Saturday after sunset and sunrise on Sunday.

Jesus died 3:00 p.m. in the daylight period. Jesus had said in John 2:19: "Jesus answered and said unto them, Destroy this temple, and in three days I will raise it up," referring to his body placed in the tomb during day period before 6:00 p.m., Wednesday. Dusk is or 6:00 p.m. is the beginning of a day.

Placed in
the tomb

Wed.	Thurs.	Fri.	Sat.	Sun.
4 – 5 pm	6 pm days end	6 pm days end	6 pm days end	5 – 6 am
1st day	start 1st night	start 2nd night	start 3rd night	empty tomb just before day break
	Start of Special Sabbath	Start of regular Sabbath		

John 20:1"Early on the first day of the week, <u>while it was still dark</u>, Mary Magdalene went to the tomb and saw that the stone had been removed from the entrance"

The Sabbath at the time of Christ was started 6:00 p.m. Friday to Saturday 6:00 a.m. Mary Magdalene came to the tomb Sunday just before 6:00 a.m. This would be the start of the fourth day, but Christ had already risen. The stone was rolled away, and the tomb was empty. Jesus was gone.

Where most religious persons go wrong is not their understanding that there is a Special Sabbath day other than the regular Saturday Sabbath in the Gospel of John; we glean more detailed information of the crucifixion.

John 19:31, KJV *"The Jews therefore, because it was the preparation, that the bodies should not remain upon the cross on the Sabbath day (for that Sabbath day was a high day), besought Pilate that their legs might be broken, and that they might be taken away* The High or <u>Special Sabbath</u> was to celebrate the Passover. In the NIV John 19:31 states, *"Now it was the day of Preparation, and the next day was to be a special Sabbath. Because the Jews did not want the bodies left on the crosses during the Sabbath, they asked Pilate to have the legs broken and the bodies taken down."*

Because of false dogma, many scholars mistakenly assumed that this was God's regular chosen day for the Jewish Sabbath on Saturday and therefore falsely preach that Jesus was put in the tomb on Friday, but this would not be three nights and three days as the Bible teaches: John 19:42. "Because it was the Jewish day of Preparation and since the tomb was nearby, they laid Jesus there". Again, some scholars misunderstand that this is for a Special Sabbath day.

We now go to the OT for clarification. *Leviticus 23:6 "On the fifteenth day of that month the LORD's Feast of Unleavened Bread begins; for seven days you must eat bread made without yeast. 7. On the first day hold a sacred assembly (Special day of rest) and do no regular work.*

Numbers 28:16 "On the fourteenth day of the first month the Lord's Passover is to be held. 17. On the fifteenth day of this month there is to be a festival; for seven days eat bread made without yeast. 18. On the first day hold a sacred assembly and do no regular work.

Since his death, Christ has become our Sabbath and in Him we find that every day is our or Sabbath or rest and our Passover. In; 1 Cor. 5:7. "Purge out therefore the old leaven that ye may be a new lump, as ye are unleavened. For even Christ our Passover is sacrificed for us".

When we accept Jesus as our savior and believe in his truth, we are spared everlasting death relating to the blood. The ancient Israelites put blood on the entrance of their home so the death angel would pass over and there was no death in the family.

Chapter 21

The Christmas Story

The Christmas story is a story a grandparent or father or mother can read to his or her children, based on the Gospel of Matthew and Luke.

The mainstream theologians consider that Jesus was born September 28–29 4 BC. There are others who consider the lambing season more logical. But just as his second coming is a mystery, we can only trust our reasoning using the scriptures. If Jesus was born in September, then we can celebrate his conception as this is when his life began in Mary's womb in December. Life begins in the womb; *Luke 1:41. When Elizabeth heard Mary's greeting, the baby leaped in her womb, and Elizabeth was filled with the Holy Spirit.*

The conception of Jesus by the Holy Spirit and the Virgin Mary gave us God's gift of love. What a great gift! We now use this date in December 24–25 to give gifts to show our love as Christians.

An angel named Gabriel was sent from God to talk to a young innocent girl in Nazareth, a town in Galilee. Her name was Mary. She was pledged to be married to Joseph a carpenter, a descendant of King David.

Gabriel the Angel told her she would have a son and she was to call him Jesus.

This is how it happened.

Gabriel appeared to Mary in our month of December and said, "Greetings, you are highly favored by God. The Lord is with you." Mary was greatly troubled by his appearance and wondered what this greeting was about. Gabriel said, *"Do not be afraid, God has chosen you to be with a child by the Holy Spirit and He will become the Savior Christ Jesus. He will heal the sick and be known as the Son of the Most High. He will reign over the house of Jacob forever, His kingdom will never end."*

"How can this be?" Mary asked Gabriel. "I am an innocent virgin?"

The angel Gabriel answered, "The Holy Spirit will come upon you on the eve, and the power of the Most High will overshadow you. Be not afraid, you will be blessed with a son." And now we celebrate Christmas Eve for it is then that God gave his gift to us.

"Your cousin Elizabeth is going to have a child in her advanced age. Although she has never given birth, she is in her sixth month," Gabriel said. *"Nothing is impossible with God." Mary then answered, "I am the Lord's servant, may I be blessed as God wishes. May it be to me as you have said?" Then the angel left her.*

Now Mary was pledged to be married to Joseph, but before they came together, she was found to be with child through the Holy Spirit.

God sent an Angel to appear to Joseph in a dream and said, *"Joseph, son of David, it is God's will. Take Mary home as your wife because what is conceived in her is from the Holy Spirit. She will give birth to a son, and you are to give Him the name Jesus because He will save his people from their sins."*

This was prophesized long ago by Isaiah the prophet: *"The virgin will be with child and will give birth to a son, and they will call him Immanuel,"* which means "God is with us." When Joseph woke up, he did what the angel of the Lord had commanded him and took Mary home as his wife. But he had no union with her until she gave birth to a son. And he gave him the name Jesus.

In those days, Caesar Augustus issued a decree that a census should be taken of the entire Roman world. (This was the first census that took place before Quirinius was governor of Syria.) And everyone went to his own town to register.

So Joseph also went up from the town of Nazareth in Galilee to Judea, to Bethlehem, the town of David, because he belonged to the house and line of David. He went there to register with Mary, who was pledged to be married to him and was expecting a child. Mary had to rest on her way, so when they arrived at the inn, there were no rooms left.

They had to stay in the barn; luckily, it was late September and the sheep and other animals still grazed outdoors at night as the shepherds watched over them. Recently, some scholars say it was in the spring, relating the time to lambing season—Jesus is referred to as the Lamb of God.

While they were there, the time came for the baby to be born, and Mary gave birth to her firstborn, a son. She wrapped him in swaddling clothes and placed him in a manger because there still was no room for them in the inn.

The shepherds were living out in the fields nearby, keeping watch over their flocks on that September night. Suddenly, an angel of the Lord appeared to them, and the glory of the Lord shone around them and they were terrified. But the angel said to them, *"Do not be afraid. I bring you good news of great joy that will be for all the people. Today in the town of David, a savior has been born to you; he is Christ the Lord. This will be a sign to you: You will find a baby wrapped in swaddling clothes and lying in a manger."*

Suddenly, a great company of the heavenly host appeared with the angel, praising God and saying, *"Glory to God in the highest, and on earth peace to men on whom his favor rests."* When the angels had left them and gone into heaven, the shepherds said to one another, *"Let's go to Bethlehem and see this thing that has happened, which the Lord has told us about."*

So they hurried off and found Mary and Joseph and the baby, who was lying in the manger. When they had seen him, they spread the word concerning what had been told them about this child, and all who heard it were amazed at what the shepherds said to them. Mary treasured up all these things and pondered them in her heart.

The shepherds returned, glorifying and praising God for all the things they had heard and seen which were just as they had been told. Jesus had been born in Bethlehem in Judea during the time of King Herod. Magi came from the east to Jerusalem and asked, *"Where is the one who has been born king of the Jews? We saw his star in the east and have come to worship him."*

When King Herod heard this, he was disturbed and all Jerusalem with him. He called together all the chief priests and teachers of the law; he asked them where the Christ was to be born. *"In Bethlehem, in Judea,"* they replied, *"for this is what the prophet has written: 'But you, Bethlehem, in the land of Judah, are by no means least among the rulers of Judah; for out of you will come a ruler who will be the shepherd of my people Israel".*

Then Herod called the Magi secretly and found out from them the exact time the star had appeared. He sent them to Bethlehem and said, *"Go and make a careful search for the child. As soon as you find him, report to me so that I too may go and worship him."*

They went on their way, and the star they had seen in the east went on ahead of them until it stopped over the place where the child was. On coming to the house (this was not in a manger in a barn) they saw the child with his mother Mary, and they bowed down and worshiped him. When the Magi finally reached the home were the infant child was located, Jesus at this point was still an infant but less than two years old.

They opened their treasures and presented their gifts of gold and of incense and of myrrh. And having been warned in a dream not to go back to Herod, they returned to their country by another route.

When the three wise men had gone, an angel of the Lord appeared to Joseph in a dream. *"Get up,"* he said, *"take the child and his mother and escape to Egypt. Stay there until I tell you, for Herod is going to search for the child to kill him."* So Joseph got up, took the child and his mother during the night, and left for Egypt, where they stayed until the death of Herod.

When Herod realized that he had been outwitted by the Magi, he was furious and he gave orders to kill all the boys in Bethlehem and its vicinity that were two years old and under, in accordance with the time he had learned from the Magi.

After Herod died, an angel of the Lord appeared in a dream to Joseph in Egypt.

"Get up, take the child and his mother and go to the land of Israel, for those who were trying to take the child's life are dead." Joseph and

Mary returned to Galilee to their own town of Nazareth. And the child grew and became strong; he was filled with wisdom, and the grace of God was upon him. Jesus began his Teaching and healing ministry at thirty years of age.

Is the Christmas Tree for Christians?

Jeremiah 10:1 "Hear what the LORD says to you, <u>O house of Israel</u>. 2. This is what the LORD says: "Do not learn the ways of the nations or be terrified by signs in the sky, though the nations are terrified by them. 3. For the customs of the peoples are worthless; they <u>cut a tree out of the forest</u>, and a craftsman shapes it with his chisel".

They had no knowledge of what God's plan was—to bring forth a Savior. Some people were using trees to carve false images to worship.

The Israelites were banned from using a tree as a symbol even though they did not understand that Jesus would become our tree of life after his work on the cross.

He was in the planted Garden of Eden, and we would become the branches. Jesus said *in John 15:5, "I am the vine; you are the branches. If a man remains in me and I in him, he will bear much fruit; apart from me you can do nothing."*

Most Christians now know that Jesus was the tree of life in the planted Garden of Eden, and when we set up and adorn a tree with lights, we are celebrating God's gift, a gift of light to the world by which we might be saved: our Savior Jesus Christ.

Jesus Christ, God's light to the world, was conceived around December 24, to be born of women in late September. God, in his love for all his children, gave us a gift; now we give gifts to the ones we love. So yes! The Christmas tree is for Christians who want to celebrate God and His Son Jesus. We read in *Hosea 14:8. Ephraim shall say, what have I to do any more with idols? I have heard him, and observed him: I am like a green fir tree. From me is thy fruit found.* The fruit or present that God would place under the tree would be Jesus his gift to Christians. *Genesis 2: 8. And the Lord God planted a garden eastward in Eden; and there he put the man ['eth-'Ha' 'âdhâm] whom he had formed.*

As no one has seen God, Jesus said, *"If you see me, you have seen the Father."*

What a great honor when an earthly father dresses up like Santa and gives gifts as God did on that day in December. The truth about this story of love can be traced back to the year 632 BC.

NIV *Micah 5:2 "But you, Bethlehem Ephrathah, though you are small among the clans of Judah, out of you will come for me* one who will be ruler over Israel [how many times since I was a child have we sung "Oh Little Town of Bethlehem"?] *among the clans of Judah, out of you will come for me one who will be ruler over Israel, whose origins are from of old, from ancient times".* This is Our Savior Jesus. Thank you, GOD.

"Therefore the Lord himself will give you a sign: The virgin will be with child and will give birth to a son, and will call him Immanuel" (Isa. 7: 14).

"For to us a child is born, to us a son is given, and the government will be on his shoulders. And he will be called Wonderful, Counselor, Mighty God, Everlasting Father, and Prince of Peace" (Isa. 9:6).

Today, some Jewish Christians who accept Christ as their Messiah believe that the birth of Christ was on day one of Nisan during lambing season. Jesus is considered the Lamb of God; they relate this back to Exodus 12:1–11 when the first Passover took place. The blood of a lamb was placed on the doorpost to save the inhabitants from death; this then relates to Jesus who shed his blood on the cross and became our Passover Lamb.

As written in *1 Corinthians 5:7, "for even Christ our Passover is sacrificed for us."*

If we look to the scriptures and what Jesus said in Matthew 24:42, "Watch therefore: for you know not what hour your Lord doth come." Could this be the reason that we can only make an educated guess as to his conception or actual birth as a man here on earth? The true Christian honors and gives thanks every day for God's Gift, his son Jesus our savior.

Matthew 11:28"Come unto me, all you that labor and are heavy laden, and I will give you rest".

Now those of us that accept Jesus the Christ as our savior, every day is our Sabbath or rest.

There has been some criticism about the authenticity of the birth of Jesus, claiming that the biblical account found in the Gospel of Luke is contradicted by the written Roman history about the period the governor of Syria Cyrenius or Quirinius was in power as he was governor around AD 11, well after the birth of Christ. Let's do a bit of research as to where or what went wrong.

The Gospel of KJV *Luke 2:1. "And it came to pass in those days, that there went out a decree from Caesar Augustus that the entire world should be taxed. 2. (And this taxing was first made when Cyrenius was governor of Syria.)."* The NIV, the *Gospel of Luke 2:1 "In those days Caesar Augustus issued a decree that a census should be taken of the entire Roman world. 2. (This was the first census that took place while Quirinius was governor of Syria.)"* We now jump ahead in this same chapter to verse 5–6: *"He went there to register with Mary, who was pledged to be married to him and was expecting a child. 6. While they were there, the time came for the baby to be born."* This raises a question.

Thus we now have cause for alarm. <u>BUT</u> when we check the word *first* in the original manuscripts written in Greek, we find that the lexicon number for the word is 4413.

The word must be an incorrect translation by the scholars or writing in error by the scribes.

Strong's no. 4413 Transliterated: protos Phonetic: pro'-tos 1 Text: contracted superlative of 4253; foremost (in time, place, order or importance):—before, beginning, best, chief(-est), first (of all), former.

Here we can see that the true translation of the Gospel of Luke should have been translated into English as 2:2. (This was before the census that took place while Quirinius was governor of Syria.) Thus we must study God's letter to us ourselves.

Some preachers try to denounce and change the now tradition of us Christians. They would Change "Merry Christmas" to season greetings. They claim the cutting down and decorating the tree in our home with gold and silver ornaments is a Pagan worship of gods. They also cite Saint Nicholas gave presents on December 6th making Santa Clause a myth.

They however support and preach the first man was the one formed and placed in a Planted Garden east of Eden, but then they also support and teach Eve ate an Apple!

They fail to grasp that by just the spoken word God created mankind male and female on the sixth day. Many are led astray by the New International Version's and other newly printed Bibles that present Act's 17: 26. From one man he made every nation of men, Some KJV that have; Act's 17: 26. From one blood he made every nation of men, [science has found there are many types of blood]. They offer in a note the proper interpretation from the Greek should reflect "The blood of the earth - soil or clay that sustains plants and supports life. There are Bibles that have Act's 17:26. From the clay he made every nation of men. [Covered in Chapter 6.]

But the man he formed from the soil and placed in the planted garden eastward of Eden was special a true representative of "Let's make man in our image"; [With no gender]. While this formed man Adam was asleep, God: formed Eve from his rib, curve or DNA to establish and keep a pure seed line to Christ.

The Christian accepts the concept of Christmas, the tree and Santa Clause.

We can feel the joy and celebrate the occasion with our family and friends by accepting this festive season; represents God as a tree and the presents are the Gospel found in the Bible; God's gift to us is our savior Jesus.

Chapter 22

Final Word

<u>Who is the Antichrist?</u>

We have read in *Matthew 24: 4. Jesus answered: "Watch out that no one deceives you. 5. for many will come in my name, claiming, `I am the Christ,' and will deceive many.*

2 Thessalonians 2:1. Concerning the coming of our Lord Jesus Christ and our being gathered to him, we ask you, brothers, 2. Not to become easily unsettled or alarmed by some prophecy, report or letter supposed to have come from us, saying that the day of the Lord has already come. 3. Don't let anyone deceive you in any way, for that day will not come until the rebellion occurs and the man of lawlessness is revealed, the man doomed to destruction.

1 John 2: 18. Dear children, this is the last hour; and as you have heard that the antichrist is coming, even now many antichrists have come. This is how we know it is the last hour.

There is a religion that has its own a religious book the Koran, in it Jesus is mentioned but they denounce Jesus as being the son of God and his death as recorded in the Holy Bible is false.

The movement has gone so far that there is now a book published as the holy bible. In it all reference to Jesus being the son of God has been eliminated could this be part of the Antichrist

Phenomena?[In the KJV there are 1,000 to 1,200 scripture linking God, Jesus and the Holy Spirit.]

There is a popular Rapture Theory being taught by many preachers they use 1 Thessalonians as their main reference: *1 Thessalonians 4: 16. For the Lord himself will come down from heaven, with a loud command, with the voice of the archangel and with the trumpet call of God, and the dead in Christ will rise first. 17. After that, we who are still alive and are left will be caught up together with them in the clouds to meet the Lord in the air. And so we will be with the Lord forever.* By their theory being raptured the Christians will escape the Tribulation which could already have begun as Christians are being beheaded and other acts of terrorism are increasing.

Will the Christians be raptured? Let us take one more look at the verse they quote to bolster their "Rapture Theory" in Revelation.

The Original Manuscripts reads: 3:10. Because you keep the word of the patience of me and you will <u>keep out</u> of the hour of trial. [This is the literal or unedited direct translation from the Greek]. The following two versions have added words for clarity.

KJV 3:10. Because thou hast kept the word of my patience, I also will keep thee <u>from</u> the hour of temptation, which shall come upon the entire world, to try them that dwell upon the earth.

NIV. 3:10. Since you have kept my command to endure patiently, I will also keep you <u>from</u> the hour of trial that is going to come upon the whole world to test those who live on the earth.

Here we find the words "keep out" and the word "from" is translated from the Greek word "ek" Strong's number 1537. [more on this to come].

The word "from" can also be translated from two other Greek words!

There are three words that are translated to the English word "from" but each has a different connotation, these three words in Greek are "ek", "apo", and "para" all can be translated to the English word "from". See listings or what the difference each word conveys of these 3 words below.

If in the verse in Revelation 3:10. The word "from" had been translated from the Greek word "apo" the word "from" would have some validity for the rapture theory or snatched away or saved. Had it not came From the Greek word "ek" but from the word; *Pronounced apo' a primary particle; "off," i.e. away (from something near), in various senses (of place, time, or relation; it usually denotes <u>separation, departure</u>.*

When the word from is translated from the Greek word "ek" to English it can be associated to how God saved Noah *from* the flood or how God parted the Red Sea to save the Israelites *from* the Egyptians, but the scriptures give this advice in Ephesians KVJ. 6:11." *Put on the whole armor of God that you may be able to stand against the wiles of the devil".*

NIV. 6:11." *Put on the full armor of God so that you can take your stand against the devil's schemes'.*

The temptations, trials or the Tribulation, the Rapture Theory is supposed to save the church and their followers [bordering on cult status] can be dismissed by understanding and validating the scripture we read in *Acts 3:21.* He [Jesus] *must remain in heaven until the time comes for God to restore everything, as he promised long ago through his holy prophets.* There is only one second or returning to earth by Jesus that can be validated by the original inspired Authors in the original scriptures.

We must also ponder and consider; Jesus in the book of Revelation was reporting on seven Churches in chapter 2 and 3! But only one of the seven churches the one in Philadelphia met with his full approval. We will now consider the three Greek words for "from".

"ek" Strong's Ref. # 1537 Romanized ek Pronounced ek - a primary preposition denoting origin (the point whence action or motion proceeds), from, out (of place, time, or cause; literal or figurative; direct or remote):KJV--after, among, X are, at, betwixt(-yond), by (the means of), exceedingly, (+ abundantly above), for(- th), from (among, forth, up), + grudgingly, + heartily, X heavenly, X hereby, + very highly, in, ...ly, (because, by reason) of, off (from), on, out among (from, of), over, since, X thenceforth, through, X unto, X vehemently, with(-out). Often used in composition, with the same general import; often of completion.

"apo" Strong's Ref. # 575 Romanized apo Pronounced apo' a primary particle; "off," i.e. away (from something near), in various senses (of place, time, or relation; literal or figurative):KJV--(X here-) after, ago, at, because of, before, by (the space of), for(-th), from, in, (out) of, off, (up-)on(-ce), since, with. In composition (as a prefix) it usually denotes separation, departure, cessation, completion, reversal, etc.

"para" Strong's Ref. # 3844 Romanized para Pronounced par-ah' a primary preposition; properly, near; i.e. (with genitive case) from beside (literally or figuratively), (with dative case) at (or in) the vicinity of (objectively or subjectively), (with accusative case) to the proximity with (local [especially beyond or opposed to] or causal [on

account of]: KJV--above, against, among, at, before, by, contrary to, X friend, from, + give [such things as they], + that [she] had, X his, in, more than, nigh unto, (out) of, past, save, side...by, in the sight of, than, [there-] fore, with. In compounds it retains the same variety of application.

If reading this book you have developed a feeling of truth for the Word and a closeness to God, Jesus and the Holy Spirit; and have a thirst to reread the Holy Bible and look for the deeper meaning and truth in His letter to you, the praise and glory belong to the Father, the Son Jesus, and the Holy Spirit.

Reading the gospel of John for the first time was a turning point for me.

I now believe in the verse in John Chapter 8:32. KJV *"And ye shall know the truth, and the truth shall make you free."-* NIV *"Then you will know the truth, and the truth will set you free.""*

My part in this book was only as a Scribe; my background makes me humble when reading what I have recorded or written in this book using one finger.

Being born in 1934 to parents who separately emigrated from a beautiful part of Sweden in 1928; they thought they were coming to a place like Banff, Alberta, with clear blue lakes, forests, and mountains; but they landed in southern Saskatchewan, a flat prairie landscape with rocky soil this is where they finally met and married. Growing up and speaking mostly Swedish. My parents spoke no English when they came to Canada. My mother worked on a farm; my father worked for the railway laying spur line railroad tracks to grain elevators. They slowly over the years learned the language.

In school grades 1, 2, and 3, I passed; but in grade 4, we were introduced to literature and the finer points of English. I failed grade 4 twice. The school sent home books on spelling, and my mom and I spent the summer months studying. The school superintendent said he would put me in grade 5 on a trial basis. I passed but had very poor grades in English all the way to grade 11.

Leaving high school in grade 11and entering a four-year apprenticeship in carpentry. Working in the construction field most of my life. I was a very poor reader. When my children were small, we would take turns reading Nancy Drew books.

My mother gave me a copy of 1611 KJV of the Holy Bible for Christmas when I was eight years old and trying over the years to read the scriptures would give up when the begat part started:

And unto Enoch was born Irad: and Irad begat Mehujael: and Mehujael begat t Methusael: and Methusael begat Lamech. (Gen. 4:8)

Listening to Billy Graham on the radio and later on in life watched *Oral Roberts, Rex Humbart, It is Written, Garner Ted Armstrong, Armor of God, Tomorrow's World*, and many others on TV. I then engaged in a "read the Bible in one year" with Ron Hembree; I did this four times and have gone through the Bible several times since. Searching for truth and understanding using purchased aids like a NIV Bible, Strong's Exhaustive Concordance and a copy of The Original Manuscripts with numbers that worked I would go to bed only to get inspiration to get up a write.

While watching the Program *To You with Love* with Allan Dunbar, he invited us listeners to tour Israel with him as a guide.

I had been sprinkled as an infant in a Lutheran Church, but when I was in Israel, I was baptized by submersion in the Jordan River.

My thirst for reading the Bible looking for more understanding really came to the forefront when I walked through the Dung Gate in Jerusalem. I was struck by such an overwhelming feeling in my body, and I said to myself I have come home.

For years after attending various churches it felt good as we sang hymns, but walking out of the door, the feeling was empty. We had really not learned anything about the Bible. Attending several weekend seminars after one was very sad when the teacher said that if you eat one slice of ham, one piece of bacon or drink a glass of wine, you will not enter heaven. Then we were told we had to give 10 percent of our gross paycheck before taxes, rent, food or anything else to the church. That did it for me.

Finding a program called *Shepherd's Chapel* on TV this increased my understanding of the Word until it was unavailable in our area. I had been writing this book for 20 + years on and off, but when I found this program, I realized that although I had attended church and read the Bible several times, I had missed the deeper story. This TV program had opened my eyes. And the search for deeper understanding of God letter intensified.

Sitting down to type, again with on finger, asking in prayer for wisdom and guidance from the Lord, I am humbled and amazed how all the sermons and teaching and book reading transfers from my fingertip to the computer with the help of the Holy Spirit to create this book.

I thank the Father, Jesus, and the Holy Spirit for the inspiration and know that <u>without their help, I could write nothing</u>.

Amen.

verncederberg@shaw.ca
Julyl 2016

About the Author

Carl Verner Cederberg is a devout Christian who has studied various versions of the Bible as well as related materials for several decades. He is also a retired construction worker. His study of the Bible began as a result of inspiration from the Holy Spirit; in 1989, he went to Israel and was baptized in the Jordan River, which is where his search for deep Biblical understanding truly began. *Key Words or Phrases That Unlock Subjects of the Bible* is his second published book.

<u>Programs</u>

The World Tomorrow
The Living Truth
The Key of David
Armour of God
Shepherds Chapel
Day of Discovery

And many more.

CPSIA information can be obtained at www.ICGtesting.com
Printed in the USA
LVOW08s0354300716

498144LV00002B/10/P